Greenhill
Books

THE MOSCOW OPTION

THE MOSCOW OPTION
AN ALTERNATIVE SECOND WORLD WAR

David Downing

Greenhill Books, London
MBI Publishing, St Paul

The Moscow Option
An Alternative Second World War

This edition first published 2005 by Greenhill Books/Lionel Leventhal Ltd, Park House,
1 Russell Gardens, London N11 9NN
and
MBI Publishing Co., Galtier Plaza, Suite 200, 380 Jackson Street, St Paul, MN 55101-3885, USA

British Library Cataloguing-in Publication Data
Downing, David, 1946–
The Moscow Option: an alternative Second World War. Rev. [ed.].
1. World War, 1939–1945 – Germany   2. World War, 1939–1945 – Soviet Union
3. Europe – History – Errors, inventions, etc.
I. Title
940.5'3

ISBN-10 1-85367-674-8
ISBN-13 978-1-85367-674-8

Library of Congress Cataloging-in Publication Data available

Publishing History
The Moscow Option was first published in 1979 by New English Library, London. A revised
edition was published in 2001 by Greenhill Books, the text of which this edition follows.

For more information on our books, please visit www.greenhillbooks.com, email
sales@greenhillbooks.com, or telephone us within the UK on 020 8458 6314. You can also
write to us at the above London address.

Printed and bound in Great Britain by
Creative Print and Design (Wales), Ebbw Vale

CONTENTS

LIST OF MAPS

Alternative Wars
AN INTRODUCTION

Human history is often perceived as a vast and immutable web of events. Behind these events stretch infinite crisscrossing threads of causation, ahead of them infinite crisscrossing threads of consequence. An historian can choose his event, and trace those threads into the past and the future.

The Russian Revolution, for example. One causative factor was clearly the strain of three years' mismanaged war. One consequence was clearly the crash industrialisation of Russia. Yet what if the Schlieffen Plan had worked in August 1914, and the Germans had won the war that year? Would there have been no Russian Revolution? And if not, would there still have been a crash industrialisation programme?

Of course the Revolution had other causes. But I think it is safe to assume that the strain of a long war helped in some way to shape the character of the upheaval. Without that strain the story would have been a different one, in detail if not in essence. And one of the details might well have been the speed of Russia's industrialisation.

History is full of such 'ifs'. What if Judas had not betrayed Jesus? What if Blücher had arrived too late on the field of Waterloo? What if the Argentine Air Force had possessed just another dozen Exocet missiles? Such questions would have seemed worthy of the asking to those present at the time, but now they seem merely speculative, interesting but irrelevant. We reserve our speculation for the present. What if Saddam Hussein has created a nuclear capability? What will happen to the Atlantic alliance if the US goes ahead with 'Son of Star Wars'? Yet in twenty years' time historians will only be analysing the consequences of such happenings if they have actually happened, for this is what we call history.

The Second World War has been dealt with accordingly. The crucial events and decisions have been pinpointed, placed in their contexts, their sources and consequences exhaustively analysed. Traditional historians mention the might-have-beens in passing. 'It is futile to speculate', they say, and then spend a guilty paragraph or two doing just that. They acknowledge the fascination, but like politicians acknowledging democracy, they prefer to keep it under control.

There is, it is true, a continually growing body of literature concerned with Second World Wars that never happened. These books can be divided into two basic categories: 'novelised' war games and speculative fiction. The war-game books usually focus on the military aspects of a hypothetical war situation of short duration. Kenneth Macksey's *Invasion*, an account of a fictitious German invasion of England in 1940, and Peter Tsouras' *Disaster at D-Day*, a re-writing of the first few days of the June 1944 invasion, are two excellent cases in point. But in such books there is rarely sufficient scope – or, presumably, desire – for investigating the underlying processes which directed the war as a whole.

In the realm of speculative fiction several brilliant works stand out, and I must acknowledge one of them, Philip K. Dick's *The Man in the High Castle* as an inspiration for this particular book. Dick's novel is set in a world in which the Germans and Japanese have been victorious, and one of the characters has written a history of a war that never happened, in which the Axis powers were defeated! In the course of the novel Dick delivers his usual quota of insights into the human condition, and contrives in the process to say a great deal about contemporary America, Nazism and much else besides. But he is not basically interested in whether his might-have-been war is also a could-have-been war; he is only interested in what would have happened if it had been.

In this book I have tried to write a history of a Second World War that both might and could have occurred. The scope – thirteen months of global conflict – is too wide for a war game. It could perhaps be considered a 'history game'; if so, I hope the emphasis is on history. It is not a work of speculative fiction in that it accepts the limits imposed by military, political and socio-economic possibility.

I have not provided the Germans with the long-range bombers they had neglected to provide for themselves. I have not widened the industrial base of the Japanese war-machine, nor blessed the invaders of Russia with an ideology of liberation. National Socialism would not have been true to its own distorted self had it desired the liberation of Slavs, even from Bolshevism. Nor could Hitler's Germany have planned ahead with any real consistency. States built around a 'romantic' solution to the stresses of advanced capitalism do not organise themselves in an unromantic manner; even the horrors of the Holocaust were perpetrated on a largely ad hoc basis. And if the Japanese had possessed a wider industrial base it is doubtful whether they would have needed to go to war at all. Such facts are 'givens', and have not been tampered with. On the contrary, the *raison d'être* of alternative history lies in the fresh light it throws on the underlying processes of real history by its shifting of the more familiar events taking place on the surface.

In this alternative war I have made only two basic changes to the normal run of events. One occurs in Chapter 1, the other in Chapter 5. The effect of these two basic changes is to give the Germans and Japanese significant military advantages without altering their fundamental historical situations. All the other changes, the entire alternative history, flow from these two. Nothing has been altered in the time prior to the first change, which occurs on the afternoon of 4 August 1941.

In the main body of the text there is no attempt to compare the 'alternative' with the 'real'. The alternative war is written as if it really happened, in the manner of a bare-faced lie 80,000 words long. For those interested in sorting out the fiction from the fact there is a Notes and References section at the end of the book, in which references are given for genuine quotations and the minor fictional characters listed. All the central characters are or were real people; they act as I believe it is reasonable to assume they would have acted in the fictional situations created.

I would like to thank Hugh Miller for his generous assistance with the medical details of Hitler's illness, Martin Noble for his friendly help in the production of the book's original publication, and record my appreciation to the late Roger Parkinson for the suggestions offered when the book was still germinating.

It is now more than twenty years since this book first saw the light of day, and I must express my gratitude to Lionel Leventhal and his colleagues at Greenhill Books for its re-emergence.

David Downing, 2001

Prologue
4 AUGUST 1941

'Somebody got lucky, but it was an accident.'
Bob Dylan

I

Churchill reached the report's conclusion. 'In our view the manufacture of atomic weapons is definitely feasible, and should be pursued on a large scale.' So far, so good. He put the sheaf of papers down on the seat beside him and stared out of the window at the awesome Scottish scenery. The western slopes of the Cairngorms were still deep in shadow, a huge black slab beneath the brightening sky. Atomic bombs and morning glory! The British Prime Minister leant back in his seat and dozed.

The train rumbled on northwards. It had departed from London's Marylebone Station the previous evening, stopping only at the small country station of Chequers to pick up Churchill. It was now 7.30 in the morning of 4 August 1941.

Also aboard the train, in varying stages of wakefulness and breakfast, were the Chief of the Imperial General Staff, the First Sea Lord, the Vice-Chief of the Air Staff and fifty other people central to the British war effort. All were *en route* to Scapa Flow, the naval base in the Orkney Islands. That evening they were to set sail in the *Prince of Wales*, Britain's newest battleship, for a meeting with the American President in one of Newfoundland's myriad bays.

Britain's warlords were carrying with them plans, schemes and dreams for the continued prosecution of the war against Germany and Italy. In his personal baggage Churchill also carried a copy of *Captain Hornblower R.N.* by C.S. Forester. He intended to read it during the voyage. A week later he would cable Oliver Lyttleton, the Minister of State in Cairo, that he found *Hornblower* 'admirable'. A number of staff officers spent several anxious hours wondering which military operation he was referring to.

The British public, ignorant of Churchill's odyssey, were busy enjoying a warm August Bank Holiday. Trains to the coast and the country were jammed as city-dwellers hurried either to enjoy the sun and the sea or visit their evacuated children. 15,000 turned up at Lords to see a combined Middlesex-Essex XI score 412-6 against Surrey and Kent. W.J. Edrich hit 102 of them and proved himself, in the words of *The Times* cricket correspondent, 'a squadron leader in the noblest sense of the word'.

The war was more than just a source of similes, however, as the newspaper's usual broad coverage demonstrated. On that morning of 4 August the daily communiqué from Cairo GHQ announced that it was 'all quiet about Tobruk and in the Libyan frontier area'. On the back page there was a picture of the new Crusader tank; this, it was hoped, would disrupt the desert calm to the British advantage. It was, *The Times* proudly stated, 'the fastest of its kind in the world'. The Crusader's chronic tendency to mechanical failure had not yet become apparent.

The campaign in Russia took up half a page. Smolensk, the Moscow correspondent reported, was still in Russian hands. As evidence he cited the theatre company which had left the capital the previous Saturday to perform for the city's defenders. It seems unlikely that they received a hearty welcome - the town had fallen to the Germans two weeks earlier.

No evidence at all was put forward for the assertion that 'scepticism is spreading through the Reich', but, perhaps in recognition of this oversight, the following day it was reported that 'in cities where the RAF raids have been most frequent an increase in the suicide rate is recorded'.

In the Far East more nations were following the United States' lead in freezing Japanese assets. The western powers were still four months away from a direct military clash with the Rising Sun, but *The Times* noted with satisfaction that 'the whole British Empire is now lined up with the United States in economic warfare against Japan'.

Roosevelt's departure from the public eye had been considerably less discreet than Churchill's. He had sailed from the New London submarine base the previous evening in the Presidential yacht *Potomac*. The need for a complete rest was the official reason given for his voyage.

The American newspapers, like their British counterparts, carried the usual mixture of war communiqués and expert military analysis. The less reputable ones were also, on 4 August, full of a noticeable side-effect of the war - the 'stocking riots' of the previous Saturday. Apparently Roosevelt's edict forbidding the processing of raw silk for non-military purposes – silk imports had plummeted with the deterioration of trade relations with Japan – had given rise to fears of a stocking famine among the women of America, and had led to full-scale battles in department stores across the country. Even the London *Daily Mirror* picked up the story, gleefully recounting the use of 'strong-arm methods' by 'husky Chicago housewives'.

Meanwhile the President, beyond the range of prying eyes or Chicago housewives, was abandoning the *Potomac* in favour of a US Navy cruiser for the journey north to Newfoundland. His staff also carried with them plans for the prosecution of the war, in their case one not yet declared. But time was growing short. Roosevelt had an interesting piece of paper to show Churchill. It was a copy of a coded Japanese message intercepted and deciphered the previous Thursday. 'To save its own life', a part of the message read, the Japanese Empire 'must take measures to secure the raw materials of the South Seas. It must take immediate steps to break asunder this ever-strengthening chain of encirclement which is being woven under the guidance of and with the participation of England and the United States, acting like a cunning dragon seemingly asleep.'

Roosevelt knew what this implied. So did Cordell Hull, his Secretary of State, who returned to work that day after six weeks' absence through illness. Some had thought his malady more diplomatic than real, evidence that Hull's hard-line approach to foreign policy was out of favour with the rest of the Administration. He quickly sought to disabuse them. The events of the past few weeks, he told the press, had offered further confirmation of 'a world movement of conquest by force, accompanied by methods of governing the conquered peoples that are rooted mainly in savagery and barbarism.' The American response must be an ever-increasing production of military supplies, 'both for ourselves and for those who are resisting . . .'

Four thousand miles away, in the north Italian town of Mantua, Benito Mussolini was delivering a farewell speech to the Russia-bound Blackshirt Division, and echoing Hull's manichean vision of the world. 'The alignment is complete,' the Duce argued. 'On the one side Rome, Berlin and Tokyo; on the other London, Washington and Moscow. We have not the slightest doubt about the issue of this great battle. We shall triumph because history teaches that people who represent the ideas of the past must give way before the peoples who represent the ideas of the future.'

In Russia, meanwhile, the bitter struggle raged on, leaving little time for such oratory. The Soviet leaders, who would have agreed wholeheartedly with Mussolini's last sentence, were for the moment more concerned with such mundane matters as the desperate battle taking place in the Yelna salient east of Smolensk; the need to halt the German panzers that were now only eighty miles from Leningrad; and the disaster looming in the steppe south of Kiev.

But in Moscow itself, the only warring capital under threat of imminent seizure, spirits were higher than they had been two weeks before. Roosevelt's envoy Harry Hopkins had only recently departed – he was now waiting for Churchill aboard *Prince of Wales* – and it had been widely assumed that he had offered bountiful American aid. More important perhaps, the good news from the central front compensated the Muscovites for the continuing flow of bad news from the more distant northern and southern fronts. The enemy was being held at Yelna! A fortnight before he had been only two hundred miles from Moscow. And he still was! Perhaps, the optimists wondered out loud, the tide was turning. Perhaps the worst was over.

Perhaps not. That night there would be a meeting of the Stavka, the supreme military-political command. The summonses would go out by telephone, and soon the long black cars would speed through Moscow's empty and blacked-out streets, through the checkpoints and the fortress walls of Stalin's Kremlin. The leaders of Soviet Communism and the Red Army would climb from their cars and walk swiftly up to the conference chamber from which the Soviet war effort was directed.

In that room, on that August night, there would be little talk of American aid; all present knew that in the months remaining before winter only the Red Army could save the Soviet Union. The discussion would be of divisions overrun, armies encircled, bridges fallen to the enemy, of days rather than years, of the struggle to survive.

In China too the war went on, but its instigators in Tokyo were now absorbed in the planning of more ambitious military projects. The American freezing of Japanese assets and a virtually complete oil embargo were proving more of a spur than a deterrent. *The Times* that day reported an article by the Japanese Finance Minister in the newspaper *Asahi*. In it he argued that Japan should go on with the construction of the Greater East Asia Co-Prosperity Sphere. Withdrawal from China would invite a catastrophe; victory and success would make 'all costs appear as nothing'. Another article, this time by the Vice-Director of the Cabinet Planning Board, urged the Japanese people to be content with the 'lowest standard of living', and to 'abolish all liberalistic individualism for the sake of the race and the nation'.

These were more than empty words. The unfortunate inhabitants of Kagoshima in southern Kyushu could, had they but known it, have confirmed as much. For their city and its bay were being used, unknown to them and most of the participants, as a training ground for Operation 'Z', the planned attack on the US naval base at Pearl Harbor. Torpedo planes flew over the mountain behind the city, zoomed down across the railway station, between smoke-stacks and telephone poles before launching imaginary torpedoes at a breakwater in the harbour. The locals, unaware that the breakwater was standing in for Pearl Harbor's Battleship Row, complained bitterly at the nerve-wracking antics of these hot-headed pilots.

II

At 11am Churchill's train was puffing along the banks of the Dornoch Firth, a hundred miles short of its destination. In Novy Borrisov, three time-zones to the east, it was 2pm, and Field-Marshal Fedor von Bock was escorting Adolf Hitler from the Army Group Centre HQ to the car waiting to take him to the airstrip nearby. The Führer, having conferred with Bock and his panzer group commanders as to the military situation on Army Group Centre's front, was returning home to the Wolfsschanze, his personal headquarters in the East Prussian forests near Rastenburg.

Watching the party make their way across the yellowed grass towards the waiting car were the two panzer group commanders, Generals Hoth and Guderian. They were enjoying a cup of the decent coffee available at Army Group HQ before returning to their own less exalted headquarters. They were also extremely confused. Why had the Führer not sanctioned a continuation of the march on Moscow? All his commanders thought it the correct course of action. If Hitler had come to argue for a different course then it would have been understandable. Mistaken, but understandable. Instead he had just listened, and then talked airily of Leningrad, the Ukraine, even Moscow itself. He had not committed himself to any one of them. He was clearly undecided. Why was he refusing to see the obvious?

While Hoth and Guderian were savouring their cups of coffee and sharing their misgivings, the Führer's party reached the Borrisov airstrip and the four-engined FW200 reconnaissance plane that was to carry it back to Rastenburg. Bock bid his superiors farewell with a characteristically unconvincing 'Heil Hitler', and the Führer, Field-Marshal Keitel and their SS bodyguard climbed aboard the plane. Within minutes the FW200 was rolling down the dirt runway and into the sky.

Rastenburg was 280 miles away to the west. The FW200 gained height and flew over the outskirts of what remained of Minsk, over the German construction gangs widening the gauge of the Molodechno railway, over fields strewn with the flotsam of war and the still-smouldering remains of villages caught in the path of the German advance. Had the Führer deigned to look down on this panorama of destruction he would doubtless have been much gratified. Perhaps he might have hummed a few bars of *Götterdämmerung*. But he didn't look down. Hitler was a nervous flier, and preferred not to be reminded of the distance separating him from *terra firma*.

About thirty miles from its destination one of the plane's four engines cut out. The pilot was probably not overly worried by this development. It would make the landing slightly more difficult, but if he had not been an extremely able pilot he would not have been flying Hitler's plane.

But worse was to come. As the dry plains of Belorussia gave way to the lakes and forests of Masurian Prussia the weather took a dramatic turn. Rastenburg was in the grip of a summer thunderstorm, and as the plane neared the airfield it was suddenly encased in sheets of driving rain.

The pilot must have considered flying on to Königsberg, a further sixty miles to the north-west, but chose not to do so. It must be presumed that a surfeit of confidence in his own ability lay behind this decision. If so, he must have felt momentarily justified as the plane touched down without apparent mishap.

But split-seconds later the pilot must have realised his mistake. The poor visibility had distorted his sense of distance. He had landed too far down the runway.

He tried to brake too rapidly. The three-engined plane went into an uncontrollable skid, slewed off the runway and careered across the wet grass. One of the wings smashed into an unfortunately placed fire-tender. With an enormous jolt the FW200 spun in a tight circle and stopped.

Seconds later airstrip staff were removing bodies from the stricken plane and carrying them through the rain to the buildings two hundred yards away. The pilot, Field-Marshal Keitel and one of the SS guards were dead. Hitler was unconscious but alive.

At first there seemed no signs of serious injury. But once the Führer had been taken indoors it was discovered that the rain pouring down his face was not rain at all. It was sweat. A heavy fever was developing, the breathing was shallow and rapid. Occasionally a spasm would seize the legs and head, arching them backwards.

The Führer was driven swiftly through the dark dripping forest to the medical unit attached to his headquarters. There, in the centrally-heated alpine chalet, he was examined by the resident staff and his personal physician, the dubious Dr Morell. They could not reach an adequate diagnosis, and soon the wires to Berlin were humming with top-secret orders for specialist assistance.

Later that evening a number of Germany's most distinguished consultant physicians arrived at the Wolfsschanze. One of them, Dr Werner Sodenstern, was considered to be Germany's leading brain specialist. He diagnosed multiple minor haemorrhages in the medulla and brain stem. They had probably been caused by the Führer's head coming into forceful contact with his padded headrest. The injuries were unlikely to be fatal, and there was no damage to the main part of the brain. There was every chance that the Führer would recover, with his faculties unimpaired. But there was no way of knowing when. No special treatment was possible or necessary. Hitler needed intravenous saline to support the blood tone, and complete rest.

Sodenstern admitted that such cases were rare, and that medical science was still trying to understand them fully. It might be days, weeks or even months before the Führer finally emerged from the coma. But the healing process had to be allowed to run its natural course. If it were hurried by either the patient or his advisers the consequences would probably be severe.

For an unknown length of time Nazi Germany had lost the political and military services of its Führer.

The eminent doctors had not been the only passengers on the plane from Berlin. Hitler's acolytes, the 'barons' of Nazi Germany, were also gathering at the scene of the disaster. The injuries might still prove fatal, in which case a struggle for the succession would have to take place. If the Führer survived it would presumably be necessary to re-arrange the delineation of authorities until such time as his recovery was complete.

Goebbels, Himmler and Boorman had arrived with the doctors, having been informed of the accident by their resident representatives at the Wolfsschanze. There had been attempts to reach Goering at Veldenstein Castle, but he was not expected back from Paris until later that evening. Colonel-General Jodl, Head of Operations in the OKW (Supreme Command of the Armed Forces) under the late Keitel and Hitler himself, was already there. Grand-Admiral Raeder, Commander-in-Chief of the Kriegsmarine (Navy or OKM), Field-Marshal Brauchitsch, Commander-in-Chief of the

Army (OKH), and Colonel-General Halder, Chief of the Army General Staff, had all been informed and were expected.

All these men wielded great power in Nazi Germany, but all were ultimately responsible to Hitler and Hitler alone. There was no complex hierarchy – just the Führer and his subordinates. Each had an empire within the empire. When their areas of authority overlapped it was Hitler who decided the boundaries. Or had done until now. In the weeks ahead his subordinates would either have to learn the art of co-operation or, more likely, leave each other well alone.

One man did have nominal authority over the others for, only six weeks earlier, Hitler had nominated Reich Marshal Goering as his successor. But it remained to be seen whether Goering had the personal stature, or indeed the inclination, to make his new-found authority more than nominal. It seemed more likely that he would delight in the trappings of power than exercise himself unduly in the wielding of it.

He did, however, take the chair in the Wolfsschanze conference room the following morning. Also present were Reichsführer SS Himmler, Generals Jodl, Brauchitsch and Halder, Grand-Admiral Raeder, Party Chief Boorman and Propaganda Minister Goebbels. Foreign Minister Ribbentrop, whom no one but Hitler could stomach, had not been invited, nor yet informed of the accident.

The records of this meeting did not survive the destruction of Berlin, but the memoirs of Halder and Raeder, who alone outlived the war, agree on all but the insignificant details. The first matter discussed – the reason for the meeting – was the Führer's condition. Should the German people, and hence the world, be informed of the accident? Such news would provide a definite morale boost for the enemies of the Reich. Could the whole business be hushed up? Did too many people know already? A compromise was decided upon. News of the accident would be released, but the severity of the Führer's condition would be played down. A broken leg, a broken arm – Goebbels's Ministry would decide the details. Hitler rarely made public appearances now in any case. Hopefully he would be fully recovered before the next one scheduled, the traditional speech to mark the opening of the Winter Help Relief Campaign on 4 September. If not, then new excuses could be dreamed up by the Propaganda Ministry. Those who knew the truth would be sworn to silence on pain of death.

The second item on the agenda concerned the replacing of the dead Keitel. It was agreed that Colonel-General Jodl should succeed him to the post of Supreme Commander of the Armed Forces, and that Colonel-General von Paulus, the Army Quarter-Master General, should succeed Jodl as OKW Head of Operations.

No other decisions of importance were taken at the meeting. No one was yet ready to cross the boundaries Hitler had laid down between them. Things would remain as they were, 'as the Führer would have wished them', and as he would doubtless expect to find them when he returned.

This, though predictable, was crucial. For in effect it offered the Army, as Hitler would never have done, *carte blanche* in the East. No one knows, of course, what the Führer would eventually have made of the confusion witnessed by Bock, Hoth and Guderian at Novy Borrisov on 4 August. He later told Brauchitsch in a fit of anger that he would have taken Kiev before resuming the march on Moscow. That way, he claimed, the Soviet Union would have been brought conclusively to its knees by the end of November. Perhaps this, like many of Hitler's later outbursts, was merely hindsight working its insidious way through his warped mind. But it is unlikely. Both his adjutant, Colonel Schmundt, and Jodl told others in the following months that Hitler had indeed set his mind on the capture of Kiev. If so his crash in the Rastenburg rain profoundly altered the course of the war, if not its final outcome.

On 5 August the newly-promoted Jodl kept remarkably quiet about his unconscious master's predilections. His reason was simple enough. He agreed with Brauchitsch, Halder, Bock, Guderian, Hoth and practically everyone else who mattered that Moscow should be the primary objective of the Army in the East. When the Army Group Centre generals declared that Hitler had not made a decision before leaving Novy Borrisov, Jodl did not contradict them. He agreed that those, like himself, who had never been undecided should now implement their decision. The march on Moscow should be resumed at the earliest possible date.

Chapter 1
'MOSCOW BEFORE THE SNOW FALLS'

Do you remember the dryness in your throat
When rattling their naked power of evil
They were banging ahead and bellowing
And autumn was advancing in steps of calamity?
Boris Pasternak

I

According to Führer Directive 21, issued on 18 December 1940, the German Army was to 'crush Soviet Russia in a rapid campaign'. With that aim in mind eight infantry armies and four panzer groups had crossed the border on 22 June 1941, destroyed the bulk of the armies facing them and advanced deep into Soviet territory. For three weeks, as the miles rolled away beneath the panzers' tracks, any doubts as to the enormity of the task had been subdued beneath the enthusiasm of conquest. In the north Höppner's two panzer corps were a mere eighty miles from Leningrad by mid-July; in the south Kleist's Panzer Group was striking towards the lower Dnieper. In the centre, astride the main Moscow highway, the panzer groups under Hoth and Guderian twice closed on huge concentrations of Soviet troops. By 16 July the tanks were rumbling through the ruins of Smolensk, already two-thirds of the way to the Soviet capital. A slice of the Soviet Union over twice the size of France had been amputated, and close to two million prisoners taken. This, surely, was victory on an epic scale.

Epic, perhaps. But not yet victory. The Soviet Union had not collapsed as Hitler had predicted it would. 'We have only to kick in the door,' the Führer had said, 'and the whole rotten structure will come crashing down.' Well, the door had been comprehensively kicked in, but the structure still stood bloodily intact. *Fall Barbarossa*, the plan for the defeat of Russia, was beginning to fray at the centre.

It had been an optimistic plan from the beginning. There were too many miles, too few roads, too little firm and open ground. This enemy was an altogether different proposition to those already crushed under the Wehrmacht's motorised heel. The citizens of the Soviet Union had a greater will to resist than had been shown by the French; they had more room to make resistance count than had been available to the hapless Poles. And there were many more of them. The Germans, outnumbered from the start, were advancing on three divergent axes towards objectives separated by over a thousand miles of often difficult terrain. And as the force of their spearheads was diluted by the growing distances between and behind them the German intelligence estimates of Soviet strength were continually being revised upwards. For every prisoner the Germans took, or so it seemed, there were two new Soviet citizens donning Red Army uniform. The German boat was taking water faster than its crew could bail. Sooner or later, unless something radical was done, it would sink.

There was only one solution to this problem. If the limbs of the Soviet Goliath could not be held down, then the blow had to be struck at the nervous system. This, after all, was the basis of panzer warfare. Death by paralysis, not by body blows. The assault had to be focused on objectives whose importance transcended their immediate value, before the Army as a whole was sucked into a war of attrition it could only lose.

But which objectives? This essentially was the question at issue during the last two weeks of July and the first few days of August. Hitler was not yet overly concerned about Russian resistance, informing the Japanese Ambassador on 15 July that he expected to be withdrawing forces from the Eastern Front some time in August. At this point *Barbarossa* still seemed to be on schedule, and this implied, according to Hitler's reading of the plan, that Army Group Centre's armour would soon be sent north and south to aid the flanking Army Groups in securing the Baltic Coast and the Donets industrial region. Hence Führer Directive 33, issued on 19 July, which ordered such a redeployment.

Brauchitsch, Halder and the Army Group Centre generals neither shared Hitler's confidence nor agreed with the proposed rerouting of the central panzer groups. It was becoming apparent to them that the grandiose aims of *Barbarossa* were not attainable in a 'rapid campaign'. They urged a continuation of the advance on the central axis. Only before Moscow, they argued, would the Russians be forced to stand and fight. And only the capture of the capital would provide that paralysing blow which alone could avert a long and costly war of attrition. They quoted the findings of the Zossen war-game of December 1940. 'In view of the paramount importance of preserving (Army Group Centre's) resources for the final, ultimate onslaught on Moscow', it had been decided, Army Groups South and North would have to make do with their own resources. For should Moscow not be attained the war-gamers foresaw 'a long drawn-out war beyond the capacity of the German Armed Forces to wage'.

Hitler, pressured even by the normally docile Jodl, wavered. Directive 34, issued on 30 July, postponed '*for the moment* the further tasks and objectives laid down (for Panzer Groups 2 and 3) in Directive 33'.

This procrastination on the Führer's part formed the background to the Novy Borrisov meeting of 4 August. The generals all clamoured for permission to continue the advance on Moscow. Hitler spoke forcibly of the need to take Leningrad, the Ukraine and the Crimea, but did not commit himself either way. He then flew off for his rendezvous with destiny on the Rastenburg airfield. Two days later Halder began to supervise the drafting of an operational plan for the capture of Moscow.

This was not a straightforward task, for the Germans' room for manoeuvre was already severely limited. Halder could not merely sanction a headlong charge towards the capital. That would have been as suicidal as continuing to advance slowly on a broad front.

The first, most obvious, limiting factor was the current disposition of the German and Soviet armies. In the central sector conditions were superficially favourable. During the first week of August both Hoth and Guderian's groups had taken strides to by-pass the heavy Red Army concentrations in the Yelna area. Hoth's reconnaissance units were approaching Rzhev, Guderian's forces had taken Roslavl and were firmly astride the road that ran through it towards Moscow. Luftwaffe reconnaissance reported that behind the Soviet line in this sector there were virtually no reserves. A breakthrough in depth would present few problems to the armoured spearheads of a renewed German advance.

But there would be problems, further back, in the rear flanks of such an advance. Here, in the Velikiye Luki and Gomel areas, there had been a build-up of Soviet strength. To charge forward towards Moscow would further stretch the German forces covering these threatened sectors. Army Group Centre did not have the strength both to advance *and* protect its own flanks. Units from the other two army groups would have to perform the latter task.

In the north the flow of battle provided Halder with a ready-made solution. On 6 August the Red Army held a line from Lake Ilmen to the town

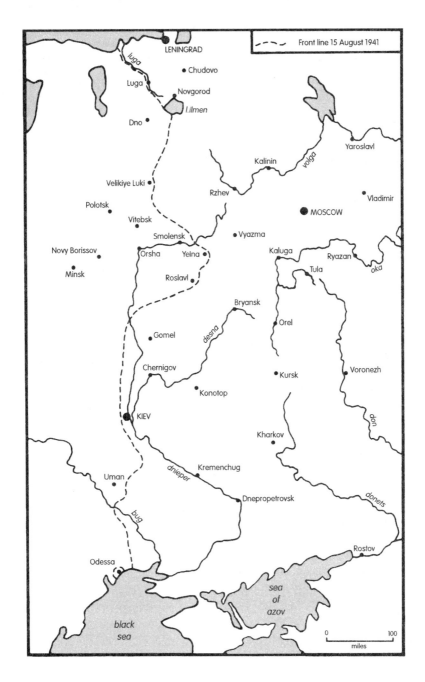

Front line 15 August 1941

LENINGRAD
Chudovo
luga
Luga
Novgorod
l.ilmen
Dno

Kalinin
Yaroslavl
volga

Velikiye Luki
Rzhev
Vladimir

Polotsk
Vitebsk
MOSCOW

Smolensk
Vyazma

Novy Borissov
Orsha   Yelna
Kaluga
Ryazan
oka

Minsk
Roslavl
Tula

Bryansk

Gomel
desna
Orel

Chernigov
Kursk
Voronezh

Konotop

KIEV
don

Kharkov

Kremenchug
dnieper

Uman
Dnepropetrovsk
donets

bug

Rostov

Odessa

sea
of
azov

black
sea

0   100
miles

I. The Eastern Front: 15 August 1941

of Luga and then down the Luga river to the Baltic coast. Here the terrain – mostly marshland and forest – was most unsuitable for the panzers, and for several weeks Höppner's Panzer Group 4 had been bogged down in positional warfare. Then on 12 August the Soviet Thirty-fourth Army launched an attack in the region south of Lake Ilmen, and one of Höppner's two corps, the 56th under General Manstein, was detached from the Luga front to deal with it. Within a few days it had done so. More to the point, 56th Panzer Corps was now ideally deployed to form the northern wing of the drive on Moscow.

In the south no such solutions presented themselves. The armoured fist of Army Group South, Kleist's Panzer Group 1, was moving away from Army Group Centre. A decisive encirclement of Soviet forces had just been completed in the Uman region, and Kleist's spearhead was now flowing south-eastwards down the land-corridor between the Bug and lower Dnieper rivers. Behind them the huge garrison of Kiev still held out against Sixth Army; further north the Soviet Fifth Army around Chernigov threatened the northern and southern flanks of Army Groups South and Centre respectively. This was a potentially dangerous situation for the Germans, and the dangers were not greatly lessened by Soviet Fifth Army's voluntary withdrawal across the Desna river in mid-August. Clearly the gap between Army Groups Centre and South had to be filled.

All this was basic strategy, second nature to the mandarins of the German General Staff. One did not advance without securing one's flanks. But Halder, unlike Hitler, did not exaggerate the problem. He intended to solve it, not let it dictate his overall strategy. One of Kleist's three panzer corps would be brought back and placed under the temporary command of Sixth Army. The newly-strengthened Army would extend its control northwards to establish a firm connection with Second Army, the southernmost formation of Army Group Centre. This shifting of Army Group South's centre of gravity away from the Ukrainian steppe would probably limit the prospects of conquest in that area, but it was unavoidable if the march on the capital was to succeed. Rather Moscow and no Ukraine than Ukraine and no Moscow. For the moment the Germans could not have both.

While Halder was thus absorbed choosing 'ends' the rest of the German Army was endeavouring to gather the 'means'. It had now been campaigning for seven weeks, longer than in France, in conditions much more wearing to both men and machines. The tanks had been worn down by the bad 'roads', their engines clogged with the ubiquitous dust; the wheeled vehicles had in many cases simply jolted themselves to pieces. An enormous flow of replacement parts and fuel was required to keep this motorised army moving, more enormous than the German transport facilities could cope with. By mid-August supply was running well below demand.

The main stumbling-block was the wider gauge of the Soviet railways. The Germans could only keep the Warsaw-Polotsk line running with the small number of engines and amount of rolling stock captured in the opening week of the attack. The rest of the railways had to be converted to the German gauge, and this would take time. Although the engineers worked around the clock to re-lay the tracks as far as Gomel, Orsha and Dno, the supplies reaching Army Group Centre in the first week of August were quite inadequate for the provisioning of a major offensive. A report from the Quartermaster General's office on 6 August reached the conclusion that a simultaneous attack by three armies on the central section was out of the question, and that even simultaneous operations by the two panzer groups would be difficult to supply. Clearly there had to be a pause of two or three weeks' duration for resting, refitting and the accumulation of essential supplies.

The more amenable supply/transport situation in Army Group North's sector further encouraged Halder in his decision to place the centre of gravity of the Moscow offensive north of the Smolensk-Moscow highway. Certainly the Valdai Hills were not ideal terrain for panzer warfare, but since an attack in that area would both dissipate the northern flank threat and be easy to supply, the disadvantages would have to be accepted. Manstein 56th Panzer Corps, now reinforced with 8th Panzer Division from Reinhardt's Corps and placed under Panzer Group 3 command, would advance eastward along the southern shores of Lake Ilmen and on to the main Leningrad-Moscow road before turning south-eastwards towards the capital. The attack would begin on 23 August.

Two days later the rest of Army Group Centre would follow suit. The other two corps of Hoth's Panzer Group 3 would strike north-eastwards towards Rzhev. From there one would continue northwards to meet Manstein's, and thus enclose several Soviet armies in a pocket around Ostashkov. The other would turn towards Moscow on the Volokamsk road as soon as conditions permitted. Guderian's Panzer Group 2 would not advance on the Bryansk-Kaluga axis envisaged in the original plan, but would pinch out the strong Soviet forces in the Yelna region with Fourth Army help and then advance astride the Vyazma and Yukhnov roads towards Moscow. Behind these panzer forces Fourth, Ninth and Sixteenth Armies (the latter on loan from Army Group North) would move forward to pick up the prisoners and tie down the ground. Halder sent out the operational orders on 14 August.

They would come as no surprise to the troops of Army Group Centre, who unlike their Führer had never considered any other objectives. Already the signs '*Moskau 240 kilometren*' were pointing the way. Morale among the troops was high, for the end was in sight. 'Moscow before the snow falls – home before Christmas' ran the popular slogan. It occurred to few that the one did not necessarily imply the other.

II

On 3 July, with the opening *blitzkrieg* twelve days old, Stalin had spoken to the Soviet people. 'Comrades, citizens, brothers and sisters, fighters of our Army and Navy! I am speaking to you, my friends!' he began. The unprecedented intimacy of this introduction underlined, as nothing else could have done, the desperation of the Soviet Union's situation. These words ushered in a new reality. Of occupied territories, of forming home guards and partisan units, of scorching the earth in the invader's path. Of total war.

As July unfolded the enemy pressed forward. All along an eight-hundred-mile front from the Baltic to the Black Sea the Red Army either died, retreated or marched west in long broken lines towards the German maltreatment camps. The towns mentioned in the official Soviet communiqués drifted steadily eastward across the maps, the first reports of German atrocities hot on their heels.

But towards the end of that horrifying month the unstoppable advance seemed, for the moment at least, to have been stopped. In the area of Smolensk the line was holding, and the inhabitants of Moscow, two hundred miles further to the east, breathed a nervous sigh of relief.

In the capital conditions were hard but not yet harsh. Strict rationing had been introduced in mid-July, and basic items like food and cigarettes were harder to come by for those in the less privileged categories. But restaurants and theatres remained open, the latter as a showcase for the burgeoning trade in patriotic plays, poems and songs. Moscow's formidable anti-aircraft defences took a fair toll of the nightly air raids and little damage had yet been done to the city. At night many slept in the recently completed Metro while the sky above the capital was awash with searchlight beams and barrage balloons.

In the Kremlin there was too much knowledge for optimism. Stavka, the supreme Soviet military-political command, met in the ancient rooms and received news of the latest disasters. There were many of them. The Red

Army had been surprised, outmanoeuvred, outclassed and outfought. Warned by the British, by its own commanders at the front, by its agents round the world, the Soviet leadership had applied Nelson's blind-eye technique with spectacularly disastrous results. The Air Force had been cut to ribbons on the ground, whole armies like lumbering mammoths had been surrounded and reduced by the German masters of the panzer art. When given the opportunity to attack, Red Army formations had charged like incoherent Light Brigades down the muzzles of the German guns. Defensively inept, offensively gallant to the point of suicide, the front line of the Red Army had practically ceased to exist.

Who was responsible for this disaster? Not the ordinary Red Army soldier. Though lacking the experience and tactical skills of his German counterpart, though frequently armed with inferior equipment, he had fought, and continued to fight, with a reckless bravery that the Germans found thoroughly depressing. Not the front-line officer either. No more than his French, British or Polish counterparts, could he have been expected to grasp the essence of panzer warfare overnight.

If anyone was responsible it was the Supreme Command. Or more simply, Stalin. Firstly for allowing the German Army to take his own by surprise, secondly for removing those leaders who did understand armoured warfare - most notably Tukhachevskiy - in the purges of 1937-8. But, these undoubted mistakes notwithstanding, it is impossible to avoid the conclusion that the fundamental reason for the Soviet defeat in the summer of 1941 was the different sense of priorities held by the political leaderships of Germany and the Soviet Union. If one state was devoting its energies to conquest and another to national construction there was an excellent chance that the former would prove a more efficient conqueror.

Stavka had to learn the hard way. Though some measures could be implemented immediately - generals like Rokossovsky, whose excellent military careers had been cut short for political reasons, could be pulled out of the Siberian concentration camps and given their uniforms back - the thorough reorganisation, re-equipping and retraining of the Red Army would take a great deal of time. And time was extremely precious.

In August it must have seemed that those lessons that needed to be learned in a hurry were hardly being learned at all. A further series of frontal attacks were launched and, like bears tumbling into pits, Thirty-fourth Army near Lake Ilmen, Twenty-eighth Army around Roslavl, and Thirteenth and Fiftieth Armies between Gomel and Krichev disappeared into historical limbo. All these attacks took place in those rear-flank areas of the projected German advance; their failure eased Halder's anxieties considerably. Only around Yelna in the central sector did the Red Army battle the Germans to an honourable draw through August, and this apparent success was to prove as fatal as the failures. The leaders in the Kremlin interpreted it, wrongly, as evidence of the continuing viability of linear defence lines, and proceeded to construct two more between Yelna and the capital. The first of these, under General Zhukov, contained five fresh armies on a line from Ostashkov to Kirov; the second consisted merely of earthworks dug by workers brought out from Moscow. On the front itself the eight armies of Timoshenko's West Front held a line from Lake Seliger to Yelna. Further south the two armies of Yeremenko's new Bryansk Front were to cover the Bryansk-Orel sector, which outdated Soviet intelligence had earmarked as Guderian's probable approach route.

All these lines were desperately thin. The potential Soviet manpower was proverbially inexhaustible, but armies need more than manpower. Only so many men could be trained and armed in the time available, and the weaponry situation was adversely affected in the short term by the removal of the armament industry to the east. The one trained and equipped Soviet army as yet uncommitted against the Germans – the thirty-division-strong Far Eastern Army – could not be withdrawn from its positions in the Maritime Provinces and along the Manchurian border until Stavka's agent in Tokyo, Richard Sorge, had confirmation of the rumoured Japanese intention to strike south rather than north in the coming months.

So, proverbially inexhaustible or not, the Red Army was outnumbered in front of Moscow. Through August Stavka waited. For the strength at its disposal to grow, for a message from Sorge, for the first welcome signs of autumn. And for the Germans to renew their attack along the road to Moscow.

III

As the sun rose slowly above the pines on 23 August, the strengthened 56th Panzer Corps moved forward from its starting line south of Lake Ilmen. There were no roads to speak of, and 8th Panzer struck east along the railway line towards Lychkovo. Some ten miles to the north 6th Panzer and 3rd Motorised Division were directed along marshy forest tracks towards Kresttsy on the main Leningrad-Moscow road. A similar distance to the south the motorised SS division 'Totenkopf' covered the Corps' southern flank against the strong enemy formations in the Demyansk-Lake Seliger area. Progress was slow but steady, the terrain offering considerably more

30

opposition than the enemy, who was still struggling to fill the gap left by Thirty-fourth Army's recent destruction.

By nightfall on 24 August 6th Panzer was astride the main road and 8th Panzer, after a short bitter engagement with a company of Soviet T-34 tanks, had taken Lychkovo and was rolling on towards Valdai. An improvised Soviet counter-attack along the eastern shore of Lake Ilmen was beaten off without difficulty by 3rd Motorised.

The following day 8th Panzer crashed into Valdai. The town, despite some recent attention from the Stukas, looked relatively normal. There was the obligatory statue of Lenin, the small cluster of administration buildings, the lines of wooden houses stretching from the centre out to the forest. Barely an hour later the leading units of 6th Panzer appeared along the road from the north. This division was directed east to take and hold the important railway junction of Bologoye; 8th Panzer was to continue south-eastwards along the main road towards Vyshniy Volochek.

In the Kremlin the threat posed by Manstein's Corps was underestimated. For days an argument had been raging as to the most probable point of the enemy's forthcoming breakthrough attempt. Opinions were divided fairly evenly between the Moscow highway and Bryansk-Orel sectors; all eyes were watching to see which it would be. Reports of a major armoured attack south of Lake Ilmen were discounted. It was only the enemy making the most of his victory over the unfortunate Thirty-fourth Army; the local Red Army commander was clearly exaggerating the scale of the attack.

By 25 August the danger was too visible to brush off so lightly, but by this time Stavka was otherwise occupied. At dawn on that day the rest of Army Group Centre, close on a million men and two thousand tanks, moved into the attack. In the Belyy area and on the main Moscow road Hoth's tanks burst through the Soviet line with all the concentrated power of long practice. 57th Panzer Corps attacked north-east towards its intended junction with Manstein, 39th Panzer Corps motored east towards Vyazma for a rendezvous with Guderian. The latter's tanks had broken through the Soviet positions on the Roslavl-Yukhnov road, with one corps punching deep into the rear of the Soviet concentrations around Yelna. The largely immobile Red Army units continued to fight hard against the slow push of Fourth Army against their front, but could do little to affect the pincers closing behind them. By 28 August Model's 3rd Panzer Division had made contact with the leading elements of 7th Panzer at Losimo and the ring was closed. Inside the pocket were the major parts of three Soviet armies.

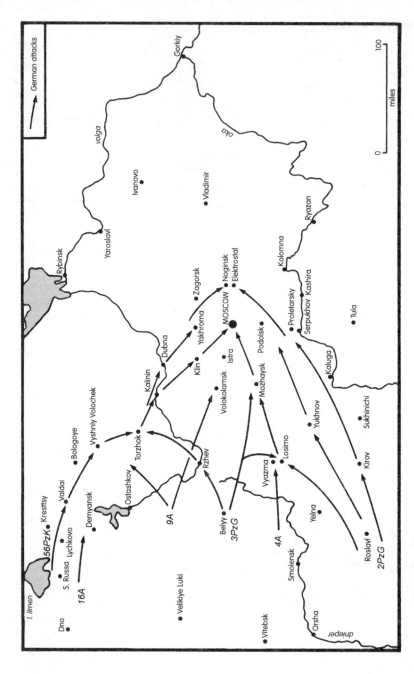

2. The Fall of Moscow

A similar ring was tightening on another five in the Ostashkov region. By the afternoon of 27 August Rzhev had fallen, and only sixty-five miles separated the closing pincers. The terrain and the poor quality of the roads continued to give the Germans trouble but the enemy, for the most part fully engaged by the infantry armies, was conspicuously absent in the rear areas. The tanks roamed through empty countryside. 'It was like France, only with less roads and more trees,' as one panzer captain put it. On 31 August the pincers met five miles south of Torzhok. Two-thirds of the Soviet forces before Moscow were now trapped in the Yelna-Vyazma and Ostashkov pockets.

Through the first week of September the German forces concentrated on reducing the encircled areas, opposing break-out attempts, and herding the surrendering Red Army soldiers towards the west. Of course the pockets covered immense areas and many Red Army units were able to keep out of the German clutches. But those which did escape, either by breaking through the thin lines to the east or by melting into the convenient forests, were in no state to interfere with the continuation of the German advance. The roads to Moscow were open.

On 2 September Zhukov was appointed Supreme Commander of the forces covering the capital. He did what he could, sending what reserves he could find into the last lines covering the city. But they were few and, most significantly, their contingency orders stressed that they were to fall back to the north and south of the capital, not into it. The fall of Moscow was beginning to look inevitable. On 4 September Stalin received the British Ambassador Stafford Cripps in the Kremlin. He seemed, according to Cripps,

> unbalanced by the tremendous strain of events. One moment he was accusing both us and the Americans of deserting him, the next moment he was stressing the importance of the aluminium shipments we were sending for the continuation of the war. After telling me that once Moscow had fallen there was no line short of the Volga that could be defended, he went on to talk with great excitement of a planned counter-attack in the south. There was none of that cold solidity which I had always assumed to be his habitual self.

The mood of the populace was also growing more apprehensive by the day. News that there was 'heavy fighting in the direction of Kalinin' meant only one thing to those trained through the years to read between the official lines. Kalinin had fallen; the enemy was less than a hundred miles distant. When *Pravda* talked about the 'terrible danger' facing the country the citizens of Moscow knew what was meant. And there were other clues than those provided by the newspapers. All over the city industrial machinery was being dismantled for evacuation or wired for destruction; from the Kremlin courtyard the black smoke of burning documents was drifting up and out across the sky.

Through the second week of September the enemy drew nearer. Manstein's corps captured the Volga bridge at Kalinin intact and fought its way down the road to Klin. Schmidt's 39th Panzer Corps crashed into Mozhaysk. Guderian's tanks took Sukhinichi and bore down on Kaluga. In the north, the centre and the south, like a tunnel looming to engulf a train, the German panzer armies closed in on the Soviet capital.

On 10 September it was announced that the Government, the Diplomatic Corps and as much as possible of Moscow's cultural and scientific assets were being evacuated to Kuybyshev on the Volga. No mention was made of Stalin's whereabouts, but it soon became known that his predecessor's embalmed body had been removed from its mausoleum for transportation to an unknown destination.

These measures were interpreted by some as the first stage of Moscow's abandonment, and those not privileged to share in the exodus sought self-preservation in less dignified ways. Shops were looted by citizens in the first throes of starvation; lorryloads of food were overturned and ransacked. The approach of the Germans induced many to burn their Party cards, and handbills suddenly appeared denouncing communism and the Jews. Stalin's portrait disappeared from many apartment walls.

The government acted decisively to quell this premature mutiny. Moscow was pronounced a part of the military zone of operations, a State of Emergency declared. NKVD squads roamed through the city shooting 'suspects' with little or no compunction.

Amidst this spreading disorder the last desperate attempts were made to provide for the capital's defence. Women, old men and children were herded to the outskirts and told to dig; young men were pressed, some willingly and some not, into workers' battalions for the defence of the main roads leading into the city proper. In Alexandrov Park, beneath the Kremlin wall, office-workers in suits practised bayonet charges. Commandeered cabs and buses carried regular units westward through the city towards the approaching storm.

By 14 September the Mozhaysk 'line' had been pierced on all the major axes and comprehensively outflanked from the north. Even the beginning of the autumn rains, which for hours, sometimes days, immobilised the German columns, could not stem the tide. Had the Germans been further from the city of decision these setbacks might have weakened their morale, but with Moscow so close it would take more than the odd shower to dampen their determination.

On the southern flank Guderian's forces had reached the banks of the Oka river on a front stretching from Kaluga to Serpukhov, and were striking east between Podolsk and Proletarskiy. Only on 15–17 September did problems arise, in the form of an attack by Timoshenko's still viable Bryansk Front armies in the region of Kirov. But this was a makeshift affair, born of desperation and conducted as such. The charging Red Army units, including cavalry, were cut down in swathes by the motorised troops deployed on Guderian's trailing flank. For the architect of the panzer arm, up with his spearhead a hundred miles further east, the matter was no more than a passing concern. He was headed for Noginsk, forty miles east of Moscow, and a meeting with Manstein.

On the northern flank the bridge at Dubna was captured by a *coup de main*, the defenders mistaking a panzer column led by captured Soviet tanks for retreating Red Army units. Then, with 8th Panzer leading, the Germans moved down the east bank of the Moscow-Volga canal to Yakhroma, before veering east towards Zagorsk to cut the Moscow-Yaroslavl railway. Now only two lines remained open between the capital and the East.

On the evening of 18 September Zhukov reported to Stalin. The Soviet leader, despite the rumours to the contrary flying round Moscow, was still in the Kremlin. Now Zhukov told him, and Stavka, that the city could not be held, and that he wished to order his remaining forces east to a line Yaroslavl-Ryazan. He was allowed to do so.

At this meeting Zhukov noticed that Stalin seemed to have recovered his former 'calm resolution'. Though reluctantly accepting that the Red Army's preservation was more important than Moscow, the Soviet leader was determined that the struggle should go on within the city limits. The NKVD battalions and the worker units would harass the Germans street by street.

The situation in the Ukraine was then discussed at length, and it was agreed that no further withdrawals should be made unnecessarily. Only the certainty of encirclement was justification for retreat. It was also decided that Stavka should leave the capital for Gorkiy while it was still possible. The option of surrender was not discussed. The members of Stavka left the meeting at 03.15 on 19 September and went home to pack their bags.

Three days and six hours later the leading units of 18th Panzer joined hands with the spearhead of 8th Panzer in the industrial village of Elektrostal, four miles south of Noginsk on the Moscow-Gorkiy railway. The previous day a special train bearing Stalin, the Stavka staff and the body of Vladimir Ilych Lenin had passed through the same spot. Moscow, though not yet fallen, was encircled and falling. In far-off Germany radio listeners were advised to wait for a special announcement.

IV

Before the outbreak of war Moscow's population had been in excess of four million, but by 22 September the calls to arms, the evacuation of industry and the exodus of the previous weeks had reduced the number of those residing in the city to roughly half that number. Now those two million people locked inside the beleaguered city had to decide whether or not to resist the imminent German occupation. Stalin had certainly decreed that they should, but Stalin was probably gone. Large detachments of the NKVD were certainly in evidence, but from the pragmatist's point of view they would prove somewhat easier to disarm than the Germans.

Nevertheless there were many prepared to continue the fight, to make of Moscow another 'Madrid'. The heritage of the revolution had deeper roots than the Germans suspected, and they had been given new life by the approach of what *Pravda* called 'the riffraff of ruined Europe'. In the factory suburbs of Moscow the German Army would learn that there was more to socialism than Stalin.

Not all who fought did so from such convictions. Some fought out of fear of the long-term consequences should they not, many had no other motivation than the momentum of the struggle. Most of them had volunteered to join the battalions raised from the Moscow working-class in the preceding fortnight; it was these battalions who would form the organisational core of the resistance, manning the improvised defence lines which stretched along the boulevards ringing the inner city.

There were others who opposed the decision to make a battleground of Moscow. Some did so from nobler motives than others. Surely it made more sense, they argued, to continue the struggle further east than to sacrifice the city and its inhabitants for no obvious military advantage. Those who wished to go on fighting should slip out of the city during the night, cross the fields and break through the thin German line to the east, and rejoin the Red Army.

Such arguments made sense to those who believed in ultimate Soviet victory; it appealed little to those who doubted such an outcome. They were much more impressed by the departure of Stalin, the media and government apparati and the Red Army than by the possibilities of death and glory. There were cries that the war had lasted long enough already. Who would benefit from Moscow's sacrifice? Certainly not the Muscovites. No, only Stalin and the hated party, now safe and warm in Gorkiy, would benefit. And they were doomed anyway, doomed by the tide of history they had so often invoked to excuse their cruelties. It would be wise to forget Stalin and his cronies, wise to rehearse heartfelt declarations of gratitude for the German liberators, and to work with these new masters for Russia's reintroduction into the family of civilised nations.

And of course there were many, perhaps the majority, of Moscow's inhabitants who intended neither to fight nor to welcome the Wehrmacht. They listened to the gunfire growing louder, they hid food in the cellars. They hoped for the best, expected the worst.

Soon they would know. To the east of the capital the Panzer Groups held the ring, to the west the infantry units of Fourth Army fought their way closer to the city. By 29 September there was fighting in the western and north-western suburbs, the next day the Germans broke through the outermost defensive ring on the edge of the built-up area. The defending forces were soon broken up into isolated units, but these continued to contest bitterly what ground they held. In the industrial suburbs of Kuntsevo and Koroshevo the workers fought for each square yard of their factories, and German casualties were high. In the boulevards of central Moscow there was less fighting, mostly lone snipers blasted out with grenades and mortar fire.

The remnants of the worker battalions retreated to the subways, to bomb sites, railway yards and the factory complexes of the south-eastern sector. In the huge State Motor Works four hundred workers were to hold out for four weeks before being wiped out to the last man and woman. Other small areas of resistance endured almost as long.

But these were isolated pockets, and overall the city was militarily secured as early as 8 October. Not long after this date the 'lions' of the Army began relinquishing responsibility to the jackals who followed in their wake. The *einsatzgruppen* began combing the city for Jews and communist officials, and received not a little assistance from Muscovites eager both to pay off old scores and to ingratiate themselves with the conquering Germans. Moscow passed out of the grim light of the war, and into the grimmer darkness of Nazi occupation.

V

In the weeks prior to Moscow's fall, Rundstedt's Army Group South had been making unexpected progress in the Ukraine. Halder had feared that this Army Group, which was outnumbered by more than two to one, would have to remain primarily on the defensive. However, some desperate Soviet attacks had presented Rundstedt with opportunities which were impossible to ignore.

After the Uman encirclement battle in mid-August one of Kleist's panzer corps had secured a bridgehead across the Dnieper around Kremenchug. This force offered no great threat to the Soviet position but Stavka, in the throes of the battle before Moscow, decided that every attempt should be made to distract the Germans from their central preoccupation. 38th Army was ordered to throw Kleist's panzers back across the river.

It was cut to ribbons. The panzers moved north through this new and inviting gap and into the rear of the Soviet forces in and around Kiev. Rundstedt, seeing his opportunity, pushed Mackensen's Panzer Corps through a weak link in the Soviet line south of Gomel, and south to join Kleist. For a few days a giant encirclement seemed possible but for once Stavka acted swiftly, ordering a withdrawal of their forces to a line from Bryansk through Konotop to Dnepropetrovsk. Only two armies were trapped when the converging pincers met at Priluki on 15 September. Army Group South disposed of these and moved slowly forward to the new line.

So by the beginning of October the Germans' situation was looking much healthier than Halder might have expected. It now seemed as if the major objectives laid down for *Barbarossa* – Moscow, Leningrad, the Ukraine – would be attained before the winter set in.

In the central sector the prime objective had already been achieved, and Halder saw no point in extending the central drive to the east, for all Manstein and Guderian's noisy canvassing. Gorkiy could probably be captured, but to what purpose? It would be better to leave Army Group Centre's weary infantry on the defensive. Then the trains hitherto engaged in transporting the pressing needs of day-to-day combat could be used to bring forward the winter equipment that was sitting in the Warsaw marshalling yards.

The panzer groups would naturally have no such respite. They would be needed for operations in the north and south, for the capture of objectives more worthy of their attention that Gorkiy. Panzer Group 3, once again comprising only 39th and 57th Panzer Corps, would be sent north for the attack on Leningrad. Panzer Group 2, which now included Manstein's 56th

Panzer Corps, was to hold the line east of Moscow until relieved by the infantry, and to extent it south-eastwards in the direction of Ryazan. One strengthened corps, to be known as *Gruppe Vietinghoff*, was to strike south along the Tula-Orel road into the rear of the Soviet armies facing Army Group South. Mackensen's Panzer Corps was to drive north-eastwards to meet *Gruppe Vietinghoff*. The rest of Kleist's Panzer Group 1 was to punch through the Red Army line in the Sumy-Konotop area and drive south-east behind Kharkov, before moving on into the Donbass industrial region.

Halder did not expect these operations to proceed smoothly. There were still a lot of Russians in uniform, and conditions were deteriorating rapidly with the approach of winter. But for once he overestimated the enemy. All the extant Soviet accounts agree that in these crucial weeks which followed Moscow's fall the Red Army came close to breaking. In order to avoid doing so it bent. According to the Soviet writer Moskalenko, then fighting in the Kursk sector:

> We thought: 'Either the war is over and we are fighting on for no reason, or it will be fought to a finish to the east of Moscow.' None of us considered surrendering – the way the Germans treated prisoners was no secret – but only a few diehards, in those dreadful weeks, wanted to fight and die where they stood. Most of us just wanted to walk away from it all. And we did, in good order, to the east.

Only the defenders of Leningrad were denied such an option. In the first week of November, over frost-hardened ground, Panzer Group 3 fought its way north through Chudovo to the southern shores of Lake Ladoga. Panzer Group 4, reinforced by the arrival of 2nd Panzer from OKH reserve, pushed forward along the Gulf of Finland coast towards Leningrad itself. The Finns, spurred on by the fall of Moscow, abandoned their reluctance to cross the old frontier. They advanced down the western shore of Lake Ladoga, joined hands with Hoth's Panzers, and ended any hopes the Leningraders had of using the freezing lake as a lifeline to the outside world. By 13 November the city was completely cut off from the rest of the Soviet Union .

Eighteenth Army moved in hopefully for the kill. It was not to be a quick or an easy one. Leningrad was doomed, but its defenders were not about to throw in an unused towel. This was not Moscow. This was the 'cradle of the revolution'. There would be no surrender.

So for three months Eighteenth Army fought its way street by street, house by house, through the spiritual centre of Soviet communism. Special units charged across the ice to do battle with the sailors of the Kronstadt Naval Base. The toll was appalling. According to Professor Hoddle in his

Leningrad: Death of a City, over half of Eighteenth Army's troops were injured or killed in the eleven-week battle. Casualties among the defenders were higher still, and there can be few who do not know the fate of the 'survivors' of the battle for Leningrad. The city and its inhabitants died, but the heirs of Lenin, Trotsky and Zinoviev exacted a high price from their conquerors.

South of Moscow the Wehrmacht was having an easier time. Two Soviet armies in the Bryansk sector failed to withdraw fast enough and were caught by the closing pincers of Mackenson's Corps and *Gruppe Vietinghoff*. In the far south Eleventh Army overran the Soviet defences on the Perekop Isthmus and occupied all the Crimea save the important fortress of Sevastopol. In the central Ukraine Kleist's main force broke through to Oboyan and swung southwards behind Kharkov. By the beginning of November the panzers were streaming down the right bank of the Donetz and into the Donbass industrial region. It was only on the Mius river that the panzer spearhead, weakened by the weather, breakdowns and its over-extended supply-lines, was halted by freshly-arrived Siberian troops.

The German military leadership was satisfied. There would be much to show the Führer when he recovered. Moscow and the Ukraine had fallen, Leningrad would soon follow. According to their calculations sixty per cent of Soviet industry had been overrun. Half of the Soviet population now lived in the lengthening shadow of the hooked cross. The Red Army was all but broken.

Perhaps there would be no Russian Compiègne, no cosy railway carriage in which the conquests and the deaths could be translated into those cold words so beloved by the politicians. But it hardly mattered. The German troops settled down to endure a winter of occupation, many of them in the relative warmth of the larger Soviet cities. The coming spring would see an end to it, once and for all. The shouts of defiance emanating from Gorkiy could be safely dismissed as empty rhetoric.

VI

Churchill was more hopeful. On 9 October he had spoken to the House of Commons in characteristic vein:

> The twisted crosses now flaunt themselves along the streets of the Russian capital. Yet, for all this, it would be a rash and foolish man who would assume the defeat of Russia. Perhaps the Nazi leaders, during those long cold Berlin nights,

the sound of British bombs loud in their ears, will remember with a chill that Napoleon too entered Moscow on the threshold of winter . . .

Stalin was also making the most of Napoleonic parallels. On 17 October he had spoken to the Soviet people for the first time since the fall of the capital. Again they listened to the slow, toneless voice, its Georgian accent more pronounced than ever, describe the tragic situation of the Soviet Union in unnervingly matter-of-fact terms. Stalin talked of huge losses, but claimed that the enemy's losses were larger still. He admitted the vast extent of the territories conquered, but reminded his audience of the still vaster expanses still available. He appealed to national pride, invoking those great Russians of the past whom Trotsky had once consigned to 'the dustbin of history'. He quoted Kutuzov's dispatch to the Tsar in 1812:

> The loss of Moscow does not mean that Russia is lost. I regard it as my duty to save my army from destruction, to safeguard its means of life and to ensure the inevitable destruction of the enemy even if this entails the evacuation of Moscow. It is therefore my intention to retire through Moscow along the Ryazan road.

'We have taken the same road,' said Stalin, somewhat inaccurately. Doubtless it would be a long and a hard one. But with this enemy - here he quoted a number of typical German *untermensch* references - there could be no dealings. Peace would only come with victory.

Chapter 2
PREMATURE CRUSADE

A dram of discretion is worth a pound of wisdom.

German proverb

I

On the evening of 16 September 1941 three fast Italian ocean liners slipped out of Taranto harbour. They were carrying fresh troops and equipment for the Axis armies in North Africa. It was a five-hundred-mile voyage to the safety of Tripoli harbour.

The liners' departure was noted by a British submarine standing watch outside Taranto, and the information relayed to Naval HQ Malta. In the early hours of 17 September the submarine *Upholder* ducked under the Italian destroyer screen and sent two of the liners to the bottom. Yet again the fallibility of Rommel's Mediterranean supply route had been crushingly underlined.

This was only one of many such disasters during the autumn of 1941 but for Admiral Weichold, German liaison officer with the Italian Naval Staff in Rome, it was the proverbial last straw. The losses at sea were becoming untenable, yet his superiors in Berlin seemed either unwilling or unable to take any measures to rectify the situation. In a desperate bid to elicit some sort of positive response Weichold lavishly doctored the loss statistics, appended his opinions, and dispatched the whole package to the Naval Command (Oberkommando der Kriegsmarine or OKM) in Berlin. It arrived on Grand-Admiral Raeder's desk on the morning of Wednesday 24 September, a propitious moment. The next day Raeder was to attend a conference of the Reich's war leaders, called by acting-Führer Goering to decide the future course of German strategy.

The conference was held at Goering's Karinhall residence in eastern Germany. The Reich Marshal was enjoying his stint as Supreme Commander and had no intention of meeting his fellow service chiefs on ground of their choosing. Amidst the looted art treasures of occupied Europe and the baronial opulence of Karinhall he expected to enjoy a definite psychological advantage.

On the morning of the 25th the other leaders arrived at the airstrip ten miles away, and were driven through the forests to Goering's ideal home by the side of the small Wuckersee. Those arriving included Jodl and Paulus for the OKW, Brauchitsch and Halder for the OKH, Raeder for the Navy, Jeschonnek as Goering's Luftwaffe second-in-command, and Minister of Armament Production Dr Todt. They were given coffee in a reception room whose walls seemed literally plastered with paintings, and then led into the dining-hall that had been prepared for the conference.

Despite the long history of personal disagreements affecting virtually all those present the prevailing atmosphere was reportedly 'workmanlike'. Halder noted in his diary, with characteristic acerbity, that 'the mood of the conference was better attuned to the matters in hand than to the preposterous surroundings'. Halder of course was always something of a foreigner to the real Third Reich, which here at Karinhall reached a rare level of warped self-expression, blending feudalism, *nouveau riche* vulgarity and technical expertise. Outside the Hall, Goering's newly-inherited SS guards stood watch among the extensive lily-ponds.

Inside the conference room Brauchitsch opened the proceedings with a report, written by Halder, on the current situation of *Fall Barbarossa*. It was as thorough and detailed as any of Halder's reports, but the gist was relatively simple. The Soviet Union had not admitted defeat, and was unlikely to do so while it commanded an army and an industrial base east of Moscow, but its offensive capacity was now virtually non-existent, and was likely to remain extremely limited throughout 1942. As things now stood Halder foresaw few difficulties in reaching the original objective of *Barbarossa* – a line from Archangel to Astrakhan – and in conquering the Caucasus during the spring and summer of 1942 with the forces presently available. It would be possible to withdraw limited air and armoured formations from the East for the duration of the winter months, perhaps even permanently.

Halder's report did not suggest alternative employment for those forces no longer vital to the outcome of the war in the East, but their possible deployment in the Mediterranean theatre had been discussed even before the invasion of the Soviet Union. In Directive 32, issued on 11 June 1941, the Führer had stated that 'after the destruction of the Soviet armed forces ... the struggle against British positions in the Mediterranean and Western

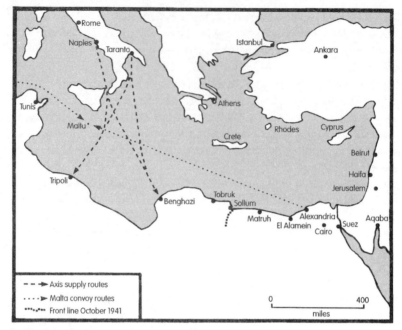

3. The Mediterranean Theatre

Asia will be continued by converging attacks launched from Libya through Egypt, from Bulgaria through Turkey, and in certain circumstances also from Transcaucasia through Iran.' These attacks were to be launched in November 1941.

This had been an over-optimistic forecast, as the report on *Fall Barbarossa*'s progress amply demonstrated. The way to the Caucasus was not yet clear, the forces necessary for operations against the still-uncommitted Turks were not yet available. The war against the British would have to be continued, for the time being, by the Axis forces in North Africa.

Here, however, there were problems. Raeder, with Weichold's report in his briefcase, proceeded to outline them. 'The situation as described (by Weichold) is untenable. Italian naval and air forces are incapable of providing adequate cover for the convoys ... The Naval Staff considers radical changes and immediate measures to remedy the situation imperative.'

Having thus struck a necessary note of urgency, the Grand-Admiral treated the assembled company to an abridged history of the German presence in the Mediterranean. He recalled how he and the Reich Marshal –

a nice diplomatic touch – had urged a greater concentration of strength in this theatre during the previous autumn, but had been unable to convince the Führer that such a course was the correct one. Hitler had wished, 'quite rightly', to deal with the Eastern threat first. Once the Russian colossus had been struck down, then, and only then, would the time have arrived for a decisive reckoning with the obstinate British. This he had told Raeder in May. Now, the Grand-Admiral argued, that time had arrived.

Raeder had done his homework. His bulging briefcase also contained a copy of the report submitted by General von Thoma in October 1940 on the situation in North Africa. Four panzer divisions, von Thoma had concluded, would suffice for a successful invasion of Egypt. General Rommel already had two at his disposal; he should be given a further panzer corps from the Eastern front. With such a force, Raeder submitted, Rommel could drive the British out of the Middle East.

Of course, the transportation and supply of these new units could not be undertaken in those prevailing circumstances described by Weichold. The island fortress of Malta must first be neutralised by air assault and then captured. This, he added, with a deferential glance in Goering's direction, was a task for the Luftwaffe. Here was a chance for its bomber squadrons and élite airborne units to write another page in their glorious history. The Navy, alas, could offer little assistance, but those U-boats which could be spared would be sent to the Mediterranean and the experience gained during the planning of 'Sea Lion' would be made available to those planning the invasion of Malta.

Raeder concluded with a review of the glittering prizes such a strategy would win. Malta's fall would lead to the capture of Egypt; the oil of the Middle East would then be there for the taking. The Mediterranean would become an Axis lake; the southern flank of the Reich would be forever secure. India would be within reach, particularly if satisfactory arrangements could be made with the Japanese at some future date. Britain, deprived of oil and empire, would be finished. America, without British help, would be unable to bring its resources to bear across the wide Atlantic. The war would be won.

None of this was particularly new, or welcome, to the OKH leaders, whose mental boundaries rarely stretched beyond the confines of continental Europe. All through 1941 they had been receiving complaints from Rommel about his supply problems, but as Halder in particular both distrusted these extra-continental activities and lacked confidence in the reckless Rommel the complaints had been happily shoved into the business-continually-pending tray. Now that the campaign in the East was all but over

Halder was reluctant to admit that the pending was over, and that this 'general gone stark mad' should be given new forces to 'fritter away'.

Still, the Chief of the General Staff had no positive alternatives to offer, and it was obviously inadvisable, as Raeder ironically interjected, to 'fritter away' the months of grace granted the Wehrmacht by its success in Russia. Halder retreated into negatives, acidly noting that he doubted the capability of the Luftwaffe and the Italians to wrest Malta from the British.

This was a psychological error in the grand General Staff tradition. Goering might not have risen to the bait of Raeder's flattery, but the Army's scarcely concealed derision was another matter. The Reich Marshal noted OKH's lack of ideas, quoted Führer Directive 32, and agreed with Raeder that he had all along been a strong supporter of a greater German commitment in the Mediterranean area. Malta would present no problem to the Luftwaffe, even with Italian assistance.

Jodl, who seems during these months to have transferred his dog-like devotion from the Führer to his deputy, concurred. Brauchitsch, as usual, went with the majority. The basic outline of Raeder's plan was accepted by the Conference.

Concrete decisions were then taken. The Navy would deploy an extra twenty U-boats in the Mediterranean; the Luftwaffe would bring Air Fleet 2 from Russia to support Air Fleet 10 in Sicily, Crete and Cyrenaica. OKH agreed to transfer a panzer corps from the Eastern front to North Africa, beginning at the end of November. General Student, who had commanded the airborne invasion of Crete, would travel with Goering and Jodl to Rome, to discuss the assault on Malta with Mussolini and his Chief of Staff General Cavallero. Strenuous efforts would be made to ensure that the island received no fresh supplies, and as the success or failure of British attempts to run in convoys from the east would largely depend on who held the Cyrenaican airfields, Rommel was to be given explicit instructions to take no offensive action that might result in their capture by the enemy. General Paulus was detailed to carry these instructions to Rommel in person.

The conference broke up, the leaders went for a walk around the lily-ponds. Raeder, aided and abetted by his habitual adversary Goering, had carried the day. The OKH leaders, though somewhat disgruntled, could find comfort in the fact that no one had challenged their handling of the war in the East. Only Admiral Doenitz, C-in-C U-boats, who was not invited to the meeting, found nothing to applaud in the Karinhall decisions. He considered the decision to move U-boats from the Atlantic to the Mediterranean the height of folly. And time would prove him right.

II

As the German service chiefs sat in comfort beneath Goering's chandeliers, Erwin Rommel was gazing down from his Storch reconnaissance plane at the vast expanse of the Western Desert. He had been in Africa for nine months, and in that time he had first pushed the British back four hundred miles to the Egyptian frontier and then repulsed Wavell's attempt to regain the lost ground by means of Operation 'Battleaxe'. The only blemish on this excellent record was the continuing presence of a British garrison in Tobruk, some seventy miles behind the front line.

Since June there had been a lull in the desert fighting, as each side sought to build up its strength; the British in order to succeed where 'Battleaxe' had failed, Rommel in order to capture Tobruk. In the meantime the Germans were laying a formidable minefield on the Sollum-Sidi Omar front line.

Rommel, though, had other preoccupations during this period. August seems to have been principally taken up with a campaign against the insect pests frequenting his headquarters. First mosquitoes, and then flies, took to pestering the panzer group commander. Fleas preferred the other officers, but the bed bugs were less particular. 'My bed is now standing in tins filled with water,' he wrote to his wife Lucie on 27 August. Three days later a more permanent solution was discovered. 'I've been free of the bugs ever since I had petrol poured over my iron bedstead, and had it set aflame. They must have been in the framework,' he triumphantly reported.

These may have been the General's most pressing problems, but they were not the only ones. A caravan *en route* from Germany for his use was sunk crossing the Mediterranean, along with some forty per cent of the other goods sent across from Italy in the months June to September. The plan for the attack on Tobruk gathered dust in Rommel's command vehicle as he waited for the arrival of the supplies necessary for its implementation.

Meanwhile, as Rommel well knew, supplies for the army facing his own were flowing into Egypt at a prodigious rate. An enemy attack could be expected sometime before the end of the year, and Rommel did not want the Tobruk garrison at his back when it came. He continued to prepare for its reduction, pestered OKH with complaints, and held on to his hopes that the British would not move first.

On 4 October General von Paulus arrived at Afrika Korps HQ with General Bastico, Rommel's nominal superior in North Africa. He brought news of the Karinhall Conference, of the decision to commit greater forces in North Africa and to attempt the capture of Malta. Rommel was pleased; he had been advocating as much for several months. He doubtless also understood Paulus's strict instructions not to risk Axis control of Cyrenaica, but was characteristically loth to abandon his intention of attacking Tobruk. Paulus did not specifically forbid him to do so, but in view of later events it seems certain that he reached the conclusion, during his two-day stay in the desert, that such an attack would constitute an unnecessary gamble. At any rate, three days after his visitors' departure Rommel received a direct order from Halder not to attack Tobruk. He was to remain on the defensive. Halder, hitherto deeply involved with events in Russia, seems to have taken this opportunity to re-establish his authority over the errant Rommel, a general whom he neither liked nor respected. But whatever his motives the decision was a sound one, as was soon to become apparent.

III

For over a century Great Britain had been staking a claim to at least a shared control of the Mediterranean Sea. The interests at stake had changed as the years passed by, but whichever they were – the overland route to India, the Suez Canal, Middle Eastern oil – they were always deemed vital to the well-being of the Empire at peace or the Empire at war.

There was of course an element of the self-fulfilling prophecy in Britain's Mediterranean obsession: the forces deployed there invited counter-concentration and hence needed reinforcement. But for all that there was little doubt in most British minds in the summer of 1941 that the defence of the Mediterranean/Middle East area came second only to the defence of the British Isles in the list of priorities. Perhaps the war could not be lost there, but it could hardly be won if the area fell to the enemy.

Whatever happened, it was likely to prove cumulative. In the worst instance the fall of Malta would herald the fall of Egypt, which in turn would lead to the loss of the Middle East oilfields. The strain on shipping resources, already heavy, would be stretched to breaking-point by the need to bring oil across the Atlantic from America. Only in Europe would the British be able to confront the Germans, and the ships which were to bring the wherewithal for a cross-Channel invasion across the Atlantic would be carrying oil instead. There would be little chance of victory.

In the best instance the capture of Cyrenaica would ensure Malta's safety; the island fortress would continue to take a heavy toll of Axis shipping, prevent supplies reaching Rommel, and hence make possible the conquest of Tripolitania and Tunisia. Then Sicily could be attacked, and the Mediterranean opened to merchant shipping. The high number of ships employed on the long route round the Cape would no longer be necessary, and a good number could be transferred to the Atlantic for ferrying across the requisites of a Second Front in Europe. Victory would be assured.

Winston Churchill was fully alive to the possibilities inherent in these two scenarios, and was naturally determined to pursue the second, more amenable one, with all the considerable vigour at his disposal. He had been much cheered by O'Connor's dazzling victory over the Italians in December 1940, and equally chagrined by the string of disasters that had followed in its wake. The Germany entry into Africa had seen all of O'Connor's gains reversed, Greece had fallen with a whimper and Crete, if with more of a bang, had tumbled after it. Then the much-heralded 'Battleaxe' offensive had clattered to a pathetic halt after a mere two days. It was more than the Prime Minister could comfortably stomach. The heads of those responsible had to roll. Heads other than his own. In mid-June Wavell received the axe he had failed to administer to the Germans. He was ordered to exchange posts with the Commander-in-Chief India, General Auchinleck.

The day after Churchill had dispatched the relevant telegrams Hitler's armies had rolled across the Soviet frontier and created a new long-term threat to the British position in the Middle East. The military seers in London had little faith in the Red Army's capabilities; rather they saw the German progress through Russia as a long approach-march aimed at the oilfields of the Caucasus, Iran and Iraq. The distances involved promised a few months grace, but not much more. The newly-named Eighth Army would have to defeat Rommel in the Western Desert, secure North Africa, and be available for redeployment in northern Iraq before the first panzers came rumbling across the Caucasus mountains. Churchill made this very clear to the newly-appointed Auchinleck in a telegram of 19 July:

> If we do not use the lull accorded to us by the German entanglement in Russia to restore the situation in Cyrenaica the opportunity may never recur. A month has passed since the failure at Sollum ('Battleaxe'), and presumably another month may have to pass before a renewed effort is possible. This interval should certainly give plenty of time for training. It would seem justifiable to fight a hard and decisive battle in the Western Desert before the situation changes to our detriment, and to run those major risks without which victory has rarely been gained.

But, much to the Prime Minister's dismay, it soon became apparent that Auchinleck had some ideas of his own. If both wished for a swift victory over Rommel, Auchinleck doubted whether the swiftness Churchill had in mind would produce victory at all. When the Prime Minister pointed to the unprecedented level of forces now flowing into Egypt, his resident C-in-C stressed the need for more, and the time it would take to absorb and condition the ones already arriving. This Churchill saw as excessive caution. He also criticised, on political grounds – there were not enough British troops fighting in the 'British' desert army – Auchinleck's deployment of British troops in Cyprus. This Auchinleck saw as excessive meddling. 'I hope you will leave me complete discretion concerning dispositions of this kind,' he tartly replied, presumably more in hope than expectation.

Auchinleck was called to London at the end of July, and subjected to the military grilling of the Chiefs of Staff and the personal magnetism of Britain's War Lord. He came out of both intact, though firmly resolved not to go through the latter again if it could possibly be avoided. He also secured sanction for delaying the long-awaited offensive against Rommel until November 1. Churchill had reluctantly concurred in the face of united military opposition.

Once back in Egypt Auchinleck got down to the more agreeable business of preparing 'Crusader', the offensive his superiors expected would drive Rommel out of Cyrenaica and perhaps Africa as a whole. They were living in a dream. Certainly Eighth Army's strength in men and arms was growing, but men and arms do not an army make. It is the relationship between them which wins or loses battles, and in Eighth Army it was a far from satisfactory one.

Tanks were being hoisted out of ships' hulls in Suez harbour, but the *savoir faire* necessary for their effective use was harder to come by. Few British generals had grasped the principles of tank warfare, most of those that had were either dead or in POW camps. Auchinleck ignored the few that were still available. To command Eighth Army, against the wishes of Whitehall, he chose General Cunningham, recent victor in the Abyssinian campaign, who knew as much about tanks as Rommel knew about prudence.

Some of Cunningham's corps and divisional commanders *thought* they understood tank warfare, but unfortunately they were under the sway of ideas propagated by the British tank enthusiasts of the '30s. This group, led by Hobart, had receive so little support or understanding from other branches of the service that they had decided, in effect, 'to hell with the rest of you', and developed a theory of armoured warfare whereby tanks would operate, and win, completely on their own. The German notion of the armoured division as an all-arms formation *centred* around the mobility of the tank was not understood at all.

So, aware of the existence of such problems but not of their precise nature, Auchinleck and Cunningham set about planning 'Crusader'. They supervised the building of the necessary infrastructure – water pipelines, extension of the railway, the creation of supply dumps, etc – and the organization and training of the growing army at their command. By the end of October Eighth Army had a better than three-to-one superiority in armour and a two-to-one superiority in aircraft over the enemy.

These figures, in Auchinleck's opinion, were subject to qualification. The tanks were mechanically unreliable, the men insufficiently trained in their use. Churchill preferred to play down the problems. While the army in North Africa trained and complained, the German armies in Russia had been closing in on Moscow. If the Soviet Union was defeated before Eighth Army so much as made a move, not only a golden chance would have been forfeited but Britain's credibility would have suffered a shattering blow. When Auchinleck asked for a further fortnight's postponement of the offensive he was refused. If the water and rail lines were not yet ready, if some of the armour had arrived without the necessary desert modifications, well, that was just too bad. Churchill noted the German successes in Russia, and he noted the quantitative disparity of forces in North Africa. He had allowed Auchinleck to wait this long only with the greatest reluctance; there could be no further extensions. The Chiefs of Staff agreed with him. Auchinleck was dissuaded from resigning by the Minister of State in Cairo, Oliver Lyttleton. 1 November it would be. The stage was set for a bigger and more disastrous 'Battleaxe'.

IV

By prohibiting the attack on Tobruk Halder had made it possible for the Panzer Group leadership to concentrate its attention on the matter of the enemy's forthcoming offensive. In mid-October air reconnaissance noticed the frantic work devoted to the extension of the railway west from Matruh and the build-up of supplies in the forward areas. The Italian intelligence network in Cairo confirmed that a major offensive was imminent.

But from 27 October onwards low cloud hindered air reconnaissance, and the sparse pickings of the German wireless intercept service were all the Axis command had to go on. Rommel accordingly deployed his forces to meet the likely eventualities. The mass of the Italian infantry remained in the siege lines around Tobruk and behind the frontier defences between Sollum and Sidi Omar. The Italian armoured and motorised divisions – *Ariete* and

Trieste – were held back to the west between Bir Hacheim and Bir el Gubi. The German light infantry 'Afrika' division (otherwise known as 90th Light) was stationed at Sidi Rezegh, ready to block either a move to relieve Tobruk from the south-east or to counter a break-out attempt by the beleaguered garrison. The two panzer divisions – the core of Rommel's striking force – were deployed a short distance apart on the Trigh Capuzzo, ready to intercept either of the likely British moves. They could fall on the right flank of a drive on Tobruk or the left flank of a British attempt to encircle the frontier positions.

Having organised his forces in such a way, Rommel waited. On 31 October it was noticed that the enemy was observing complete radio silence, and the Axis forces were placed on full alert.

At dawn the following day 'Crusader' began. Led by the five hundred tanks of the 7th, 4th and 22nd Armoured Brigades a huge column of transport rolled across the frontier between Gasr el Abid and Fort Maddalena. This was 30th Corps, under General Norrie; its task was to seek out and destroy the German armour and then proceed to the relief of Tobruk. On its right flank the 13th Corps, mostly made up of infantry formations, was to pin down and then envelop the enemy troops holding the frontier positions.

This may have looked good on the map-table, but if so it is hard to believe there was a map on it. For one thing the two corps were pursuing separate objectives on diverging axes, for another 13th Corps, with very little armour of its own, was dependent on the disappearing 30th Corps for flank support. The result should have been predicted. The British armour was doomed to dispersal.

Unaware of what the fates had in store, through 1 November the British armoured brigades advanced steadily across the desert wastes and into the enemy rear without meeting any resistance. German reconnaissance patrols were sighted slipping away to the north. By evening 30th Corps had reached the vicinity of Gabr Saleh, on a front thirty miles wide facing north-west. Here the plan began to go awry. The low cloud still hindered air reconnaissance, and Cunningham had little idea of the whereabouts of the German panzer forces marked down for destruction. It had been assumed that they would find him, but they hadn't. By morning on the following day there were still no dust-clouds on the horizon, and the British commander was in a dilemma.

It had been foreseen, and a dubious contingency plan prepared. Norrie, Cunningham's one commander with experience in handling armour, had doubted whether Rommel would seek battle at Gabr Saleh. If not, he had argued, the British should drive on to Sidi Rezegh, the key to Tobruk. Then the Axis commander would have no choice.

On the morning of 2 November Cunningham compromised. Fatally. 7th Armoured Brigade would move north on Sidi Rezegh, but alone. 4th Armoured Brigade would have to stay at Gabr Saleh to protect 13th Corps' left flank, and 22nd Armoured Brigade would have to secure 30th Corps' left flank against the threat of the *Ariete* division, which its reconnaissance screen had discovered in the Bir el Gubi area. The British armour was divided up.

Thirty miles to the north Rommel was concentrating his armour and waiting for accurate intelligence of the British movements. When the skies cleared sufficiently that evening for air reconnaissance he could hardly believe his good fortune. He ordered General Cruewell, commander of the Afrika Korps, to take his two divisions south towards Gabr Saleh against the isolated 4th Armoured Brigade. As darkness fell the German tanks rolled forward into the clear desert night, lights extinguished and wirelesses turned off.

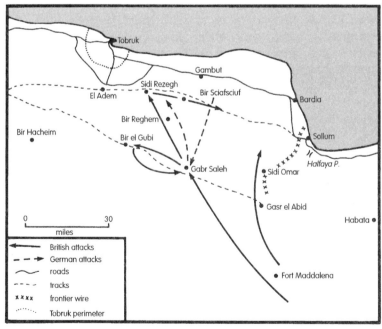

4. Crusader – The First Four Days

At dawn on the 3rd they were spotted by the RAF. Cunningham immediately ordered 22nd Armoured Brigade back from Bir el Gubi to Gabr Saleh. It had twice as far to travel as the German panzers.

An hour or so after dawn the hastily breakfasting soldiers of 4th Armoured Brigade spotted the dust-clouds they had searched for in vain the previous day. At around 06.30 Cruewell launched a concentric attack on the sprawling leaguer around Gabr Saleh. 15th Panzer moved in from the north as 21st Panzer, which had taken a longer wheel round to the east, attacked from the south-east. The British tank crews, high on gallantry but low on tactical sense, rushed out to do battle in their Stuarts. Fast and reliable, but thinly armed and, since they ran on aviation fuel, liable to flare up, the Stuarts were no match for the Panzer IIIs. Soon the desert was littered with flaming wrecks as the experienced panzer commanders pressed home their advantage. By 09.00 between ninety and a hundred Stuarts had been destroyed for German losses of around fifteen, and the remainder were withdrawing in disorder to the south. Cunningham's dispersion of his armour had claimed its first victim, and the German panzer force was astride the central position of the battlefield.

Towards noon the second victim arrived. 22nd Armoured Brigade had already lost twenty-four tanks in a foolhardy attack on *Ariete* the previous afternoon, but the lesson had apparently not yet been digested. The inexperienced brigade simply charged the German veterans, who proceeded to give a demonstration of what 4th Armoured Brigade should have done that morning. The tanks were held back and 22nd Armoured Brigade, rather than finding itself in a tank-to-tank encounter, found itself staring down the long barrels of the German 88 mm anti-tank guns. By 14.30 another hundred British tanks were smouldering on the gravel wastes around Gabr Saleh and Cruewell had accounted for two of Norrie's three armoured brigades.

During the afternoon, news of these disasters percolated through to Cunningham at Norrie's HQ twenty miles to the south. He now had to decide how to save 7th Armoured Brigade, which for twenty-four hours had been engaging the *Afrika* division in the neighbourhood of Sidi Rezegh airfield. It was now out on a distinctly precarious limb, for should Rommel order Cruewell north it would be caught between the hammer and the anvil. 7th Armoured Brigade would have to be withdrawn to the west, where it could join up with the strong elements of 13th Corps – the New Zealand Division and the 1st Army Tank Brigade – which had been moving north behind the frontier defences. In the meantime Cunningham was hurrying forward his armoured reserves, a process hardly helped by the incompletion of the supply infrastructure. As Auchinleck had feared, Churchill's haste was becoming Cunningham's defeat.

In the Axis camp there was jubilation as news of Cruewell's victories came through. But Rommel was not one to meditate on success. He ordered Cruewell to bring the panzer divisions north, as Cunningham had feared. They were to cut off 7th Armoured Brigade's escape routes to the east and the south.

It was a race against time, and one which the British brigade all but won. 15th Panzer, wheeling in from the south-east between Bir Reghem and Bir Sciafsciuf, crashed into the rear echelons of the withdrawing British armour at first light on 4 November, and a savage mêlée ensued. Honours, for the first time in 'Crusader's' ill-starred career, were fairly even, each side losing some thirty tanks. But the battlefield belonged to Cruewell and that evening, as the panzer force re-concentrated among the wreckage of war on Sidi Rezegh airstrip, Rommel was planning his next stroke.

What were the alternatives? One was to use the breathing-space offered by the temporary demise of the British armour to attack Tobruk. But this would take time, and allow the enemy to regroup and regain his balance. Another was to pursue 7th Armoured Brigade and to complete its destruction. This though offered only tactical gains, and Rommel was more interested in a strategic breakthrough. Furthermore there was the problem of the frontier troops to be considered, for while Cruewell had been breaking up 30th Corps the other British corps had been slowly enveloping the Sollum-Sidi Omar line. Rommel decided to strike out for the frontier with his entire armoured force. If he could get behind the British line there was a possibility of cutting off both 7th Armoured Brigade and the whole of 13th Corps from their supply bases.

On the morning of 5 November the three hundred tanks of the three Axis armoured divisions moved south-east towards Gabr Saleh and the frontier. In the process the *Ariete* division, on the right flank of the advance, overran the vast British supply depot south of Gabr Saleh and captured most of the fuel earmarked for the British conquest of Cyrenaica.

Rommel intended to push 21st Panzer north along the far side of the frontier to Halfaya Pass while 15th Panzer rolled up the near side. The British forces would be broken up, the road into Egypt forced open. But at this moment Auchinleck arrived on the scene to stiffen the wavering Cunningham's resolve, and the German advance soon ran into trouble. Eighth Army, thanks to Auchinleck's earlier insistence, had tank reserves; the Germans did not. On the evening of 5 November 21st Panzer ran into the newly-refurbished 4th and 22nd Armoured Brigades near Sidi Omar, and was halted in its well-worn tracks.

15th Panzer was faring almost as badly in its battle with 13th Corps, losing several tanks and making negligible progress. At the far northern end of the front 7th Armoured Brigade had already broken through the Italian infantry and reached the safety of the British lines. In the far south the South African division continued to block the advance of *Ariete*.

By the following morning it was obvious that the battle of movement was over, but Rommel was reluctant to admit as much. He brought 15th Panzer south to aid 21st Panzer, whereupon the British fed in their arriving reserves to help 4th and 22nd Armoured Brigades. A battle of attrition developed in the area around Sidi Omar.

This could only be to the Germans' disadvantage – their fighting strength was rather more finite – and Rommel, bowing to the inevitable, finally disengaged his armour on 9 November. 'Crusader' was over. In eight days of battle the British had transformed a crushing superiority in armour into virtual parity, and had moved the front line not a single mile to the west.

V

As Cunningham's battered force began to lick its wounds behind the line it had crossed with such misplaced enthusiasm nine days before, the Chiefs of Staff in London pondered the consequences of Eighth Army's failure. There would be no moving of forces east to stem a German onslaught through Anatolia or the Caucasus; the armour gathered so assiduously with such eventualities in mind was now gathering sand in the desert. And Malta. The task of sustaining the island was now one of herculean proportions. With the Luftwaffe back in Sicily, with German airfields ranged either side of 'Bomb Alley' between Crete and Cyrenaica, the convoy route from Alexandria could only be used in the direst emergency and at the greatest risk. The naval forces at Gibraltar, weakened even as the Chiefs conferred by the U-boat sinking of their only carrier *Ark Royal*, were little better placed to succour the island. The British, though still unaware of the planning energies then being devoted to Malta's capture, had to reckon with the possibility that the island would be bombarded and blockaded into submission.

In the German war-camp there was room only for celebration. Halder congratulated himself on restraining Rommel, the latter bathed in the warm glow of desert success. In Rome General Student studied maps of Malta and lectured his officers on the lessons they had all learned in Crete; in Karinhall the Reich Marshal eagerly anticipated the plaudits of a slowly recovering Führer. In the last week of November several trains of flat-cars rattled through Belorussia carrying 39th Panzer Corps west towards Germany and its new tropical equipment. The war was going well for the Reich.

But not for the British Empire. Its severely stretched forces in the Middle East were about to receive another shock. For as the armies in North Africa settled once more into relative immobility, other armies eight thousand miles to the east were being set in motion. The rising sun was about to fall on His Majesty's Empire in the East.

Chapter 3
SAYONARA

At midnight, the bright sun.
from the Zenrin Kushu

I

In the vast expanses of the northern Pacific Ocean, according to the *Kaga* Chief Air Officer, 'not even a bird flew'.

Nor a reconnaissance plane. On the afternoon of 1 December no American pilot looked down upon the six carriers and their powerful escort as they battled their way through the heavy seas and dense fog. And on the ships' decks were stacked crushed empty oil cans; down below the accumulating refuse was neatly piled away. No trail of rubbish would be thrown overboard to indicate this fleet's passage.

Pearl Harbor was now eighteen hundred miles and six days away. *Kido Butai*, the First Air Fleet, was taking Japan to war. Its commander, Admiral Nagumo, stood on the *Akagi* bridge and fretted. 'Will it go well?' he repeatedly asked his Chief of Staff. *Daijobu* – 'don't worry' – was Admiral Kusaka's inevitable reply. The two of them watched the anti-aircraft gunners at target practice, shooting the brightly-coloured kites that darted to and fro in the grey sky above.

Below-decks the four hundred pilots of *Kido Butai*'s planes wrote poems and letters, painted watercolours and spent time in their cockpits so as not to lose the feel of the controls. Beneath them the miles slipped by.

Two thousand miles to the west the battleship *Nagato* rode at anchor in the calmer waters of Kure Bay. In his quarters the Commander-in-Chief of the Combined Fleet, Admiral Yamamoto, played Japanese chess with one of his staff officers. Another of them, Captain Kuroshima, the author of *Kido Butai*'s attack plan, was in the Operations Room with Chief of

Staff Admiral Ugaki. They were bent over the huge map of the Pacific, taking stock of Nagumo's progress. It seemed as if everything was going to plan.

That same day, in wintry Berlin, the Japanese Ambassador hurried down the Wilhelmstrasse and through the dark portals of the Foreign Ministry. He had news for von Ribbentrop. A telegram had arrived from Tokyo the previous night; it had ended with the words: 'War may come quicker than anyone dreams.' One can safely assume that Ribbentrop, a man who thrived on drama rather than thought, was suitably impressed.

The following afternoon Yamamoto cabled Nagumo the confirmation he was waiting for. *Kido Butai* was to 'climb Mount Niikata', to attack as planned.

It was an aptly-coded message. In substituting Niikata, the highest mountain in the Japanese Empire, for the United States, the world's leading industrial power, Yamamoto symbolised the immensity of the task facing Japan's armed forces. To some Japanese it would seem like military madness, but few doubted that it was a national necessity.

II

For over a decade Japan had been drifting towards war with the other Great Powers who had East Asian interests to defend. The international division of spoils in China and South-east Asia, and Japan's need to change it for domestic reasons, lay at the root of the conflict.

Japan's rise to a position among the leading rank of capitalist powers had been too swift. The same depressing scenario that has haunted the underdeveloped world throughout the present century haunted the heirs of the Meiji Restoration. The two great gifts of western civilisation – medicine and mechanisation – had provoked vast changes in Japanese society, reducing available land while raising the population, and sending the excess millions into the cities in search of a living. But the growth of capital had proved unable to keep pace with the growth of population or its aspirations. Britain had faced similar problems in the nineteenth century and had carved an empire to solve them. The United States had used its open frontier as fuel for growth. But for the Japanese, searching for solutions in the middle of a world-wide depression, things were not so easy. Every effort to increase exports met with new import barriers, every attempt at emulating the western penchant for empires produced only moral rebukes and the threat of worse.

The problems were acute, but those Japanese whose job it was to solve them lacked either the wisdom or the resolution to do so. The country's political institutions were immature, the democracy introduced in 1924 already knee-deep in corruption. The God-Emperor, though theoretically omnipotent, was supposed to keep himself aloof from such mundane matters as the problems of Japanese society. Real power was held, but not much exercised, by the twin pillars of the Army and Navy.

As in Weimar Germany the failure of the centre implied the rise of Right or Left. The latter, though growing more significant through the '30s, had no more roots in Japanese society than the centre; there was no strong tradition of radical materialism, no large socialist or communist parties seeking a compromise between economic growth and social justice.

The Right, on the other hand, could offer a traditionalist anti-materialism to those suffering material hardship and visions of a strong Japan to those suffering from the effects of Western competition. As in Germany little more than lip-service was paid to the anti-plutocratic elements of this 'ideology'; what really mattered was that a militant nationalist policy could turn attention away from the formidable problems at home. *Lebensraum* on the Asian mainland would provide new land for the inhabitants of the crowded Japanese islands, new markets for Japanese products, new sources of raw materials for a country which had next to none of its own. All the young men who might join revolutionary groups would enter the armed forces instead; they would be purified in the service of the nation rather than corrupted in the godless ways of alien materialism. They would become modern Samurai, the heirs of past Japanese glories.

All would be cloaked in the familiar phrases. The Greater East Asia Co-Prosperity Sphere would bring justice and order to the war-torn mainland; the Japanese Army would assume that burden of exporting civilisation previously borne by the white races.

Yet time for the completion of this glorious endeavour was not unlimited. China, the obvious centrepiece of the Sphere, was apparently sorting out its own problems. Both Chiang Kai-Shek's nationalist movement and the Communist Party were growing yearly stronger at the expense of those warlords who for decades had held the country in splintered chaos. The Japanese had taken Manchuria in 1932 and granted it a fictional independence as Manchukuo; if they were to save the rest of China from disorder it would have to be soon, before the Chinese saved themselves.

1937 seemed an opportune year. Europe was preoccupied with the imminence of its own catastrophe, the United States absorbed in contemplation of its isolationist navel. Only the old enemy to the north presented a military threat, and this had been much reduced by the signing of the Anti-Comintern Pact with Germany and Italy the previous year. Imperial Japan took the irreversible plunge. An incident at the Marco Polo bridge near Peking was deliberately allowed to get out of hand, and within weeks the Japanese Army was marching south towards Shanghai, the Yangtse valley and the conquest of China. Or so it thought.

But the Chinese did not submit, preferring to withdraw deeper and deeper into the vastness of their country. Soon, to the annoyance of the Japanese, they were receiving help from the United States, Britain and France.

The two European powers could be ignored. They were far away, they were weak, and they were otherwise involved. But the Americans were a different proposition. Their enmity, though clearly hypocritical – as the future Foreign Minister Matsuoka said: 'And what country in its expansion era has ever failed to be trying to its neighbours? Ask the American Indian or the Mexican . . .' – was also dangerous. No one was as aware of the Japanese Armed Forces' dependence on the United States as the leaders of the Japanese Armed Forces. The Navy, which protected both Japan and its overseas armies, was built largely with American scrap-iron and ran on American oil. The threat was real. Though the Japanese knew that the United States was as yet both unwilling and unable to fight a war in the Pacific, the threat could not be ignored. The need for haste in the subjugation of China was more apparent than ever.

The outbreak of war in Europe improved the situation, in that it diverted Western forces and attention. The Nazi-Soviet Pact was a shock but in the long-term beneficial to Japan; it neutralised the Soviet Union almost as effectively as a German attack would have done. But there were also new problems to consider, most notably those concerning the Dutch East Indies, Japan's only alternative source of oil. If the Netherlands fell to the Germans who would assume control in Batavia? Japan was not at this time considering herself for the vacant appointment, but she was determined that no one else should secure it. Through the first half of 1940 Japanese diplomacy became very insistent on this issue. The United States, misinterpreting these cries of alarm emanating from Tokyo as evidence of fresh aggressive designs, proceeded to retaliate.

Roosevelt and Hull had long been both admonishing the Japanese and supplying their armed forces with the materials they needed to do the things they were being admonished for. In the summer of 1940, with Germany victorious in the West and Japan seemingly more voracious than ever in the East, the American administration deemed it time to act. Two steps were taken, one to weaken Japan and one to strengthen the United States. Roosevelt restricted the sale of oil and scrap-iron to foreign governments and firms, and decreed the creation of a 'two-ocean navy', one that would ensure US superiority in both Atlantic and Pacific by the end of 1942. The message was crystal-clear.

Imperial Japan and the United States were now trapped in a vicious spiral of measures and counter-measures that could only end in war. The former had grown used to the latter's complaints and to the feeling that there was nothing much behind them. Now, suddenly, the gloves were off and the firsts were very visible. In two years' time those fists would pack a formidable punch, while the Japanese, thanks to the new restrictions, would be less well-equipped to fight than they were now. Speed, which had been advisable before, was now imperative. If there was to be a war with America it had to start soon, while there was still some hope of victory. If there was to be an acceptable peace that too had to come soon, while Japan was still bargaining from a position of strength.

The negotiations for peace, and the preparations for war, went on. The political leaders sought a formula that would both avoid the fatal collision and keep alive Japan's dreams of empire on the mainland. Would a pledge to move no further south satisfy the Americans? Would they then allow Japan a free hand in China?

The answer was no. The Americans did not care about, or wish to understand, Japan's predicament. Like authoritarian parents scolding a child they saw only consequences, not motivations. Having delivered the scolding and the threats they simply turned their self-righteous backs. And not only metaphorically. For through the spring of 1941 the US Navy was becoming increasingly embroiled in the distant Atlantic.

Here was the chance, perhaps the last chance, for Japan to strike. A neutrality pact was signed with the Soviet Union in April; Japan's rear was formally secured. Yet still the leadership held back from the ultimate step. The Army was ready for war but the Navy doubted if it could be won. The politicians wondered whether the negotiations would proceed more smoothly if the sword was more visible. They pushed towards the brink, trusting in Roosevelt and Hull to pull them back with concessions.

Then, out of the blue as far as the Japanese were concerned, the Germans invaded the Soviet Union. Things were moving too fast; the world was being rearranged and the Japanese were not making the most of the opportunity. If they did not act soon then either an all-powerful Axis or an all-powerful Soviet-American bloc would be standing in their way, re-asserting the supremacy of the white man. At two Imperial Conferences, on 25 June and 2 July, the long-delayed decisions were finally taken.

In the north the Army would wait. 'In case the German-Soviet war should develop to our advantage, we will make use of our military strength, settle the Soviet question and guarantee the safety of our northern borders.' The Kwangtung Army, in 'friendly' Manchukuo, would be strengthened. Its staff would draw up plans for the invasion and administration of Siberia.

They would only be contingency plans. Overall the Army did not much like the enormous distances, the difficulties of terrain and climate involved. And there was no oil in Siberia. The Kwangtung Army would only move in if and when the Soviet Union was decisively beaten by the Germans.

For the moment then, Japanese attention was focused on the south. Now was the time to raise the stakes, while the Americans were involved in the Atlantic and awaiting with trepidation the outcome in Russia. In July the Japanese Army took over the rump of French Indo-China.

The gamble failed. The US Government, far from turning a blind eye to this latest indiscretion, announced a freezing of Japanese assets in the United States. The British and, more significantly, the Dutch East Indies administration, soon followed suit. There would be no more oil to power Japanese expansionism.

In Tokyo the worm wriggled on the end of its own hook. From here on each turn of a Japanese propeller reduced the precious stocks of fuel oil. The Navy joined the Army in arguing for war. As it would take both six months to prepare the politicians were allowed that much time to find an acceptable alternative. They failed. Konoye asked to meet Roosevelt, but was refused. A grim fatalism gripped the rulers in Tokyo. One word expressed it all. *Sayonara* – 'so be it'. It was no longer a drift towards war – it was a countdown.

III

In December 1941 the Japanese Army comprised fifty-one divisions. Twenty-two were engaged in China, fourteen were occupying Manchukuo, and five were based in the home islands. This left ten for the conquest of South-east Asia. Clearly quality, rather than quantity, would be the key to the early Japanese successes.

The Japanese had learnt two valuable lessons in China. One was the use of aircraft in a ground-support role. The other was the art of retaining mobility in difficult conditions. It was frequently impossible to move heavy vehicles or guns away from the few reasonable roads and so the Japanese, if they wished to avoid costly frontal attacks, had been forced to devise lighter equipment. Light tanks were constructed, with the emphasis on mobility rather than firepower. Light mortars were developed for the troops to carry. Bicycles were flown into China by the thousand. The Japanese Army became masters of mobility in areas where a western army would hesitate to move at all. The extra training in jungle warfare and amphibious landings which took place in the months preceding Pearl Harbor thus honed an already sharpened weapon.

Their prospective opponents were in a sorrier state. Between them the British, the Dutch and the Americans could muster over 350,000 troops in the threatened areas, but this numerical superiority had little significance. The western-officered native units, which made up more than half the total, were badly trained and equipped and hardly bursting with enthusiasm at the prospect of fighting their fellow Asians on behalf of the White Man's Burden in South-east Asia. The European and American troops were not much superior. More highly motivated perhaps, but little more experienced in modern warfare, and not at all in its tropical form.

These limitations were serious enough; the failure to perceive them was catastrophic. It was widely assumed that the Japanese, like other Asians, would prove indifferent warriors – who had they ever beaten but decrepit Tsarist Russia? – and therefore not too much of a problem. The Japanese had acquired, not undeservedly, a reputation in the West as the Asian mimics of the white man's ways. From this it was assumed, quite wrongly, that they were incapable of initiatives of their own. All Western intelligence of Japanese strategic thought, weaponry and fighting ability was perceived through the distorting lens of racism. It echoed the German mistake in Russia, and it was to have equally disastrous consequences. No one *dreamed* that the Japanese had developed the finest fighter aircraft of the war. The British fully expected to hold Hong Kong, where they had only four planes, for the three months it would take for reinforcements to arrive! McArthur, the US C-in-C in the Philippines, talked of setting the 'paper cities of Japan' ablaze with his *nine* B-17 bombers! He was so confident of holding Luzon that he decided to spread his forces out and so hold the entire archipelago.

A similar optimism was, more understandably, displayed in Allied naval circles. There was virtual parity in capital ships – eleven Allied to ten Japanese – and capital ships were what naval warfare was all about. Or so everyone, including most of the Japanese, still believed. Unfortunately for the Allies it was no longer true. Carriers were now the key to the world's oceans, and the Japanese had ten to the Allies' three in the Pacific area.

Six of Japan's, armed with over four hundred planes, made up Admiral Nagumo's First Air Fleet, the most powerful naval strike force the world had ever seen. It was, like the rest of the Japanese Fleet, a highly-trained, disciplined and coherent force. It saw itself as the heir to a great naval tradition; it had never suffered defeat. It eagerly anticipated new laurels, to add to those won at Russian expense in 1904–5.

Both Army and Navy were thus strong in width and capable, as was soon to be seen, of delivering blows of stunning force. In the short run they were more than a match for anything the Western powers could throw against them.

But there was no strength in depth. For all its qualities the Japanese Armed Forces could not overcome the limitations of the Japanese economy. Like the Wehrmacht the sword of the Rising Sun was a virtually finite resource when compared with those of its enemies. Each hack or slash would have to be definitive. Victory would have to be swift, or in the long run defeat would be by a thousand cuts. And this victory, given the inconceivability of conquering the enemies' homelands, would have to be primarily psychological. If the enemy could not be destroyed then his will to fight on had to be.

Was this possible? The Japanese military leaders preferred to ignore the question. They had to try. *Sayonara*.

Wars are easier to begin than to end. The Japanese strategy for the opening months was obvious. A secure source of oil was the number one priority, therefore the Dutch East Indies and Borneo had to be taken and held. The communications between these islands and Japan had to be secured, therefore South-east Asia had to be taken in toto from the Dutch, British and American forces stationed there. The only serious threat to this catalogue of conquest was the US Pacific Fleet sitting in Pearl Harbor. That had to be destroyed. It could only be destroyed by a surprise attack. Surprise was only possible at the commencement of hostilities. *Ipso facto* the war would have to begin with an attack on Pearl Harbor.

With the American fleet accounted for, and South-east Asia incorporated in the Greater East Asia Co-Prosperity Sphere, a vast defensive perimeter would be created, running from Burma around the East Indies and New Guinea and north across the Pacific to the Aleutians. This would then have to be defended against the inevitable counter-attack. The enemy would be repulsed, and would realize that eventual success would cost an exorbitant price. He would thus sue for a reasonable peace. So ran the theory. So, almost, would run the reality.

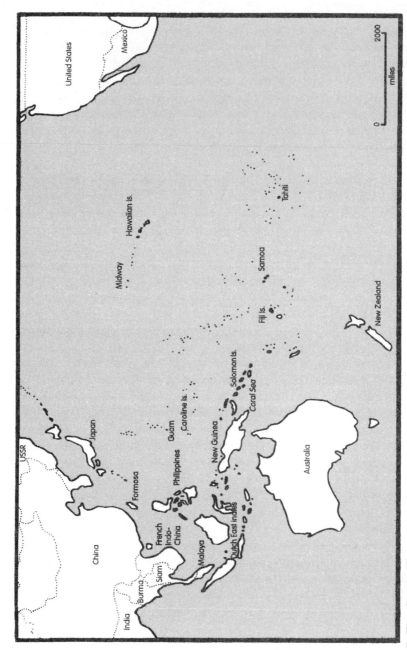

5. The Pacific Theatre

IV

At 07.53 on 7 December Flight Leader Mitsuo Fuchida stared down from his cockpit at the blue waters of Pearl Harbor. It looked uncannily like the model he had spent so many hours studying in the *Akagi* operations room. Nothing was moving. The planes on Hickam Field were lined up wing-tip to wing-tip; the capital ships of the US Pacific Fleet stern to bow along 'Battleship Row'. 'Tora tora tora,' he radioed the anxious Nagumo – surprise had been complete. Behind Fuchida the sky was full of *Kido Butai*'s planes, the pilots waiting to begin their attack. He fired the blue signal flare; they peeled off from the formations and flew down into war.

An hour or so later Pearl Harbor was full of burning, keeling ships. Four of the nine capital ships were sunk, another four badly damaged. Nearly two hundred planes had been destroyed. Operation 'Z' had succeeded.

Across the Pacific to the west other Japanese forces were moving into action. In the South China Sea thousands of soldiers watched from their landing-craft as the shorelines of northern Malaya and southern Thailand grew closer and more distinct. Others waited on the Indo-Chinese frontier for the order to march on Bangkok.

In Formosa Japanese airmen waited for the sky to clear. Their targets were the US air-bases in the Philippines, and the bad weather was to prove a blessing in disguise. For unknown to the cursing Japanese pilots the US planes had been sent aloft on receipt of the news from Pearl Harbor. They would barely have touched down again before the delayed Japanese arrived overhead to catch them helpless on the ground.

By 10 December the US air strength in the Philippines had been virtually destroyed, and the first Japanese troops were wading ashore in northern Luzon. On the same day Japanese reconnaissance planes discovered the two British capital ships – *Prince of Wales* and *Repulse* – which Churchill had optimistically sent east as a deterrent. Within two hours they were no more than bubbles on the surface of the South China Sea.

In four days the Japanese had sunk six and severely damaged four of the eleven capital ships ranged against them. Masters of the sea and masters of the air, they were now ready to assert their mastery on land against the isolated colonial armies of South-east Asia.

Chapter 4
WINTER

London/Washington DC

Optimism is the content of small men in high places.

F. Scott Fitzgerald

The two wars, Asian and European, were now inextricably linked in the Pacific Ocean. It remained for either Germany or the United States to close the circle of global war in the Atlantic.

Both hesitated. Roosevelt was unsure whether the American public's new-found fury, born in the trauma of Pearl Harbor, would stretch to include the greater menace bestriding continental Europe. He hoped the Germans would take the initiative and so render the problem academic.

In Berlin opinions were divided. Goering and the Army leaders, though convinced that war with America was inevitable, saw no need to hasten the evil day. Raeder disagreed. The need to respect the United States' purely nominal neutrality had hitherto placed severe restrictions on German action in the Atlantic. Now, with war inevitable, and with British and American naval strength depleted by the demands of the war with Japan, those restrictions had to be lifted.

Raeder acted on his opinions. On the evening of 8 December, without consulting his fellow Nazi barons, the Grand Admiral authorised German vessels in the Atlantic to attack any American ships engaged in activities prejudicial to the Reich's war-effort. The following day U-186 sank an American destroyer off the coast of Iceland.

This was all Roosevelt needed. On 10 December the United States of America declared war on Germany and Italy.

The attack on Pearl Harbor cast a ray of sunshine through the growing darkness of Churchill's winter. The continuing German successes in Russia, the failure of 'Crusader', the accelerating debacle in the Far East ... all were compensated for by the American entry into the war. Within hours of the American declaration of war on Germany the British Prime Minister was inviting himself to Washington.

Roosevelt did not wish to see him immediately, but was too tactful in saying so. Churchill ignored the hint; he was afraid that the American service chiefs might reach some conclusions of their own if his visit was delayed. On the night of 11 December he made the long journey north through blacked-out Britain to the Clyde, and there boarded the new battleship *Duke of York* for the cross-Atlantic voyage. This time he did not read *Hornblower* en route; he and the Chiefs of Staff were too busy drawing up plans for the continued prosecution of the war.

The strategy outlined during the voyage comprised five basic elements. They were:

1. The need to translate the enormous industrial potential of the anti-Axis alliance into military strength.
2. The need to maintain communications, first and foremost those between the three Great Powers engaged in the struggle, and secondly those connecting these powers with their armies and raw material sources overseas.
3. The continuance of the war against Germany by those means presently available: strategic bombing, encouragement of subversion in the occupied territories, propaganda, and blockade.
4. The retention of vital positions in the Far East, notably Singapore.
5. The tightening of the military ring around Axis-occupied Europe, by increasing aid to the Soviet Union, and by conquering North Africa and opening up the Mediterranean.

Point 1, the realisation of military potential, was no problem for the United States. Two weeks after Churchill's arrival Roosevelt announced the grandly-titled 'Victory Programme'. In 1942 the US would produce 45,000 tanks, 45,000 aircraft, 20,000 anti-aircraft guns, 15,000 anti-tank guns and half a million machine-guns. And these figures would be doubled in 1943.

Point 2 was rather more problematic. The enemy, though doubtless impressed by all this prospective production, could find consolation in the difficulties likely to be encountered in its transportation. For by the end of 1941 Allied communication lines were looking distinctly tenuous.

Allied naval commitments seemed to be ever-expanding. They now included protecting the major convoy routes to Britain, Russia and the

Middle East, holding off the rampant Japanese in the Pacific and Indian Oceans, and keeping a watchful eye on the remnants of the French fleet in Dakar and Casablanca. And while the commitments expanded the fleets shrank. The back of the US Pacific Fleet had been broken at Pearl Harbor, and Churchill's wish to reinforce the survivors with the *Prince of Wales* and *Repulse* had been rudely dashed by the sinking of the two ships on 10 December. From the east coast of Africa to the west coast of America the Allies had lost any semblance of naval superiority.

Nor was this the worst of it. The British Mediterranean Fleet had suddenly become disaster-prone. First *Ark Royal* had been sunk, then Force K sailed into a minefield and lost three cruisers, and finally two battleships in Alexandria Harbour – *Queen Elizabeth* and *Valiant* – were disabled by Italian frogmen. The only capital ship still afloat in the Mediterranean was the battleship *Barham*, and this was badly needed in the Indian Ocean.

Only in the Atlantic were the Allies holding their own, but here too the situation was soon to take another plunge for the worse. Balked by improved British radar in the latter half of 1941, Admiral Doenitz, the German U-boat Chief, was now busy organising 'Operation Drumbeat', a calculated carnage of those American merchant ships still sailing, alone and unescorted, the East Coast and Caribbean sea-routes.

The imminent success of this enterprise would place an additional strain on the already serious Allied shipping situation. By January 1942 the British had lost both the option of sending ships through the Mediterranean and thirty-five per cent of their pre-war merchant tonnage. Thus there were more miles to cover and less ships to cover them. As a result only forty to fifty thousand troops could be dispatched overseas each month, a figure that barely covered the natural wastage through injury and illness. Even this level of transportation had only been sustained by the borrowing of American ships, a practice which would now have to cease. For the Americans, though naturally in a better situation than the British, had barely enough ships to meet their own needs, and this number was to be further depleted by 'Drumbeat's' ominous roll. To sum up this picture of Allied marine gloom, by February 1942 there was barely sufficient shipping to form the necessary convoys and barely sufficient naval forces to protect them. Further setbacks would be calamitous.

The hopes expressed in Point 2 could be generously described as optimistic; those expressed in Points 4 and 5 were merely naïve. The chances of stemming the Japanese onslaught in South-east Asia were slim indeed; already their forces were racing down the Malay peninsula towards

Singapore and island-hopping their way towards the East Indian oil-wells. Perhaps Burma could still be held, but little else.

Churchill, however, had as much misplaced faith in the garrison of Singapore as he had previously had in the ill-fated *Prince of Wales* and *Repulse*. He brushed aside suggestions that reinforcements bound for the island should be redirected to Burma. As a consequence both would fall to the enemy.

This sad process was still unfolding; the situation in North Africa could better be described as unravelling. The failure of 'Crusader' and the need to send troops to the Far East had set in motion that course of events most feared in London. Malta was now in direst peril. Should it fall Egypt would surely follow. And the threat from the Caucasus was likely to loom larger with the coming spring. It was now not so much a question of tightening the ring around Axis Europe as of holding it desperately shut. Any hopes of a joint Anglo-American landing in North-west Africa would have to be placed in cold storage for the indefinite future.

So where should those forces that were available be committed? To the British it was obvious – in the Middle East and the Indian Ocean. These were the areas of potential crisis; these were the areas that had to be held. The enemy still held the initiative; in Russia, the Middle East, the Far East. His armies were still moving forward, and they had to be stopped. Until such time as they were, all else was clearly secondary.

Unfortunately the Americans, as Churchill and his party discovered on reaching Washington, were unaware of the escalating peril. Their service chiefs, who considered the military initiative a god-given right, were understandably loth to admit that it rested with the enemy. Consequently they had devised plans for utilising an initiative they did not possess. The East Indies would be held, North-west Africa invaded. As soon as possible.

Churchill, with rare tact, explained that the failure of 'Crusader' had rendered a North-west Africa operation inadvisable. There was not enough shipping, he explained, to countenance this operation, the supply of the Middle East and the retention of footholds in the Far East.

The Americans were not convinced that the general situation was as lamentable as the British said it was. But, amidst the prevailing honeymoon spirit, they agreed to put their disagreements aside for the time being. Churchill was reasonably satisfied. He was confident that time and a few more unexpected jolts would produce a more realistic approach. And the British representatives on the new Combined Chiefs of Staff Committee would naturally be on hand to hasten their new ally down the road to wisdom.

Kuybyshev

Better to turn back than to lose your way.
Russian proverb

One crucial decision *was* taken by the British and Americans in Washington. They would continue with, and seek to expand, the programme of economic and military aid to the Soviet Union. Philanthropy was not the motive. The Western allies had realised that only the Red Army could hope to tie down the bulk of the Wehrmacht for the year it would take to bring the resources of the United States to bear. Any additional strain imposed on Anglo-American shipping was a small price to pay for keeping the Soviet Union in the war.

If it could be done. In early January Stalin's government moved further east to Kuybyshev on the Volga, and so rejoined the rump of the administration and the foreign diplomatic corps. Kuybyshev was situated closer to the centre of unoccupied Russia; it was also likely to remain unoccupied rather longer than Gorkiy, which was little more than a hundred miles from the front line.

The Soviet military situation was far from enviable. The Red Army, its ranks thinned by the autumn battles, its morale lowered by constant retreat and the loss of the capital, its supply channels thrown into confusion by the loss of the Moscow railway node, had only been saved from complete disaster by the early arrival of winter and the transfer of some eighteen crack divisions from the Far East. These fresh troops, accustomed to the rigours of winter, had been deployed mainly in the Mius, Voronezh and Vladimir sectors. There were not enough of them to throw the Germans back but, with the help of the conditions and an enemy reluctance to mount any determined attacks, they had succeeded in stabilising the line.

But for how long? It was glumly recognised that winters do not last for ever, even Russian winters. It seemed highly unlikely that the Red Army would be able to cope with a renewed German offensive once conditions again became conducive to mobile operations. And so the measures being taken in Kuybyshev, like those under discussion in Washington, were primarily long-term defensive measures. Stalin too was playing for time. If the Soviet Union could somehow avoid the knock-out punch, then there was a good chance of winning the bout on points.

These points were now being totted up out of reach of the rampant Wehrmacht, first and foremost by the enlarging of the industrial base east of the Volga.

This process had been underway since the early '30s. The Soviet leadership had, unknown to the Nazi devotees of the *blitz* solution, demonstrated a rare prescience. Stalin had been preparing for this war for over a decade. By 1941 a substantial proportion of Soviet industry was located east of Moscow, and as the war began more industrial concerns were shifted, machine by machine, in the same direction. As the panzers rolled through Belorussia, Soviet trains rolled east across the steppe carrying tank factories, steel mills, diesel plants and other vital equipment to the Volga, Ural, Siberian and Central Asian regions.

In the winter of 1941–2 this process went on, as those areas likely to be overrun in the coming spring and summer were denuded of industrial plants necessary for the continued prosecution of the war. This exodus even took precedence, in terms of rail capacity, over the movement of supplies to the hard-pressed troops in the front-line.

The major problem involved in this evacuation of industry was the time consequently lost to production. For example the huge aircraft factories of Voronezh, moved east in November and December, could not be expected to resume full production until May. The same applied to the Moscow aviation industry. Overall, only that thirty-five per cent of aircraft production already situated in the Urals would be turning out planes in the first five months of 1942. It was going to be a thin year for the Red Air Force, no matter how promising the prospects might be for 1943.

Industry could at least be evacuated; mines and agricultural land were not so mobile. New sources of production would have to be found. The food situation was difficult rather than impossible, largely because the loss of vast producing areas had been matched by the loss of most of the mouths they usually fed. The oil situation, though, was potentially critical. The probably imminent loss of the Caucasian oilfields – currently contributing eighty-six per cent of the Soviet output – could only be compensated for by the rapid expansion of the recently developed fields in the Volga and Ural regions. The story was the same with most of the mineral products. Old mines had to be reopened or expanded, new sources prospected and exploited. In certain crucial cases – aluminium, lead, the high-octane fuels and quality blending agents necessary for the production of aviation fuel – insufficient sources were available. The necessary quantities would have to be brought in from abroad.

But the Soviet Union's greatest problems in this period concerned transportation. The Red Army had few motor vehicles and had lost the means of producing many more. The railways suffered from a different malaise. The radial network was centred on the capital, and the loss of the

Front line January 1942

0   100
miles

Konosha

Tikhvin

Vologda

Kirov

Bologoye

Rybinsk
Yaroslavl

Kalinin

Kalyazin

Ivanovo

Vyazma

Vladimir

Gorkiy

Kazan

MOSCOW

oka

Ryazan
Tula

Ulyanovsk

Orel

don

Penza

Syzran

Kuybyshev

Tambov

volga

Kursk

Voronezh

Saratov

Kharkov

Stalino

donets

Stalingrad

Rostov

6. The Eastern Front: January 1942

Moscow nub had severely weakened the ability of the Red Army to switch its troops from front to front. To move an army from Tikhvin to Rostov now took four times as long as it had previously taken. The north-south line furthest to the west in Soviet hands ran from Yaroslavl to Gorkiy before winding its way interminably south to the Don at Liski. It was a single-track line for most of its length, with a correspondingly low carrying capacity.

In December work had begun on a new track, running from Kazan to Stalingrad down the west bank of the Volga, but on reflection the Soviet leaders decided that the line was rather too close to the front line, and top priority was then given to the construction of a north-south line between the Volga and the Urals, running south from Balezino to Chkalov via Izhevsk and Ufa. Further south the line connecting Orsk to Guryev on the Caspian was completed in March, so allowing the transport of Baku oil by tanker and rail to the Ural region. Through the extremes of a continental winter thousands of Soviet men, women and youths worked in merciless conditions to lay these miles of track.

The one compensating feature in this desperate outlook, and one for which the Soviet planners could claim the credit, was the country's continued accessibility to the outside world. The Konosha-Kotlas railway, built during 1940-1, and connecting Murmansk and Archangel to the Urals area by way of Kirov, was an invaluable resource. Even should the Finns and Germans make a more determined effort in the Far North and capture Murmansk, the thin line from Archangel, running through the pine forests south to Konosha, would probably prove beyond their reach.

Already it was in heavy use. The first Allied convoy had docked in Murmansk harbour the previous September, and had been followed by others at roughly fifteen-day intervals. In mid-October Cripps and Hopkins had met Stalin in Gorkiy and taken away the Soviet Union's Christmas list, and in the succeeding months British and American ships had been loaded with everything from lump sugar to aluminium, from field telephones to lard, that would keep the Soviet Union in the war.

Unfortunately this route was only viable through the perpetual darkness of the Arctic winter; the perpetual light of summer would give the Luftwaffe and Kriegsmarine units stationed in northern Norway too much of an edge. So the other two major ingress routes were of considerable importance. One ran up the new Trans-Iranian railway from Basra to Mianeh, thence on by road and another railway into the Caucasus. The other consisted of American ships flying the hammer and sickle and sailing under the eyes of the Japanese and into Vladivostok. Clearly neither offered a long-term guarantee. A German advance into the Caucasus, a shift in Japanese policy, and there would be a cork in each bottle.

Still, perhaps the Germans would not reach Baku, perhaps the Japanese Navy had its hands full enough already. The Americans continued to load ships in Chesapeake Bay. The one commodity they could not hoist aboard the freighters was determination. If the Soviet Union could continue the war – would it?

The answer was yes. German policy in occupied Russia had more than made up for any shortage of Soviet resolve. If a *modus vivendi* could ever have been reached with Stalin, if the rifts could ever have been deepened between the Soviet people and its leadership, then by December 1941 such possibilities no longer existed. There were too many frozen corpses swaying on village-square gallows. There could be no peace with such an enemy. The cost of war could not exceed the cost of submission.

The depths of bestiality plumbed by Hitler's aryans were naturally most apparent in the occupied regions. And here the fight was only just beginning. Stalin's speech of 3 July 1941 had decreed the formation of partisan units in those areas overrun by the enemy and those soon to suffer a similar fate. Deep in the forests and marshes of European Russia bases had been prepared, albeit inadequately, for the struggle to come. And, as the Germans advanced, these bases acted as focal points for the thousands scattered in the panzers' slipstream. For weaponry these proto-partisans could rely on the enormous tonnage of discarded arms littering the vast fields of battle.

In late 1941 and early 1942 many trained officers were parachuted into occupied territory to organise the raw material into efficient partisan units. In this first winter of the war little action was taken against the occupying power, only selective raids calculated to elicit German reprisals and so cement the local population's loyalty. For similar reasons there were many executions of those inclined to collaborate with the new masters. Most of the time the partisans were too busy establishing their bases and arranging for supplies, and to the German field commanders they were as yet little more than a minor irritation.

Given time they would become more, much more. 'Given time'. How often must Stalin have muttered those words? The crippled Soviet engine was firing fit to burst on its remaining cylinders. It would get there, given time. Stalin, pacing the floor of the Governor's Palace in Kuybyshev, could only watch its painstaking progress and wait. Armaments, railways, foreign aid, partisans. All would prove their worth. 'Given time'.

WINTER

Tokyo

Unless you enter the tiger's den you cannot take the cubs.
Japanese proverb

In Tokyo and Berlin the problems confronting the planners were the reverse of those troubling their counterparts in London, Washington and Kuybyshev. The Germans and the Japanese had the initiative but not the resources in depth; they had to maximise the advantages offered by the one before the threat implicit in the other could be brought to bear against them. But while the German military chiefs had reached agreement on the broad outlines of their strategy for the first half of 1942, the Japanese had yet to take the necessary decisions.

It was becoming urgent that they did so. The first phase of the strategic blueprint drawn up in November 1941 was nearing completion. As February passed into March the Japanese forces had either reached or were approaching those military frontiers deemed necessary for the defence of the Co-Prosperity Sphere. Inside those frontiers there remained a few pockets of resistance, but they were isolated and soon to be reduced. Then the Rising Sun would hold sway over the oceans and islands from the Andamans to the International Date Line, from the Kuriles to the Arafura Sea. On the Asian mainland the Army would reign supreme from Rangoon to the northern borders of Manchukuo. Except, of course, for China. And this, surely, was the time to settle the China 'Incident' once and for all, while the world was held at arms' length by Japanese control of the seas.

This had been the original plan, but the sweeping victories had increased the appetite for more. Now it was argued that to hand back the initiative to the enemy was both temperamentally impossible and strategically unwise. The most should be made of the current Japanese superiority, in expanding further the perimeters of the defensive shield, in hindering the enemy's attempts to create a countervailing force.

So it was decided that offensive operations would continue. But in which direction? There was no shortage of alternatives. To north, south, east and west new prizes studded the horizon. Which should be pursued?

To the north lay the half-crippled Soviet Union, fully engaged in a life-and-death struggle with Japan's German ally. The Red Army forces in the Far East were known to be weak, and there was every chance that they would grow weaker still. The Japanese Army leadership was eager for action against the old enemy; memories of the costly border skirmishes in 1938–9 still rankled. But in early 1942 there were not the troops available for a full-scale invasion of Siberia; the most that could be expected of the Kwangtung Army's sixteen divisions was the conquest of the Soviet Maritime Provinces. Nor were climatic conditions propitious, particularly in view of the appalling terrain involved. The Army was willing to wait for spring, perhaps even summer. By then the Germans would have finished off the job west of the Urals and the Japanese could take Siberia virtually unopposed.

The Naval General Staff was not considering action against the Soviet Union, for the simple reason that its role in such an endeavour would be minimal. It was much more concerned with the likely American use of Australia as a base for mounting counter-offensives against the Japanese positions in South-east Asia. The island continent should be conquered, so as to avert this probable danger. But unfortunately for the Naval General Staff the Army vetoed the idea, claiming that there were insufficient divisions available for such a daunting task.

Yamamoto's Operations Chief, Captain Kuroshima, was more interested in the possibilities of a westward drive into the Indian Ocean. This would serve a valuable double purpose. In negative terms it would secure the Japanese rear for a showdown with the Americans in the Pacific, in positive terms it would push the British out of the Indian Ocean and make possible a link-up between Japanese and German forces in the Middle East area. The latter, as we shall see, was discussed by the two powers involved in February, with important consequences. But for the moment Kuroshima was also stymied by the Army's opposition. There were not enough troops available for the conquest of Ceylon. In any case, it would be better to wait for the post-monsoon period in autumn, when an advance from Burma into Bengal could divide the enemy forces in the area. Kuroshima had to be satisfied with a mere raid into the Indian Ocean, to be carried out by *Kido Butai* in late March and early April.

Yamamoto himself, though theoretically subordinate to the Naval General Staff, was in practice the decisive voice in Japanese naval circles. And to him all these options evaded the real issue. In his opinion the strategic situation in March 1942 could be usefully compared with that existing in March 1905. In both cases a surprise blow delivered at the end of the previous year (Port Arthur/Pearl Harbor) had proved disabling but not decisive. In the former case the disabling had opened the way for the decisive battle – Tsushima. So it should be in the latter case; the Japanese Fleet should seek out and destroy the American Pacific Fleet while it was still weak from the losses suffered at Pearl Harbor.

For when all was said and done Nagumo's dawn strike had given the Americans a severe shock, but little else save a thirst for revenge. The oil-storage facilities had not been damaged, the American carriers had not been in port. And it was carriers that held the key to the Pacific. For the moment the Japanese had a numerical superiority of more than two to one, but this would swiftly vanish as the more productive American dockyards swung into top gear. In six months to a year the Americans would have enough carriers to build an impenetrable screen of their own across the Pacific; another year and a new fleet could be built behind that screen which the Japanese could never hope to match. The conclusion to be drawn was obvious. This American snowball effect must never be allowed to gather momentum; those carriers now afloat must be destroyed without delay. The Japanese Navy should strike east, in search of another Tsushima.

In February 1942 Admiral Ugaki, Yamamoto's Chief of Staff, shut himself away with an endless supply of green tea and meditated on the problem. He emerged four days later with the word – 'Hawaii'. This choice of target was, like all the others, disputed. The Army refused to supply the necessary troops. Ugaki's naval colleagues considered the difficulties involved to be almost insuperable. The Naval General Staff disliked the whole idea, and put forward a new plan for cutting the Australia-America sea-route by seizing Fiji and Samoa. It seemed as if the Japanese Navy would never make up its mind.

Yamamoto decided to cut the Gordian knot. Ugaki's plan, for all its over-ambition, was at least a step in the right direction – east. Yamamoto forcibly declared his backing for a diluted version of the plan. It was not necessary to invade Hawaii; the tiny island of Midway, a thousand miles to the west, would prove a sufficiently certain bait for the US carriers. These, and not a few extra acres of sand and coral, were what concerned Yamamoto. He was ready to allow a minor operation beforehand to clear the Coral Sea and secure Japanese communications with the Solomons and New Guinea; he also promised Kuroshima that a westward move would be contemplated after the destruction of the American fleet. But he was adamant that the Midway operation should have top priority, and his prestige was enough to decide the issue. The Naval General Staff huffed and puffed and eventually acquiesced. For the rest of March and most of April planning went ahead for the decisive encounter with the US Pacific Fleet.

The size of the forces to hand seems to have gone to the heads of the Japanese planners. In nearly every department they possessed a numerical superiority over the enemy, and in many the qualitative advantage as well. Ten aircraft carriers against four or five, ten modern battleships against the none-too-modern survivors of Pearl Harbor, twice the number of cruisers and destroyers. Moreover most of the crews – particularly the air crews – had by far the greater experience of combat.

The Japanese planners were all too aware of these facts. It was almost as if the certainty of victory encouraged the securing of it in the most complex and interesting manner. The vast armada at their disposal was split into no less than nine combat groups, all of which would perform separate roles in the unfolding of the masterpiece. Two groups, an occupation force and its support, were to attack the Aleutian Islands and thus provide a diversion in the northernmost reaches of the Pacific. This would draw off, it was assumed, a substantial portion of the US forces. They would be ambushed by a third Japanese group waiting in the north-central Pacific. Meanwhile the remaining six groups would be proceeding towards Midway. A submarine cordon would arrive first, followed by the main carrier force. The latter's planes would bombard Midway and then wait for the Americans to come charging up from Pearl to their doom. Behind the carriers would come the Midway occupation force, its support, an independent cruiser squadron, and the main battle-force under Yamamoto himself. By the time the Americans reached Midway most of the Japanese Navy would be waiting for them.

It does not, now, take much acumen to spot the fatal flaw in this plan. The whole detailed process rested on the one assumption, that the Americans would be surprised. To assume the opposite – something the Japanese refused to do until it was impossible not to – would have produced some very different conclusions. If the Americans were not caught unawares then the Aleutian diversion merely dispersed Japanese strength, and it would be the Americans rather than they who would do the pouncing around Midway. On carriers moreover three hundred miles ahead of any possible support.

Some of these fears were expressed when Ugaki put the plan through a series of war-games in mid-April. In one exercise a number of Japanese carriers were sunk by an unexpected American strike, but Ugaki, in his role as umpire, hastened to undo this decision by rewriting the rules. Some of the participating admirals were not so easily put off. Vice-Admiral Kondo, just back from the Java Sea, and Rear-Admiral Yamaguchi, who had commanded carriers at Trincomalee and Pearl Harbor, were not impressed by the plan. They disliked the widespread dispersion of forces, and argued that at least the carriers should be wielded as a cohesive force. Nagumo's Air Operations Officer, Commander Genda, strongly endorsed their views. The plan should be rooted in a carrier-centric premise. As it now stood a few carriers had merely been appended to a plan rooted in the traditions of the battleship era.

This was perceptive thinking, but Yamamoto's haste had blunted his receptivity. He remained adamant; Operation Midway would commence on 25 May. The die had apparently been cast. Captain Kuroshima, however, had been much interested by the criticisms, which had served to focus some of his own dissatisfaction with the plan. He began to ponder an alternative of his own, merely, so he thought, as an enjoyable recreation.

But Kuroshima's scribblings were to be of greater value than he guessed. For in late April Yamamoto was reluctantly forced to abandon Ugaki's plan. The reason – the only conceivable reason – was the Japanese discovery that their staff code had been broken by the Americans. Certain circles had suspected as much for several weeks, but only at this late date had they received confirmation.

The first hint had been vouched to Admiral Nagumo during his sojourn in the Indian Ocean. An aide had pointed out to the Admiral that the marked course of the two British warships just sunk by his planes suggested that they were heading for the precise point at which the Japanese Fleet had agreed to rendezvous. Nagumo had studied the chart and agreed that it was a strange coincidence. It had to be, or the staff code had been broken, an unbelievable hypothesis. Nagumo tucked his moment of concern into a small corner of his report and thought no more about it. Neither did two other commanders in different theatres who noticed similar 'coincidences'. Only an eagle-eyed young staff officer in Tokyo, one captain Yorinaga, drew the possible connection as he sifted through the various reports. He too thought it inconceivable that the code had been broken. But could it have fallen into enemy hands?

Each Japanese warship carried a codebook weighted with lead to take it swiftly to the bottom should disaster strike. Yorinaga went conscientiously through the record of those few Japanese ships sunk since the war's beginning, and had soon narrowed his attention down to one. Submarine I-124 had last broadcast its position on 19 January, as standing sentry outside Darwin harbour in northern Australia. It had been assumed sunk, but where? Suppose it had been depth-charged either in or just outside the harbour? Yorinaga examined the available oceanographic charts and found that the water in-harbour was a mere 140 feet at the deepest point, quite within the limits of a thorough salvage operation.

In the middle of April Yorinaga took his suspicions to Rear-Admiral Fukudome, the Naval General Staff Chief of Operations. The latter was impressed and, without informing Yamamoto and the Combined Fleet Staff, decided to test Yorinaga's theory. Information was relayed in code by Japanese warships in the Pacific pertaining to imaginary problems with the water-distillation plant on Guam. A week later one of Japan's agents in Hawaii reported that the information had come through. The code had indeed been broken.

Yamamoto was informed of this by Fukudome on 28 April. He had no choice but to accept that the details of the Coral Sea and Midway operations, which had been flooding the Pacific radio waves for several weeks, were now known to the enemy. The former was postponed indefinitely, the latter would have to be rethought. Or so Yamamoto believed. But to his surprise it was discovered that Kuroshima had an alternative plan half-drafted. With the Coral Sea operation off, Yamamoto decided to advance the schedule for the Midway operation.

Berchtesgaden

He is a giant who has many dwarfs about him.
Yiddish proverb

In January 1942 the German military leadership had a new variable to consider: the recovery of its supreme commander, Adolf Hitler. For over twenty weeks, since the crash-landing on Rastenburg airfield, the Führer of the German Reich had lain in a fluctuant coma, oblivious to the war raging on his behalf. Now apparently the lesions were fully healed and Hitler, though still physically weak, was mentally ready to take up the reins he had let fall the previous August.

But he was determined to take no unnecessary risks. Once before, in later November, he had seemed on the verge of a complete recovery, and had attempted, against Dr Sodenstern's advice, a premature comeback. There had been a recurrence of haemorrhaging in the medulla area, and he had succumbed once more to the coma. This time the Führer was determined to take things more slowly. His recovery offered further proof of that path marked out for him by destiny, but the narrowness of the escape had emphasised the frailty of the physical form which destiny had selected as its vessel. With so much still to accomplish it would not do to tempt the fates a second time.

Convalescing at the Berghof, amidst the Wagnerian splendour of the winter mountains, Hitler had a super-abundance of time in which to think about the war and the way it had been conducted in his absence. He was not completely dissatisfied. Naturally certain errors could have been avoided had he been personally at the helm, but overall his service chiefs had performed as well as could have been expected. They were, after all, with the exception of Goering, only professional soldiers. And by and large they had only needed to implement the plans bequeathed by himself.

On 17 January Hitler was informed of the broad strategic decisions taken at Karinhall the previous September, and of the subsequent implementation of specific measures relating to those decisions. He agreed with the general line of strategic thought. Had he not suggested as much himself in the June conversations with Raeder and in Führer Directive 32? Certain details jarred slightly, as he informed Goering on 23 January. Hitler did not fully share OKH's conviction that the Soviet Union had been comprehensively defeated. It would, he noted in passing, have been better to conquer the Ukraine before advancing on Moscow. He was also rather surprised that operations on the Eastern Front had been suspended in December. Could not the German soldier fight better in any weather, any terrain, than the *untermenschen*? Clearly the Army's education in the National Socialist spirit was far from complete. When fully recovered he intended to take the matter firmly in hand.

As for Africa, the Führer agreed to the transfer of 39th Panzer Corps, but would countenance no further reinforcement of Rommel's army. All the remaining panzer strength would be needed for the drive to the Urals and the conquest of the Caucasus. As for Malta, Hitler admitted to the gravest doubts about an operation which rested on such a high level of Italian involvement. Particularly as regards the Italian Fleet. At the first sight of the British Navy the Italian ships would scuttle back into their harbours and leave the Germans isolated on the island!

Goering was very reassuring. He agreed with everything the Führer had said concerning Russia. But what could you expect? Brauchitsch was a clown, Halder a conceited prig. And none of the generals knew how to take orders, even when they were the correct ones! But there was no need to worry about Malta. The Luftwaffe had fully learnt the lessons of Crete, and the force involved was much larger and much better equipped. He had just returned from a meeting with Generaloberst Student in Rome, and Student had assured him that the Italian troops were excellent, far superior to the rabble in North Africa. As for the Italian Navy – even they would find it hard to run away from the British forces still afloat in the Mediterranean. No, the only real problem as regards the Malta operation was the lackadaisical Italian attitude towards fuel and other supplies. It would be useful if Hitler could prod the Duce into more dynamic action when the two leaders met in February.

Goering was not Hitler's only visitor. As was his usual practice, Hitler preferred to see his acolytes one at a time, just in case they all disagreed with him. Raeder was the next military chief to ascend the Berghof road, and he was full of grandiose plans to cheer the Führer on his road to complete recovery. After tactfully reminding Hitler of his decision to settle accounts with the British in the Middle East once *Barbarossa* was completed, the Grand-Admiral eagerly outlined his 'Grand Plan' for the conquest of that region through concerted German and Japanese offensives. Talks had been proceeding in Tokyo and Berlin, and though, as Raeder had to admit, no concrete plan of action had yet been agreed, there seemed every possibility that the two great Axis powers could join hands 'in the Arabian area' some time that summer. Already the Japanese were expressing interest in Ceylon and Madagascar, and Raeder's Chief of Staff, Admiral Fricke, had dispatched all the information the Germans possessed with regard to suitable landing points. It was quite possible that the Japanese intended first to crush the Americans in the Pacific before turning west, but this would present no problems. Admiral Oshima had assured him that such an operation would still allow adequate time for the planned summer rendezvous in the Indian Ocean.

Hitler was greatly taken by the 'Grand Plan' – it appealed to his sense of drama – and he told Raeder how impressed he had been by the Japanese attack on Pearl Harbor. It was unfortunate that Germany's other ally lacked a similar sense of resolution. Hitler then talked at length of the Japanese national character – a subject of which he had his usual cursory acquaintance – and explained to the captive Admiral how Pearl Harbor exemplified the 'devil' tactic in *kendo*, a surprise thrust followed by lightning retreat.

Raeder eventually steered his Führer back to more pressing matters, and outlined the latest developments in the Atlantic. He did not trouble Hitler with Doenitz's fury on learning that twenty per cent of his available U-boats were being transferred to the Mediterranean, but contented himself with reciting the latest encouraging statistics. Hitler was apparently not much interested, in either the Mediterranean or the Atlantic. He merely seized on the westward drift of the conversation to pour scorn on the American declaration of war. How, he asked, could the United States, led by Roosevelt and his Jewish financiers, expect to wage war on the German Reich? It was ridiculous.

The British, of course, were another matter. But the Karinhall decision-makers had, unwittingly, hit on their Achilles heel. This was not, he assured Raeder, the Suez Canal. It was the Persian and Iraqi oil-fields. With the capture of these and the Caucasian fields neither Britain nor the Soviet Union would have sufficient oil to sustain their hopeless struggles. The British might try to bring oil across the Atlantic, but the U-boats would make

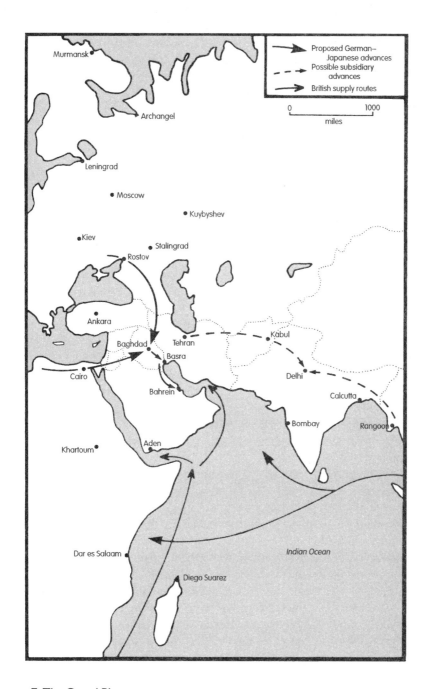

7. The Grand Plan

mincemeat of the tanker fleets. 'It is the economic aspects which are crucial in war,' he told the Grand-Admiral.

He said the same thing to Brauchitsch three days later, and accused the hapless Army Commander-in-Chief of almost destroying the Russian campaign by attacking Moscow, 'a mere geographical concept'. The Army had been fortunate to take the more vital Donbass region before the winter set in. As it happened the ordinary German soldier had saved the day. But what really mattered, what lay at the root of the Army's strategic errors, was the lack of National Socialist spirit at the highest levels. This would have to be put right in the coming year. In the meantime Hitler wished to know the Army's intentions for the spring campaign in the East. He did not tell Brauchitsch that General Jodl, back with his old master, was already drawing up a plan to Hitler's specifications for future comparison. The Commander of the all-powerful German Army left, as usual, with his tail firmly between his legs.

On 'Heroes Memorial Day', 16 March, Hitler spoke to a larger audience, addressing the German nation for the first time in eight months. He thanked destiny for his miraculous recovery from a 'serious accident', seeing in the former – the recovery, not the accident – further evidence of Fate's interest in the mission he and the German *volk* were struggling to fulfil. As regards the Russian war – 'we have succeeded where another man failed one hundred and thirty years ago'. The war would be over this year. Russia would be crushed without mercy; Britain would come to realise the futility of continued resistance. The United States was no military threat. Hitler derided the 'Victory Programme' – 'these people who think they can buy strength, who think they can mass-produce will-power'. Forgotten, apparently, was the dictum that in war the economic aspects were crucial.

And not only forgotten in speeches. Hitler might belittle Roosevelt's efforts, but had Germany been engaged in such a thorough-going armaments programme of her own there would have been more solid grounds for the Führer's confidence. The one visitor whom Hitler did not enjoy receiving was Dr Todt, the Minister of Armaments and Munitions. He brought only problems to the Berghof, problems that were not only of little interest but that also seemed to admit of no instant solutions.

Which was very unfortunate, not to say profoundly irritating. Hitler – and here he exemplified the essence of that ideology he thought he had created – thought in terms of weeks or in terms of decades. In both cases he could make instant decisions, on the one hand shifting a platoon in southern Russia, on the other peopling the empty Ukrainian steppe with sturdy German settlers. But the space in between the present and the distant future interested him not at all. Planning for the coming year or the year after that – the sort of timespan relevant to armament production – was always conspicuous by its absence. Hence the decisions that had *not* been taken in 1939-40 were, by 1941-2, coming home to roost. There were no long-range bombers for attacking the new Soviet centres of industry east of the Volga, not enough U-boats for winning the Battle of the Atlantic, not enough production capacity in the artillery, tank and ammunition sectors.

It was the low production which most worried Dr Todt, and which most irritated Hitler. It was the Armament Minister's responsibility to secure the necessary capacity and materials, Hitler told him. Yes, said Todt, but the Reich Marshal had taken most of everything for the Luftwaffe and his Four-year Plan. Could not Hitler intervene to put matters right?

But Hitler was reluctant to enter the jungle he had created, and which he preferred to rule from the outside. There was no need to worry, he told Todt. The war would soon be over, and there was sufficient strength to bring it to its victorious conclusion. Why worry about 1943? Then they would be rebuilding Berlin, not waging war. Todt was sent away to muddle on as best he could.

Only in one respect did Hitler concern himself with the intermediate future. Only one programme was planned meticulously in advance. At the end of March SS Reichsführer Himmler visited Hitler at the Berghof. He recounted the successes of the *einsatzgruppen* in occupied Russia, the deadly blows they had dealt the Jewish menace. Hitler was not overly impressed; his brush with death had convinced him that this programme, his greatest contribution to the purity of humankind, should be accelerated lest Fate should take a further hand. He ordered Himmler to step up the exterminations in eastern Europe, and to prepare new squads of *einsatzgruppen* for action in North Africa and Palestine in the coming summer. There would of course be no point in transporting these Jews back to Europe; facilities for their disposal would have to be created on the spot.

The Führer was back at his blood-stained helm.

London

In January Churchill had been hoping that time, British advice and a few more unexpected jolts would help his American allies down the road to realism. In the matter of the jolts he was not to be disappointed. Through February and March they came thick and fast as the Japanese contemptuously shrugged aside Allied resistance in South-east Asia. The pitiful remnants of Western naval power were crushed in the Battle of the Java Sea, and the islands of the South China Sea dropped one by one into the Japanese hand. Singapore, with its impregnable defences facing south, was taken from the north. The US Army in the Philippines was herded into the Bataan peninsula for a long, heroic and futile siege. Sumatra, Borneo, Celebes, Java, Timor, Wake, Guam – one after another the sparks of resistance were extinguished. In Burma General Iida's Fifteenth Army took Rangoon on 8 March and pursued the retreating British northwards towards Mandalay.

Four thousand miles further west Auchinleck was attempting to shore up the British position in the Middle East. The forces holding the northern front in Iran and Iraq were still negligible; no units could be spared from the Western Desert, particularly now that Rommel had received large panzer reinforcements. On Malta the population suffered from shortages and the almost hourly attentions of the Luftwaffe. There seemed little chance of a convoy getting through, every chance of an Axis invasion.

As March gave way to April the situation looked profoundly ominous. Wherever the Western allies looked they saw the growing strength of the enemy and the inadequacy of the forces ranged against him. If to those who strolled though London's St James Park the air was redolent with spring, to those in the war-rooms below-ground nearby the new season offered only a drying of the ground in Russia and blue skies and calm seas in the Mediterranean. New blows were about to fall, and there was precious little with which to blunt or avert them.

In the Indian Ocean *Kido Butai* was nearing Ceylon; in the Mediterranean the signs of an invasion force being readied for an assault on Malta were unmistakable. In the Arctic Ocean the days grew relentlessly longer, endangering the convoys which struggled to meet the desperate needs of the Soviet Union. In the Atlantic the toll exacted by Doenitz's U-boats had still not reached its awesome peak. In India the Congress Party rejected the British offer of post-war independence; it was, said Gandhi, 'a post-dated cheque on a falling bank'.

Amidst this situation of escalating danger, Harry Hopkins and General Marshall visited London with American plans for the continued prosecution of the war. These showed a remarkable lack of realism. Eager to get into the fray, the US Chiefs of Staff had set their hearts on an invasion of continental Europe in 1943, to be preceded by 'raids' in the second half of 1942. They admitted that the necessary American troops could not reach England before September, but asked for a binding statement of intention from their British allies. This way a 'dispersion of Allied strength' could be avoided.

Churchill was naturally reluctant to contradict flatly the ally he had so long awaited, but his 'acceptance with qualifications' of the 'broad principles' of the American plan was further qualified by the less diplomatic British Chiefs of Staff. They patiently explained to their American guests that the 'dispersion' of British strength served a valuable purpose, that of containing the enemy. Holding the ring had to have priority over all other considerations. If the Axis powers could be successfully contained through the coming summer, then, and only then, could serious attention be paid to the possibilities of a cross-Channel assault. Naturally such an operation would have to be undertaken at some time, but putting a date to it was neither practical nor useful at the present time.

The Americans were not happy with this 'over-cautious' approach. They considered Britain's problems in India, which were much in evidence during these days, to be caused purely and simply by the British desire to hold on to an outdated Empire. They doubted the possibility of that German-Japanese link-up in the Indian Ocean which the British feared so much. They stressed the need to relieve Russia's burden by landing troops in France. Above all they wanted action.

They would soon have it. The storm was about to burst. On the evening of 12 April, as Hopkins and Marshall were sipping their pre-dinner cocktails at Chequers, a message was handed to the British Prime Minister. German parachutes were opening in the skies above Malta.

Chapter 5
THE FALL OF MALTA

There I was, trapped. Trapped like a trap in a trap.
Dorothy Parker

I

At three o'clock in the afternoon of Sunday 12 April one Lieutenant Johnston, commanding an anti-aircraft battery in the outskirts of Kalafrana on Malta's south-eastern coast, was the first British soldier to see the armada of Ju52 transport planes approaching the island from the east. Like all of Malta's defenders he had been vaguely expecting such a sight for several weeks, and definitely awaiting it since noon on that day. But still, somehow, it was a surprise. 'There were so many of the wretched things. And for those of us who'd been in Crete it was like having the same ghastly dream all over again.'

Lieutenant Johnston's battery claimed one of the low-flying transports but there was no time for rejoicing. Scores of others flew overhead as the accompanying fighters zoomed down on the British anti-aircraft positions. Had Johnston and his comrades had the time to watch, they would have seen the lines of paratroopers tumbling from their planes and floating down to the ground in the two miles of countryside stretching west from Hal Far airfield. Other British gunners stationed around Hal Far could not believe how low the Ju52s were flying. 'They were barely three hundred feet up. The parachutes hardly had a chance to open before the Jerries hit the ground.'

But hit the ground they did, in most cases safely. The area chosen was sparsely defended, and the troops had time to regroup and recover the weapons containers that were parachuted down amongst them. In Crete the dropping zones had been badly chosen, and the troops had been spread out too widely. As a result many had been dead before they reached the ground. But on Malta the drop was concentrated, the zones chosen well.

The vanguard *fallschirmjager* of 7th Airborne Division unpacked their heavier guns and mortars and prepared to move off towards their pre-assigned targets. They laid out large swastika flags on the ground as markers for the planes still to come. The invasion of Malta was underway.

II

This airborne assault was the culminating blow of a campaign that had already lasted four months. It had begun with the virtual doubling of Luftwaffe strength in the Mediterranean at the end of the previous November. Luftflotte X, whose responsibilities covered a vast area – including supporting Rommel, protecting the Axis Mediterranean supply-route, protecting Italian oil shipments *en route* from Roumania through the northern Mediterranean, and attacking the British rear areas in Egypt – had been joined by Luftflotte II, fresh from its successes in the skies above Moscow. The new Air Fleet, mustering some 325 planes, was deployed exclusively in Sicily, with orders to neutralise Malta's capacity to interfere with Axis shipping and to weaken the island's ability to withstand the planned invasion. It comprised five bomber groups of Ju88s, one group of Stukas, one of Me110s and four of Me109fs.

This formidable force got off to an unfortunate start in January and early February, mostly due to the employment of mistaken tactics. Field-Marshal Kesselring, in overall command of the Mediterranean Luftwaffe formations, ordered continuous raids by small groups of planes. Such tactics, he felt, would give the defenders no rest. But Kesselring overlooked the fact that it would also give them the chance to concentrate their forces. German losses suddenly climbed alarmingly.

Nor were the raids doing much damage. Malta's defences were highly dispersed, and the prevailing Luftwaffe gospel of pinpoint bombing ensured that each target destroyed exacted an inordinate cost in planes.

New tactics were called for, and in early February Luftflotte II's Chief of Staff, Air-General Deichmann, decreed a changeover to area bombing by massed bomber formations. The areas chosen were not particularly large, but they were hard to miss. The first chosen were the Grand Harbour, with its naval installations, and the three principal airfields at Hal Far, Luqa and Takali. For three weeks practically the entire Air Fleet was engaged in attacking these targets.

The new tactics worked well. Enormous damage was inflicted, yet the cost to the Luftwaffe was negligible. The last remaining seaworthy ships were forced to evacuate Malta; the submarines had to remain submerged through the daylight hours. Dockyard work was brought to a virtual halt; even in the underground workshops it was continually interrupted by power breakdowns and light failures. The airfields were kept barely functional by civil labour and the local troops, but in any case the planes which used them were being slowly consumed by the battle above.

During the last fortnight of March the German bombers shifted their attentions to secondary targets – camps, barracks, store depots and roads. Anti-aircraft positions were subject to almost continuous attack, particularly those in the south-eastern corner of the island. It seemed to the Maltese garrison and population that the sky was rarely clear of the enemy for more than ten minutes.

The scale of the air assault, and the losses involved, naturally created enormous difficulties for the island's political and military leaderships. None of the losses could be replaced. Not one convoy had docked in Valletta's Grand Harbour since the previous September. Cunningham's failure to win back the Cyrenaican airstrips in 'Crusader' had led to the cancellation of the convoy planned for early January; only one merchant ship, the *Breconshire*, had tried to slip through unescorted at the end of the month with a cargo of much-needed fuel oil. Caught by German bombers operating from those very airstrips, the ship had been severely disabled and now sat, leaking oil, in Tobruk harbour.

In mid-February another attempt had been made, this time involving three merchant ships, but it was no more successful. Mercilessly attacked by German planes from Crete and Cyrenaica for over four hundred miles, the three merchantmen went down one by one, leaving Admiral Vian's destroyers to guard an empty sea.

By this time the situation on the island was serious, and was recognised as such in London. Churchill, as we shall see, was reluctant to pester Auchinleck into a desert offensive, but was ready to order Admiral Cunningham (the General's brother) to push through a convoy 'regardless of the cost in naval vessels'. This was easier said than done, though Cunningham was characteristically willing to try. The next convoy, containing six merchantmen and aptly-code-named 'Essential', would be protected by virtually the entire Mediterranean Fleet. Not that this, in March 1942, amounted to very much. Only three cruisers and seven destroyers could be found to protect the convoy against the battleships of the Italian Navy and the might of the Luftwaffe.

It was not enough. The Italian Fleet put in an appearance, but failed to bring the inferior British force to battle. Vian's destroyers cloaked the convoy with smoke, and Admiral Iachino, not for the first time, refused to expose his capital ships to the dangers of a British torpedo attack. The Luftwaffe was not so easily deterred. Once again the merchantmen succumbed to its bombs as their escort pumped flak into the clouds. The first ship was sunk due south of Cape Matapan, the last eighty miles short of Malta. A British destroyer went down with them. At nightfall on 17 March a disconsolate Cunningham turned back for Alexandria.

The failure of 'Essential' was a crippling blow. On Malta the situation deteriorated day by day. Flour, bread, sugar, coal, benzine and kerosene were either running short or not running at all. Even drinking water was in short supply. Rationing and the communal 'Victory Kitchens' ensured that the hardships were shared, but that was small comfort as they grew harder to bear. All in all, Malta's life-support system was stretched to the limit. Although it was estimated that the island could hold out until the end of April, there is no doubt that its ability to resist an invasion had been growing steadily weaker since the middle of March.

In the purely military sphere the shortages were also taking their toll. The *Breconshire*'s failure in January had left the stocks of aviation fuel dangerously depleted, a situation only saved, ironically, by the shortage of planes to use them up. By the end of March only six Hurricanes remained of the island's fighter force.

Ammunition was also a pressing problem. There was enough for small arms and the light anti-aircraft guns, but not for the vital heavy anti-aircraft weapons. Since these latter guns, together with the now largely non-existent air force, formed the backbone of the island's air defence it was unlikely that any serious opposition could be offered an airborne assault while it was still in the air. Malta's survival would have to be fought for on the ground.

Through 1941 the garrison had been steadily increased despite the calls of other theatres, and by August consisted of some thirteen infantry battalions and the King's Own Malta Regiment, altogether some 23,000 men. It had been intended to raise the numbers still further but the Luftwaffe's grip on the Central Mediterranean made reinforcement impossible.

Up until January 1942 the plans for thwarting an invasion rested, in the worst British tradition, on an almost exclusively static conception of defence. A line of fortifications – the Victoria Lines – was built from east to west so as to cut off the north-western corner of the island, and the coastline of the remaining two-thirds was fortified. Anti-tank and anti-personnel mines were sown on and behind the beaches, wire was laid in profusion, and an anti-tank ditch excavated. Concrete and mutually-supporting pill-boxes were built in three parallel lines inland from the coast. Others were scattered around the all-important airstrips. Only a few companies were allotted a mobile role; these would counter-attack in the event of an enemy threat to the airfields. The rest of the garrison was supposed to sit inside its defences and wait.

General Beak, who arrived in January to take over the military command, did not think much of these arrangements. He wanted a considerably enlarged mobile reserve. But at the end of the month the Luftwaffe offensive moved into top gear, and most of the garrison's time was taken up with repairing damage done by the bombing. There was little time for training exercises, or for the implementation of Beak's ideas. The island's defence would have to rest, in the great tradition of Rourke's Drift, on the thin red line and a wall to put it behind. Unfortunately the British were wearing khaki now, and the Ju52s would not be dropping Zulus.

III

The invasion of Crete the previous May had been a costly affair for Student's XI Airborne Corps. Out of 22,000 troops committed over 6000 had been killed, and 3764 of those had been members of the Airborne Corps. The losses in experienced officers and NCOs had been particularly high. It seemed to many as if the *fallschirmjager*'s days of glory were now at an end.

Student had disagreed, and for several months had been awaiting the opportunity to prove the doubters wrong. Now, with Malta, he had been given his opportunity. The mistakes made during the Cretan operation – inadequate reconnaissance, wrong choice of dropping zones, the inadequate preparation of the Greek airfields – could, he believed, have been rectified. In the Malta operation they would be rectified.

This time round the *fallschirmjager* would be dropping with their Italian allies, a less disheartening prospect than might have been imagined by those used to decrying the efforts of the Italian infantry in the desert. Italy, like Germany and the Soviet Union, had taken an early interest in the possibilities of airborne assault, and experiments in the new form of warfare had been proceeding since the late '20s. The Italian parachute battalions raised during the previous decade – by 1942 expanded into the *Folgore* and *Nemba* divisions – were well-trained, and possessed of a high *esprit de corps*. If the Germans were to be let down by the Italians, it would not be by the airborne troops.

The preparations for 'Operation C3' (the Italian designation) had begun in late November under the overall supervision of Student. It was recognised that it would have to take place by mid-April at the latest, for both Rommel and the Army in Russia would be demanding the return of their air strength by that time. The invasion could not take place much earlier on account of the conditions at sea.

The forces available were certainly large. 30,000 men were to be lifted in by air and another 70,000 by sea; an invasion force which outnumbered the British garrison by four to one. Four hundred Ju52s and two hundred Savoia 82s would drop the paratroopers and bring in the other airborne troops once an airfield had been captured. There were also over five hundred gliders available, most of them either the standard DFS230s or the newer Gotha 242s. The former, which had been used in Crete, carried only ten men, the latter either twenty-five men or the equivalent in hardware. There were also thirty of the aptly-named Me321 'Gigants'; these could transport either two hundred men, a 75 mm anti-tank gun, or a small tank. They had to be towed by a troika of Me110s.

In Crete the gliders had gone in first, their silent approach maximising the element of surprise. But in the case of Malta surprise was considered highly unlikely, and in any case the nature of the terrain – most notably the stone walls which cut the island into tiny segments – made it impossible to land the gliders anywhere outside the airfield areas.

The one outstanding advantage Malta had over Crete was the short distance the troops would have to be carried. Each transport plane could be expected to make the thirty-minute run four times each way in the course of a day. In the two runs envisaged on the afternoon of the invasion some 12,000 troops could be dropped.

The amphibious operation presented more difficulties. For one thing the six Italian divisions involved were of dubious quality, for another it was doubted in some quarters whether the Italian battlefleet would defend their passage with sufficient resolution. There were also the usual anxieties about insufficient oil supplies.

But for all this, there was no lack of confidence in the Axis camp. The Prince of Piedmont, the conservatively competent nominal commander of the operation, expected it to be successful. Student was also optimistic. His subordinate, Major Rancke, had submitted glowing reports on the state of the *Folgore* Division; the size of the forces involved in the operation was almost overwhelming. Student saw no flaws in the plan. Kesselring did expect problems with the amphibious operation, but did not anticipate any with the more vital airborne invasion. Only the Italian generals commanding the six infantry divisions expressed deep pessimism, but their doubts were swept aside by Mussolini's military supremo, Marshal Cavallero. He was hoping for the laurels.

One major source of all this confidence was the thoroughness of the reconnaissance operation. Every square inch of Malta had been caught by the camera's eye; the type and position of all but the most expertly camouflaged defence positions had been noted and taken into account. As Student said later: 'we even knew the calibre of the coastal guns, and how many degrees they could be turned inwards.' The invaders had a very clear idea of what they were invading.

Armed with all this information the German-Italian Planning Staff in Rome had drafted their plan of attack. The area chosen for the initial assault was in the south-eastern corner of the island, for the coast in this section, though rockier and steeper, was known to be less well defended. At around noon on the chosen day intensive attacks would be launched on the anti-aircraft positions in this area and, as the last bombs fell, the airborne troops would drop from their transport planes in the areas north and west of their primary objectives, Hal Far airfield.

By this time the amphibious operation would be getting underway. The spearhead force – 8300 men, artillery and tanks carried in self-propelled craft – would beach that night in the Marsa Scirocco Bay, within easy linking distance of the airborne troops. On the following day continuous flights of transport planes would bring in more troops to the captured Hal Far airfield, and the bulk of the invasion fleet would be pulling in to secure beaches. The Luftwaffe would be controlling the skies and, aided by the Italian Navy and German U-boats, the sea. Conquering the rest of the island would be no problem.

IV

The initial drop went well. Over Crete the pilots had over-compensated for the strong offshore winds and dropped the troops too far inland, but here the winds were light and onshore and no such mistake was made. By 15.00 nearly 4000 German and Italian paratroopers had been dropped into the intended zone west of Hal Far. Only a dozen or so transport planes had been downed by the AA fire, and most of the troops had safely reached the ground. Once there they swiftly regrouped and, closely supported by the diving Stukas, began to consolidate and expand their bridgehead.

In the other major dropping-zone, between the Birzebbugia-Tarshin road and Hal Far, the Axis losses were heavier. The anti-aircraft positions, more numerous and better camouflaged, claimed a healthy number of the Ju52s, and the defenders' machine-guns killed some five per cent of the 7th Airborne Division's 3rd and 4th Battalions before they hit the ground. But again the drop was well concentrated, and soon the other ninety-five per cent was consolidating its position, one unit setting up a north-facing road-block as the others moved east into the rear of the coastal defences and south against the northern perimeter of Hal Far airfield.

As the invaders began to put down roots in Malta's stony soil the island's civil and military leaders were meeting in Sir William Dobbie's office in Valletta's Government House. For many weeks they had been expecting the worst, and here it was. The island's air force was virtually nonexistent, and no help could be expected from the Royal Navy until the following day. In any case the scale of naval assistance was unlikely to offer any panaceas. Vice-Admiral Syfret, commanding Force H at Gibraltar, had only the small carrier *Argus*, the battleship *Malaya*, the cruiser *Hermione* and eight destroyers available for the rescue mission. The US carrier *Wasp* was also docked in the shadow of the Rock, but her employment in such a dangerous undertaking required the assent of Washington. No one had thought to secure this permission in advance. It was the early hours of 13 April before Syfret could begin his thousand-mile journey east to the embattled island.

The enemy was at sea by dusk on the 12th, the Italian troop-carrying craft moving round Cape Passaro escorted by the Italian Battlefleet. They had a mere seventy miles of ocean to cross, and the only threat to their passage was that offered by British submarines. One of these, the *Upright*, had observed the invasion fleet assembling outside Syracuse harbour. It had radioed the information to Valletta and was now shadowing the convoy south.

On Malta itself darkness fell with the battle for Hal Far airfield well underway. Seven miles away in Valletta Generals Beak and Dobbie were struggling to make sense of the confused information at their disposal. Beak decided on caution. He would commit his small mobile reserve against the bridgeheads, but would not move any other units from their present positions until such time as he knew the landfall of the armada coming down from the north.

He had, like his predecessors on Crete, got the priorities wrong. It was the airborne threat that had to be countered, and immediately. If the Axis troops gained control of Hal Far they could bring in heavy equipment and

97

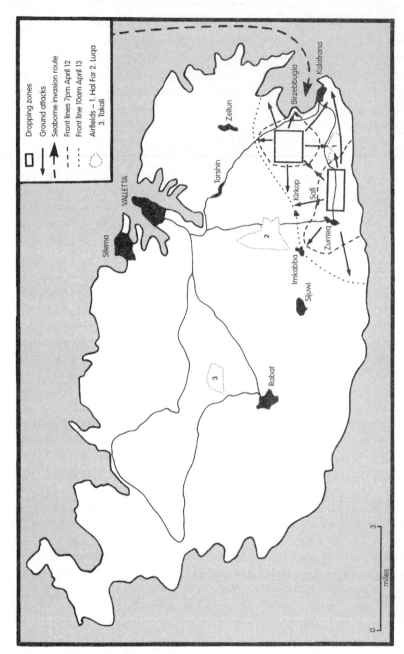

8. The Fall of Malta

large troop reinforcements by glider and transport plane. Sooner or later the respective forces would be equalised, and from thereon the odds would rise against the defenders. Already, with the second mass-drop around 16.30, there were almost 9000 Axis troops on the island, over half of them German. And the battle for Hal Far was not going well for the incumbents.

By 21.00 the bridgehead west of the airfield was four miles wide and over a mile deep. The *Folgore* units on the northern and western flanks had taken the village of Safi and were ensconced in the outskirts of Imkabba. On the eastern flank the *fallschirmjager* of 7th Airborne's 1st and 2nd Battalions had reached the western and southern perimeters of the airfields, and were working their way around the latter towards the Kalafrana road. To the north of the airfield the 3rd and 4th Battalions were holding, with some difficulty, the Tarshin road and closing in on Birzebbugia and the southern beaches of the Marsa Scirocco. The two bridgeheads were now less than a mile apart.

The fighting continued through the night. The German troops poured mortar fire into the 231st Infantry Brigade's positions in and around Hal Far. In the early hours the airfield was the scene of bitter hand-to-hand encounters as the forces from the two bridgeheads squeezed the British defenders out to the north and east.

Another mile to the north-east similar struggles were taking place for the coastal stretch around Birzebbugia. The village itself fell just before midnight; further to the south the Kalafrana flying-boat base was overrun soon afterwards. The beaches between the two were cleared in the succeeding hours in circumstances which could only be described as chaotic, for it was at this time that the amphibious invasion force arrived in Marsa Scirocco Bay.

It had been realised by the Axis planners that their time-table was a tight one, and that Marsa Scirocco might not be cleared of the enemy before the first landings took place, but it was felt that leaving the amphibious operation any later would allow the Royal Navy time to intervene. So at 03.00 on 13 April the first Italian boats sailed into a hail of fire from the British guns on the northern arm of the bay, and soon afterwards those troops fortunate enough to survive this enfilade clambered on to mine-strewn beaches and into the British-German inferno raging above them. Not surprisingly the Italian losses were incredibly high; something in the region of forty per cent of the first wave did not survive to see the dawn. Much of the equipment, including most of the light tanks, followed the boats to the bottom of the bay. It was not an easy baptism of fire for the inexperienced Italian infantry.

Dawn brought relief to the invading force. As the sun rose the Stukas and Messerschmitts filled the skies once more. General Beak had received news of the Italian armada's destination soon after 02.30; he had then issued the orders that a more adventurous spirit would have issued six hours before, thinning the garrison's deployment across the rest of the island and moving his strength into the south-eastern sector. It was too late. With daylight the movement of troops became more and more hazardous, as the German planes launched strike after strike against the unprotected British columns. Though the leaders in Government House were loth to admit it, the battle for Malta had already been lost.

Hal Far had been finally cleared by the Germans just before dawn, and although the airfield was still under fire from the north and the runway in need of repairs, the Axis command could now begin to send in its gliders. Lieutenant Johnston, still holding out with two hundred others on the peninsula south of Kalafrana, watched them wafting in soon after 09.00, 'sinister and silent'. He had seen the DFS230s in Crete, but not the enormous Gigants, 'like bloated birds'. The gliders, score after score of them, belly-flopped down on to the grassy expanses of the airfield, disgorging their troops and – in the case of the Gigants – howitzers, several 75 mm guns and seven Panzer IIs.

By mid-morning the Axis bridgehead comprised – Lieutenant Johnston's party apart – the entire south-eastern corner of the island. The dividing line ran from the coast south of Sijuwi through Imkabba and Kirkop to the Marsa Scirocco coastline south of Zeitun. All along its eastern half fierce fighting was taking place as the British tried to force their way back into Hal Far and the Germans attempted to clear the northern arm of the bay. The latter were more successful. In Syracuse a satisfied General Student was preparing to leave for the bridgehead.

At 11.00 Syfret's Force H was two hundred miles to the west of Malta. On the bridge of the cruiser *Hermione*, the Admiral was sifting through his apparent options. They seemed pitifully few. On paper his fleet was far inferior to that of the Italians; for contesting the skies with the all-powerful Luftwaffe he had sixty-five Spitfires aboard the *Wasp* and the slow *Argus*. If he attempted to interfere with the troop transports moving across the Malta Channel in daylight he was likely to incur what in any circumstances would be regarded as unacceptable losses. The Western allies could certainly not afford to lose a carrier like *Wasp* with the situation in the Atlantic so precarious. Yet the Italians were unlikely to be fool enough to shift their transports by night once they knew the Royal Navy was in the vicinity. Syfret could bombard the

German bridgehead by night, but he doubted whether this would make much difference to the outcome of the land battle. Whatever he did the risks were likely to outweigh the benefits. Successful naval activity beneath an enemy-held sky was just not on the cards.

By noon the need for a decision was growing more acute. Rounding Cape Bon, Force H was spotted by long-range Axis reconnaissance planes. Surprise, always unlikely, was now out of the question. What, thought the Admiral, should he do?

In London, too, there was agonised indecision. The reports from Malta suggested that the Germans had already secured the airfield they needed. The Chiefs of Staff remembered only too well that the seizure of Maleme had proved the beginning of the end on Crete. Was the battle for Malta already lost? And, if so, was there any reason to risk Force H and the remains of the Mediterranean Fleet? Would it be better for Syfret to fly off his Spitfires and return to Gibraltar?

Churchill, with his usual never-say-die attitude, was extremely reluctant to abandon Malta if any hope still remained. But as the afternoon wore on, and as Syfret's fleet sailed deeper into the jaws of the Luftwaffe, the situation reports coming from the island grew more and more alarming. The last of the Hurricanes had been shot down that morning, Marsa Scirocco was now ringed by the invading forces, the approaches to Hal Far were jammed with hovering German and Italian transport planes. General Beak estimated that over 25,000 Axis troops would be on the island by nightfall.

This was only a slight exaggeration. Minute by minute the Junkers, Savoias and gliders touched down to disgorge men and equipment. Two-thirds of the airborne component was now on Malta. The village of Imkabba had finally fallen to the *Folgore* division, and 7th Airborne, with its few light tanks, was more than holding its own on the Tarshin road. The Luftwaffe fighters and dive-bombers continued to pin the defenders to the ground. The battle was clearly going the invaders' way. By nightfall the struggle for Luqa airfield was beginning.

At 21.15 Syfret's Gibraltar Fleet rendezvoused with Vian's cruisers and destroyers fifty miles south of the island. Both fleets had been heavily attacked throughout the afternoon, but no ship had yet been lost. The orders from London were to bombard the enemy disembarkation area under cover of darkness. If the enemy fleet intervened Syfret was to use his discretion; he was not, however, to be deterred by the threat of heavy losses should the situation ashore warrant them. But the carriers were not to take part in the attack. They were to return to Gibraltar; their planes would be flown off to Takali airfield at first light.

Syfret duly took his ships in to attack Marsa Scirocco, and the German-Italian beachhead was bombarded with the necessary vigour through the early hours of 14 April. The Italian Fleet did not intervene – it was back in Sicily, preparing to escort the day's convoy – but the threat of air attack forced Syfret to withdraw his fleet a decent distance to the east in the hours before dawn.

And that, more or less, was that. Through the night the exhausted Axis airborne troops had been wresting most of Luqa airfield from the debilitated and despairing grasp of the British infantry. In London it was realised that the battle was lost, and Syfret was ordered out of the danger area. The Chiefs of Staff reached the unpopular but wise decision not to attempt an evacuation by sea. The experience with Crete had shown just how costly such an evacuation could be, and this time round the odds were stacked even more heavily against the British. It was a fact of life in April 1942 that ships were more precious than infantry.

As if to demonstrate the correctness of this British decision the Luftwaffe heavily attacked the two withdrawing carriers that morning. *Wasp*'s flight deck was hit by several German bombs, and the resultant blaze was impressive enough to convince the Luftwaffe pilots that the American carrier was on her way down.

On the island the full-scale battle lasted several more days. In the caves, grottoes and underground workshops sporadic resistance was offered for several weeks. But, as with Crete, the issue had been decided the moment the invaders secured a functional airstrip. Malta had been a lost cause since the early hours of 13 April.

Student was promoted Colonel-General by a pleased Führer; Mussolini, not to be outdone, promoted nearly everyone who had set foot on the island. The Duce also toyed with the idea of a triumphal visit, but decided to wait for the more tantalising occasion of an entry into Cairo.

Chapter 6
'THE PYRAMIDS ARE LARGER THAN I IMAGINED'

The ship seems to be heading inevitably for the rocks.
General Brooke, 31 March 1942

I

As the last pockets of Maltese resistance were systematically extinguished by the Axis invaders, General Erwin Rommel sat in his captured British command vehicle, cursed the flies, and pored over maps of the Western Desert and Lower Egypt. With Malta occupied Axis control of the central Mediterranean was assured, and the free passage of supplies to *Panzerarmee Afrika* was at last an enduring reality. Now Rommel could afford to look east and only east, towards Egypt and the glittering prize of plentiful oil in the deserts beyond.

Soon the Luftwaffe formations that had doomed the British forces on Malta would be joining the army in North Africa, and Rommel would have parity in the air with the enemy. The three divisions of 39th Panzer Corps – now redesignated II Afrika Korps – had arrived in Cyrenaica late in February; by now they were reasonably accustomed to the climate and the terrain. The peculiarities of desert battle could of course only be learned in combat, but Rommel was confident that the divisions' level of experience and training would see them through.

He had great hopes of the new commanders. General Rudolf Schmidt, commanding II Afrika Korps, was a solid leader with a wealth of panzer experience. He was also, as luck would have it, an old friend of General Cruewell, commander of the original Afrika Korps (now I Afrika Korps). The two new panzer division commanders had both been regimental commanders in France, and their swift rise to divisional command testified to their excellent records. General Balck had commanded Guderian's spearhead regiment in the drive to the English Channel and a panzer regiment in Kleist's Panzer Group 1 in the Ukraine. He had recently succeeded General Stumpff as commander of 20th Panzer Division. General Manteuffel had led 7th Panzer Division's panzer regiment in the drive on Moscow, and had taken over command of the division when General Steiner was killed outside Volokamsk. Rommel, of course, knew many of 7th Panzer's officers and men, having himself led the division in France. So *Panzerarmee Afrika*, even with its growing size, remained something of an old boy's club, and the wealth of shared experience and common thought-patterns would serve it well in the often disjointed desert fighting of the coming weeks.

Rommel himself was certainly confident. His letters to his wife Lucie brimmed with breathless anticipation of the struggle ahead. To take but one example:

> Dearest Lu
>
> I'm fine in every way. Things are working out as I hoped. Now that Malta has fallen our supply difficulties are over. And that seems to have cured my stomach troubles! Soon you will be hearing big news in the Wehrmacht communiques. The troops are in good fettle, and I'm more than ready to go! We're all hoping to strike the blow that ends this war.

II

Rommel's good cheer was Churchill's gloom. The enthusiasm engendered by the American entry into the war had faded as the immediate dangers to the British position became steadily more apparent. America would take time to gird its collective loins, maybe too much time. The Japanese had already swallowed up the Far East, and were now at the gates of India and the Indian Ocean. In Russia the situation, though obscure, was clearly critical. Only in North Africa was the line holding. But for how long?

As recently as February Churchill had seen no reason why it should not hold indefinitely. There were, as he never tired of exclaiming, over 600,000 British, Dominion and Imperial troops in North Africa and the Middle East. This surely was enough to stem any German onslaught, whether from the west or the north or both. It was possible that General Auchinleck was correct in asserting that no offensive action could be launched until the summer. Churchill, mindful of his own role in pushing 'Crusader' to its premature demise, was reluctant to press his Middle East C-in-C on this point. But there could be no question of a further retreat; the Egyptian frontier would have to be held until such time as an offensive could be launched.

This uncharacteristic realism on the Prime Minister's part had suffered not a little strain as the Axis designs on Malta became evident through the month of March. Churchill had been understandably unwilling to see the island fall while Eighth Army watched impotently from the sidelines. Less understandably he urged an offensive in the Western Desert, 'regardless of the risks', as a means of averting the threatened calamity.

Auchinleck, who possessed an occasionally debilitating surfeit of realism, had considered this 'senseless'. And had said so, as diplomatically as possible. He and his staff in the Middle East had argued that a desert offensive, with Eighth Army palpably unready, would do nothing to save Malta and would probably result in the loss of Egypt.

> We feel that to launch an offensive with inadequate armoured forces may very well result in the almost complete destruction of those troops, in view of our experience in the last Cyrenaican campaign. We cannot hope to hold the defensive positions we have prepared covering Egypt, however strong we may be in infantry, against a serious enemy offensive unless we can dispose of a reasonably strong armoured force in reserve, which we should not then have ... We still feel that the risk to Egypt incurred by the piecemeal destruction of our armoured forces which may result from a premature offensive may be more serious and more immediate than that involved in the loss of Malta, serious though this would be.

The Chiefs of Staff in London, after much heart-searching, had reluctantly agreed. Brooke had seen 'no possibility of holding on to Malta unless the Italians make a complete hash of the enterprise. Unfortunately the strong German involvement makes this extremely unlikely.' Britain's resources were too few and too precious to expend on causes already lost.

And so Malta fell, with Eighth Army still intact on the Egyptian frontier. It would need to be, for despite Churchill's habitual optimism it was virtually all that stood between Germany and the oil that both sides needed to continue the war. Ninth Army in Syria and Tenth Army in Iraq and Iran were both of little more than corps strength; the former would most likely join Eighth Army in the defence of Egypt, leaving the latter's three half-trained and ill-equipped Indian divisions to stem a German surge across the Soviet-Iranian border.

The weakness of this northern flank, and Rommel's increased panzer strength, worried General Brooke more than it apparently worried Churchill. Brooke began to wonder whether Eighth Army's deployment on the Egyptian frontier was either tactically or strategically wise. In its present position Eighth Army could always be bypassed and encircled by panzer forces moving round the open desert flank. Tactically it might make more sense to pull the Army back to the El Alamein position, where its left flank could be anchored to the northern cliffs of the Qattara Depression. Strategically even this might prove insufficient. Eighth Army would still be a long way from the ultimate zone of decision, the oilfields of southern Persia. These were threatened from the north as well as from the west. Perhaps it would be wiser to give up Egypt altogether, to pull Eighth Army back behind the Suez Canal, or even the Jordan.

But such notions, however sensible from the military point of view, were political anathema to the British leadership. Only five months before they had been advertising 'Crusader' as the offensive that would drive the Axis out of North Africa; now they could hardly surrender the same area to the enemy without a fight. Or even conduct tactical withdrawals. Auchinleck was promised another two infantry divisions for the northern front, but for better or worse Eighth Army was to wait for Rommel on the Egyptian frontier.

III

The fate of Egypt was of interest not only to Germans, Italians and British but also, surprisingly enough, to the Egyptians, many of whom were hopefully awaiting an Axis victory. They were not looking for new rulers, but for the independence which they naïvely, if understandably, expected from the all-conquering Rommel.

British rule was unpopular. It was not so much tyrannical as possessed of that huge unconscious arrogance which only centuries of empire-building can produce. Britain was fighting for the world, and the world, including the Egyptians, would have to make the necessary sacrifices. If this meant being bombed, invaded and forced to suffer basic shortages then that was just too bad. The British Empire had no time to consult with the people it was saving from dictatorship.

This attitude – and British policy in Palestine vis-à-vis Jewish immigration – generated a marked lack of loyalty to the Allied cause among the Arab populations of the Middle East, Egypt included. Nascent rebellions in Syria and Iran and a real rebellion in Iraq had already been crushed in 1941. Egypt was occupied by a rather larger army, and armed rebellion was, for the moment, out of the question. But help, in the form of *Panzerarmee Afrika*, was on the way. If the British were too busy to consult the Egyptians the Axis powers were not.

King Farouk had come to the throne in 1937, and had soon installed the pro-Axis Ali Maher-pasha as his Prime Minister. Maher had no desire to bring Egypt into the war, and refused to declare war on Italy merely because Italy had declared war on Britain. This was naturally unacceptable to the British, who removed him as inconspicuously as possible.

But Ali Maher would not go away. He maintained close contact with the King, and the two of them remained the Axis's chief supporters in Egypt. They also kept in surreptitious touch with the Axis powers, particularly Germany. The King's father-in-law and Ambassador to Tehran, Zulficar-pasha, told his German counterpart in April 1941 that Farouk and his nation would 'like to see Germany's liberating troops in Egypt as soon as possible'. He further conveyed the King's sympathy and respect for Hitler and Germany, and wished them every success in the war with England.

This was far from the only contact between the Axis and the Egyptians. General Aziz Ali el-Masri-pasha, who had been Egyptian Chief of Staff under the Ali Maher Government, had contacts with the Abwehr. In early 1941 Admiral Canaris's organization tried to help him out of Egypt and into Axis-held territory, but the British caught him boarding his plane and sentenced him to a mild prison term.

Aziz Ali el-Masri also had links with the so-called Free Officers Group, which was made up of young and indignant lieutenants and majors like Gamel Abdul Nasser and Anwar as-Sadat. This group, whose contacts with the Italians in 1940 had borne little fruit, were now establishing new contacts with the more impressive Germans.

All this clandestine anti-imperialism might well have come to nothing had Egyptian popular opinion been better disposed towards the occupying power. But as the shortages of food and basic goods became more marked, and pro-Axis propaganda more intense, the popular mood swung in the opposite direction. In January 1942 the students of Al Azhar University rampaged through Cairo calling for Rommel and the return of Ali Maher. Farouk, attempting to ride this tide of nationalist fervour, sought a showdown with the British. He demanded the resignation of his Foreign Minister, who had just broken off relations with Vichy France at British insistence. This caused the entire Egyptian Government to resign. The British, fearing that Farouk would fill the new vacuum with Ali Maher, surrounded the King's Abdin Palace with armoured cars and presented him with two alternatives. He could appoint the pro-British Nahas-pasha or he could abdicate.

Farouk chose the former and the British, content with such sensible behaviour, promptly forgot the matter. They would have done better to keep it in mind. Farouk's humiliation was Egypt's humiliation, and anti-British feeling deepened and spread. Major Nasser, one of the Free Officers later hanged by the British for collaborating with the Axis, wrote in his diary:

> As for us, as for the army, this event has been a deep shock; hitherto the officers talked only of enjoyment and pleasure. Now they talk of sacrifices and defending dignity at the cost of their lives ... You see them repenting of not having intervened in spite of their obvious weakness to restore the country's dignity ...

Nasser and his fellow Free Officers did more than repent; they began to plan for the not-too-distant future when, they hoped, Rommel would burst through the western gates of Egypt.

IV

Oblivious to this plotting behind them in Egypt, but only too aware of Malta's fate and the new panzer units in front of them, the men of Eighth Army waited through the last two weeks for Rommel's blow to fall. General Cunningham was still their commander; Auchinleck, though not entirely satisfied with his performance in 'Crusader', had been loth to dismiss him for what he saw as Churchill's mistake. Cunningham's naïve handling of the British armour had been at best overlooked, at worst misunderstood. Auchinleck, who made few mistakes of his own, was very good at persevering with others who did.

Eighth Army, despite the battering of the previous November and the calls of the embattled Far East, was a stronger force than it had been six months before. It was still divided into two corps, the 30th under Norrie and the 13th under Godwin-Austen. The former now comprised two armoured divisions, boasting 650 tanks, of which 165 were the powerful new American Grants. The latter comprised two infantry divisions, both almost completely motorised, and the 32nd Army Tank Brigade. The 1st Armoured Brigade was in reserve, the 2nd New Zealand Division *en route* from Syria. There was also 70th Division and 1st Army Tank Brigade ensconced, none too comfortably, in Tobruk.

The British had conserved their Middle Eastern strength well during the months of Japan's Far Eastern onslaught but their deployment of it left much to be desired. The force in Tobruk was an heroic lamb laid on the altar of Imperial prestige. Should the Germans attack the fortress in strength – as they were virtually certain to do – there was little chance of successful resistance and none at all of escaping to fight another day. Auchinleck wanted to abandon Tobruk, the Navy was fed up with the losses involved in supplying it, but Churchill and the Chiefs of Staff had convinced themselves that its port facilities should be denied to the Germans for as long as possible.

The rest of Eighth Army sat astride and behind the frontier defences, which had been greatly improved in the preceding months. Minefields and barbed wire had been laid and draped in a profusion previously unknown in the desert theatre. 13th Corps' infantry and 'I' tanks were deployed immediately behind these killing grounds, in some cases accommodated amongst them in 'boxes'. 30th Corps' armoured units were deployed further back.

Little, it seemed, had been learnt from the 'Crusader' battle. Rather than dividing the front into two command areas, north and south, it was again divided into infantry and armour, static and mobile, front and back, with no thought of the confusion such arrangements would inevitably give rise to. Wherever the Axis forces attacked they would be engaging infantry and armour controlled from two separate headquarters.

Even more serious was Cunningham's continuing failure to concentrate his armour adequately. He saw this as flexibility, it was merely incompetence. Auchinleck specifically enjoined him to ensure that no chance be given the enemy to destroy the British armour piecemeal, but such a chance was to be offered just the same. The British commanders, as Rommel said after the war, could not seem to grasp the peculiar conditions of mobile desert warfare. It was much akin to naval fighting; there was little point in relying on fixed positions, little to be gained from controlling space *per se*. If the British had been literally at sea they would have had no trouble grasping the point. Unfortunately they were only metaphorically at sea, and grasp it they could not.

The German attack on the frontier positions, when it came, would be concentrated against either the British right flank, centre or left flank. Which would it be? The former was considered unlikely. Along the coastal strip the terrain was difficult, the defences deep, and there was no obvious objective upon which an encirclement could be anchored. It would be like punching air. Auchinleck expected Rommel to try and punch a hole in the centre of the British line. Such an attack, if successful, would effectively cut Eighth Army in two, and give the German commander a good opportunity of encircling and destroying one of the halves. Cunningham thought Rommel would attempt a 'Crusader-in-reverse', a long right hook around the trailing British southern flank and a straight drive for the coast between Buq-Buq and Sidi Barrani. If this move proved successful the whole British army might be forfeit.

Both these options were certainly open to Rommel, and the deployment of the British armour had to take both possibilities into account. 1st Armoured Division was placed east and south of Bir el Khireigat, 7th Armoured Division an ominous twenty miles further south. In theory a German attack in the centre could thus be hit in both flanks, while one in the south would give the British armour time to concentrate. It sounded better than it was.

V

At dawn on Monday, 8 May, dense formations of German bombers and dive-bombers swooped down on the Tobruk perimeter defences, and as the clouds of smoke and dust drifted up into the blue sky detachments of infantry from 14th Motorised cut the wire along the south-eastern sector and pushed forward into the front-line defences. Within two hours a wide breach had been made, and the sappers and engineers were called forward to clear channels through the minefields and bridge the anti-tank ditch.

In April 1941 some forty German tanks had broken into these defences before being repulsed by strong counter-attacks. Rommel was determined that there would be no recurrence of this setback; he had committed the whole of the recently arrived II Afrika Korps to the attack, while the more experienced I Afrika Korps kept watch on the frontier sixty miles to the east. At around 09.30 the tanks of 7th and 20th Panzer moved forward across the bridged anti-tank ditch and fought their way north towards the 'King's Cross' road junction. By mid-afternoon they had broken through the inner minefields with only light losses and were engaging the Matildas and Valentines of 32nd Army Tank Brigade around 'King's Cross' and astride the Pilastrino Ridge. In these engagements tank losses were heavier, and one British anti-aircraft crew who had the temerity to use their 3.7" AA gun against Balck's tanks – the Germans had been using their similar 88 mm AA guns in an anti-tank role since Arras in 1940 – claimed several victims before being overrun by German infantry.

By late afternoon the disparity of forces was becoming too much for the defenders. Manteuffel's leading tanks had broken through to the harbour area and were gaily shooting up British naval vessels; Balck's division was in undisputed possession of the ridge and the road junction. The Luftwaffe filled the sky.

General Scobie, commanding the garrison, realised that the unequal contest could not be prolonged indefinitely. In fact it was only his desire to inflict enemy losses that prolonged it through the night. By morning there was no choice but to raise the white flag. Tobruk had followed Malta into the Axis bag.

Rommel had no time for celebrations. 'Fortress Tobruk has capitulated,' he signalled the Panzer Army. 'All units will reassemble and prepare for further advance.' The Italian *Brescia* and *Trento* infantry divisions were set in motion for the frontier; II Afrika Korps refuelled, refitted and set out for its pre-arranged assembly area west of Gasr el Abid. The new offensive was set to begin four days hence, on Saturday, 13 May.

The inability of the British commanders to think and act at Rommel's pace continued to haunt Eighth Army. Cunningham expected that his German counterpart would require at least a fortnight to prepare his next attack, despite plentiful past experience to the contrary. As darkness fell on 13 May he had no idea that the long columns of I Afrika Korps and XX Italian Corps were beginning their long night-march around his southern flank, following their route by compass, the moon, and the dim marker lights in gasoline cans. In the early hours of 14 May Cruewell's Corps, with Rommel and his armoured command vehicle in close attendance, were refuelling south-east of Fort Maddalena, still unsighted by the British.

Further to the north, around Gasr el Abid, dawn broke with a ferocious artillery barrage and air strike as II Afrika Korps, fresh from its desert battle baptism at Tobruk, attacked the centre of the British line in the sector held by 150th Brigade of the 50th Infantry Division. 1st Army Tank Brigade was ordered south to help the hard-pressed infantry by 13th Corps Commander Godwin-Austen. He also suggested to his fellow corps commander, General Norrie, that 1st Armoured Division might also care to lend a hand.

Cunningham, as fortune would have it, received news of II Afrika Korps' attack and garbled reports of a German armoured attack in the far south at the same time. Mindful of Auchinleck's instructions not to send his two armoured divisions off in separate directions he decided to leave them where they were, and await identification of the main enemy effort. This, though understandable, was a mistake. Cunningham should have concentrated his armour at this point by withdrawing 7th Armoured Division northwards; by postponing such concentration until he had more information, the British commander gave Rommel exactly the chance which he wished to deny him.

The Panzer Army commander was, as usual in such situations, in his 'Boy's Own' element. His plan, such as it was, was to strike north with I Afrika Korps across the British rear and see what happened. If II Afrika Korps broke through the British centre there was a good chance that the two corps between them could cut off and destroy the southern half of Eighth Army. Or, more optimistically, if I Afrika Korps reached the coast then the entire British Army would be trapped. The next few days would provide the answers.

For Cunningham too. As the sun rose in the sky that morning more ominous news came in from the south. 151st Brigade, holding the positions around Fort Maddalena, reported itself under strong attack from the *Ariete* Division. The 3rd Indian Motor Brigade, which had been deployed some ten miles to the east of Fort Maddalena, reported that it had been overrun by 'an entire bloody German armoured division'. From 7th Motor Brigade there was no news at all. In fact it had been crushed by 21st Panzer, headquarters and all.

The next in line to face this southern onslaught was 4th Armoured Brigade, which should by this time have been falling back to link hands with 1st Armoured Division. But Cunningham had ordered it to stay where it was for the moment, and around 10.45 the Brigade suddenly found itself under attack from the south and south-west as 15th and 21st Panzer closed in for the kill.

Here the Germans received their first, though not too serious, setback. The new Grant tanks, of which German Intelligence knew next to nothing, proved a worthy foe for the panzers. Though the British brigade lost more than forty tanks, nearly a quarter of its complement, the Germans lost close to that number themselves, and the British managed to withdraw northwards in reasonable order. The German divisions followed, but soon found themselves counter-attacked as 2nd Armoured Brigade appeared out of the north to bolster the shaken but still intact 4th Armoured Brigade. For the rest of the afternoon and early evening the two sides slugged away at each other, the 88s on the one side and the Grants on the other taking an occasional victim. Night fell with 15th and 21st Panzer in leaguer ten miles south of Bir el Khireigat. Further to the east 90th Motorised, which had earlier overrun the small supply depot at Habata, was now threatening the huge one at Misheifa.

During that afternoon a bolder man than Cunningham might have been tempted to bring 22nd Armoured Brigade into the battle against I Afrika Korps, in the hope of gaining a decisive victory. But the British commander was too worried about the situation developing on the frontier, where Schmidt's Corps was proving too powerful for 150th Infantry Brigade. By nightfall mixed elements of 14th Motorised and 20th Panzer had secured a bridgehead to the west of the minefields, and a full-scale breakthrough was threatening. Cunningham decided that 22nd Armoured Brigade should attack this bridgehead at first light on the following day.

At the opposing Command HQ Rommel was worrying about his overextended supply route. The Italian motorised division *Trieste* had not yet taken Fort Maddalena, and I Afrika Korps' supplies were still having to be carried right round the southern end of the British line. During the night Rommel considered sending the as-yet-uncommitted 7th Panzer south to help *Trieste*, but then decided that II Afrika Korps could be relied on to open a fresh route through the centre during the coming day.

Cunningham was not so confident, and the night passed with endless conferences among the British commanders which only served to increase their general confusion. In truth the British position at this juncture was far from untenable. The bulk of the armour was still intact and Rommel's drive for the coast had been, temporarily at least, halted. 1st Armoured Brigade had been called out of reserve and was being deployed to the west of Misheifa, between 90th Motorised and the coast. There was a distinct possibility that the German attack could be ground down by a resolute defence, if only the British could react swiftly enough to whatever Rommel pulled out of his hat.

By dawn on 15 May they were already one step behind. Rommel, aware of the twenty-mile gap separating the two armoured engagements, had made use of his mobility. Before first light he had pulled 21st Panzer south and then directed it east towards the frontier, leaving 15th Panzer to tie down 4th and 2nd Armoured Brigades. Simultaneously Schmidt was funnelling 7th Panzer into the bridgehead. Cunningham had unwittingly directed 22nd Armoured Brigade into a trap. Around 08.00 it was still assembling to attack the bridgehead when 21st Panzer loomed out of the south to hit the brigade in the flank. A large number of British tanks were driven back on to the waiting 88s of 7th Panzer and 14th Motorised. The division broke up into uncoordinated segments, lost almost half its tanks, and took no further part in the battle for almost thirty-six hours. Yet again the Germans had managed to concentrate against dispersed British armour.

All was not yet lost, however. Units of 2nd Armoured Brigade, pushing south in an attempt to outflank the long-gone 21st Panzer, had inadvertently driven a wedge between the two German corps and struck hard at the unsuspecting *Ariete* Division. 21st Panzer, by now almost immobilised by lack of fuel, could neither go to the Italians' aid nor close the gap. 15th Panzer was also low on fuel and ammunition, and fully occupied holding off the British armour to its north. So Rommel's main priorities for the rest of the day were to reseal the gap, concentrate his two corps on a line facing north, and get supplies through to 15th and 21st Panzer. For the moment there could be no full-scale exploitation of the gap presented by 22nd Armoured Brigade's temporary demise. Only 7th Panzer could be pushed north towards Bir el Khireigat, and this division was halted by the stern resistance of 1st Army Tank Brigade and the 2nd South African Brigade. On the frontier 20th Panzer and 14th Motorised were struggling to widen the breach through the minefields for the supply columns.

By nightfall on 15 May the 'front' ran in an L-shape south from the coast to Gasr el Abid and then east to the area of Habata. British armour losses had been heavier than the German, and the tank ratio now stood at roughly five

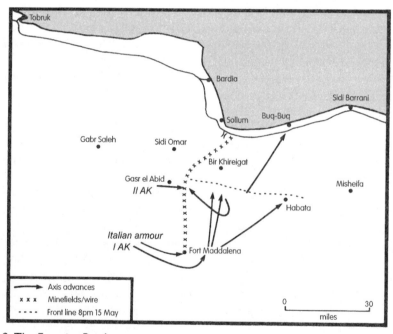

9. The Frontier Battle

114

to six. Cunningham reported to Auchinleck that he doubted whether a German breakthrough to the coast could be held off indefinitely. He wondered whether it would be wise to pull back to the Alamein positions which, Churchill notwithstanding, had been appreciably strengthened in the preceding months. Auchinleck decided to come and assess the situation on the spot the following morning. In the meantime he 'advised' Cunningham to move 1st Armoured Brigade, which had been 'harassing' 90th Motorised for the previous twenty-four hours, west to the area of Bir el Khireigat. 5th Indian Division could take its place north of Habata.

Through the night of 15/16 May the supply columns drove east across the gravel wastes to replenish the German right wing. Behind them rumbled the tanks of 20th and 21st Panzer. Rommel intended to deliver the decisive stroke that morning – a three-panzer division attack towards the coast at Buq-Buq. Eighth Army, he believed, was as good as dead.

Auchinleck, arriving at Cunningham's HQ around 08.30, and receiving the first reports of Rommel's attack, came to a similar conclusion. Eighth Army had to retreat. Fortunately 1st Armoured Brigade had not, for reasons unknown, received the order to move west, and with the newly arrived 5th Indian Division was fighting a resolute delaying action.

Cunningham's mental condition gave less cause for satisfaction. The strain had been too much, and Auchinleck effectively assumed direct command of Eighth Army that morning, Cunningham being officially relieved some days later.

What could be saved from the wreck? The two infantry divisions, with the exception of 50th Division's 150th Brigade, had suffered relatively few casualties. The South African Division was ordered out along the coast road, while 50th Division's other two brigades would retreat across the rear of the German armour. The armoured brigades in the north would fall back slowly to provide cover as the South Africans withdrew through the narrowing gap between the panzers and the sea.

Rommel, naturally enough, was determined to close the gap. In this he was to be disappointed. Despite all the efforts of the panzer crews their progress was slowed by the prodigious efforts of the RAF. On 16 and 17 May, as Auchinleck later categorically stated, 'Eighth Army was saved by the RAF.' When Balck's leading panzers reached the coast two miles east of Buq-Buq at 15.45 on 17 May only a few stragglers remained to the west.

But there was ample compensation for Rommel. The enemy was in full retreat, having suffered severe losses in supplies and equipment. His victorious Panzer Army was now not much more than two hundred miles form Alexandria. Egypt, he believed, was in his grasp.

VI

During the next few days, as 90th Motorised reconnaissance units moved east along the coastal road in the wake of the retreating British, the defenders and population of the Egyptian heartland prepared themselves for the inevitable onslaught. The proud remains of the British Mediterranean Fleet sailed from Alexandria on the night of 19 May; around the harbour the demolition gangs awaited the order to destroy the port installations. The town itself seemed like a ghost town, the effects of a strict curfew compounded by the absence of army units, most of whom had been sent either west to the front or south-east to Cairo for possible evacuation.

In the capital itself streets were jammed with traffic from the front, from the country districts, from Alexandria. It was impossible to find space on the densely-packed trains leaving the main station for Palestine. On the roads leading east and south away from Cairo long convoys carried non-combat personnel towards the Suez Canal, Suez itself and the Upper Nile valley. On an open stretch of ground between the British Embassy and the GHQ buildings a number of bonfires were consuming maps, codes, reports, documents of every kind. Cairo seemed to be echoing Moscow.

In the Abdin Palace a nervous King Farouk was closeted with ex-Prime Minister Ali Maher. The King had promised the British authorities that he would move to Gaza when the time came, but he had no intention of doing so. The Germans had also offered him sanctuary; the Abwehr had promised to spirit him and Ali Maher away to Crete. The two Egyptians had refused this offer. They would 'disappear' in the near future, they told their Axis contact, and resurface only to welcome the 'liberation of our country'.

In the barracks of the Egyptian Army the plotting was also proceeding, though with little apparent effect. The Free Officers were trying to inveigle the powerful leader of the Muslim Brotherhood, Sheikh Hassan el Banna, to join them in mounting a coup. He advised them to wait for further Axis successes. When Rommel reached Alexandria, he told Anwar as-Sadat, then they would act together to free Egypt of the accursed British.

While these two were sitting in Banna's tree-shaded mansion in an expensive Cairo suburb, the British were busy building defensive positions on the outskirts of the capital, around Mena to the north-west and near the Pyramids to the west. Auchinleck was still in the desert, supervising Eighth Army's retreat into the El Alamein positions, but messages were flashing back and forth between him and his deputy in Cairo, Lieutenant-General Corbett, concerning the defence of central Egypt. Though Auchinleck did not wish to alarm his already despondent army, he was determined to prepare for the worst. A plan to flood large areas of the Delta was being drawn up, a line of defences under construction between Wadi Natrun and the coast near Alexandria. If the worst came to the worst Auchinleck intended to pull Eighth Army back through Egypt step-by-step, half of it to the line of the Suez Canal, the other half up the valley of the Nile where it could threaten the flank of any German advance into Sinai and Palestine.

There was always the chance that such a retreat would not prove necessary. Eighth Army, though weak in the all-important armour, was drawing back in good order to the Alamein line. The 2nd New Zealand Division was already there, having arrived from Palestine the previous week. The 10th Armoured Division, though lacking tanks and training, was on the way. These movements naturally left the 'northern front' thin to the point of invisibility, but the Germans had not yet renewed their advance in Russia and more divisions were expected from England. The risk had to be taken.

The Prime Minister, whose political position in London was showing signs of deterioration as the military disasters accumulated, fully backed Auchinleck in his resolve to stand and fight at El Alamein. He further suggested, in a typical telegram, that the troops should be given a firm order to 'stand or die where they stood'. This he thought would inspire them. Brooke, though naturally sharing the sentiment, thought that such a categorical order might well cost Britain the entire Eighth Army, which was considerably more precious than Egypt. He approved Auchinleck's policy of demanding the best while preparing for the worst, and won Churchill round to his point of view.

In Washington, Roosevelt shared his ally's alarm. When Churchill asked for help he immediately ordered that 300 new Sherman tanks, one hundred self-propelled guns and a considerable number of aircraft be sent forthwith to the Middle East. If Egypt fell while they were *en route*, then they would be unloaded at Aqaba or Basra rather than Suez.

In Rome the Duce was eagerly anticipating the triumphal march into Cairo that his ally's army had made possible. It had long been agreed that Egypt, and indeed the whole of the Middle East, was in the Italian 'sphere of influence', and Mussolini intended to make the most of it. Accordingly, in the staterooms of the Foreign Ministry, Count Ciano was supervising his staff in the difficult task of preparing a declaration of Egyptian independence which legitimised a virtual Italian annexation. The Rome newspapers were full of the 'two thousand year friendship between Rome and Egypt'. Cleopatra's problems with Octavian were not mentioned.

The Germans, while happy to reaffirm their ally's primacy in public, were hard at work subverting it in private. The Italians had not been told of the Abwehr's contacts with Farouk and Ali Maher – both detested them – and were not to be granted the singular authority they wanted in Cairo. Instead there was to be a German military government headed, for the moment, by Rommel, and an Italian civil government. Naturally, while the war lasted, the former would have priority powers. The latter, on the other hand, would carry the can for the Egyptian economy, itself unlikely to be strengthened by the German refusal to accept any agreement on either the division of war booty or the control of resources. Given that both Germans and Italians recognised that their good behaviour in Egypt might well prove the key to a decisive Arab uprising against British rule east of the Suez Canal, these 'arrangements' showed a characteristically remarkable lack of political acumen. Once again the arrogance and the greed would prove too strong, and the ideological poverty of the 'New Order' would prove its own undoing.

Still, the Axis leaders were never noted clairvoyants, and in the early summer of 1942 the bright glow of military success blinded them to all else. The Führer, arriving at the Wolfsschanze to preside over the new campaign in Russia, told Jodl that he would make Rommel a Field-Marshal on the day his forces entered Cairo.

VII

On the afternoon of 22 May the leading echelons of *Panzerarmee Afrika* loomed out of a sandstorm in front of the El Alamein 'line'. Rommel was determined to attack on the following day, regardless of the fact that most of the Italian infantry and armour was still strung out along the two hundred miles of coast road from Sidi Barrani.

He had problems with the German armour as well. The two Afrika Korps had started the frontier battle with 665 tanks, and had lost over 150 in the process of winning it. More disturbing, a further 90 had broken down in the succeeding pursuit, leaving around 430 for the conquest of Egypt. Supplying even this number was subject to growing difficulties as, for reasons best known to the Italian supply organisations, fuel and ammunition was still being unloaded at Tripoli and Benghazi rather than the much closer Tobruk. Consequently both were short. Only water was plentiful, following 90th Motorised Division's opportune capture of the British supply point at Habata.

The speed of the advance was also causing difficulties. The armour had outstripped its air cover. But Rommel, who wished to slice through the

Alamein position before Eighth Army had time to compose itself, had no intention of slowing the pace. If the panzers had to fight for a day or two under an enemy-held sky then so it would have to be. Such problems tend to solve themselves when an army is going forward.

The problems confronting Auchinleck, whose army was going backwards, were of an altogether more serious nature. Eighth Army had lost more tanks in battle and retreat than the Panzer Army. 7th Armoured Division, now comprising 4th and 1st Armoured Brigades, had only 235 runners, and over two-thirds of these had been 'borrowed' from the now-skeletal 8th Armoured Brigade in reserve. 1st Armoured Division had only 135 tanks, 95 to 2nd and 40 to 22nd Armoured Brigades. For the first time in North Africa the British armour was outnumbered.

In infantry it still possessed a small numerical superiority. Four under-strength divisions were in the line. The greatly depleted 50th Division was inside the Alamein perimeter with the twenty-five tanks remaining to the 1st Army Tank Brigade. One brigade of the 2nd New Zealand Division was manning the Deir el Shein 'box' some fifteen miles inland from the coast; the other two were further back in the area of Alam el Onsol. The 1st South African Division held the Bab el Qattara and Deir el Munassib 'boxes' ten miles further south. At the far southern end of the line the weak 5th Indian Division was deployed in and behind the Naqb Abu Dweis position, a mile or so north of the cliffs which tumbled down into the Qattara Depression. All these units, with the exception of the New Zealanders, were weak in anti-tank guns and heavy artillery and low on morale. They had become somewhat accustomed to defeat.

Auchinleck, expecting Rommel to break through his right centre, had placed his armour behind and to the north of Ruweisat Ridge. He hoped to use it against the flank of a northward German swing to the coast. He had also formed the 5th and 6th New Zealand brigades into mobile battle-groups on the German pattern – lorried infantry with anti-tank guns capable of all-round defence. The relative success of this measure in the days to come would serve to emphasise the poverty of British tactics in the preceding months, and again bring into question Auchinleck's perseverance with the unfortunate Cunningham.

Rommel's hunger for speed precluded adequate intelligence of the British dispositions. He had to guess, and he guessed wrong. Unaware that he was now facing Auchinleck rather than Cunningham he expected the British armour to be further south than it was, ready to block a right hook by the panzer divisions. But Auchinleck had guessed his adversary's intentions correctly, and the two Afrika Korps, advancing along either side of Miteiriya

119

Ridge on the morning of 23 May, soon ran into unexpectedly stiff resistance. II Afrika Korps, trying to work its way around the Alamein perimeter towards the coast, ran headlong into the New Zealand battle-groups and the Grants of 2nd Armoured Brigade. The Germany advance slowed dramatically. Further south 15th Panzer spent the whole day overcoming the 4th New Zealand brigade in the Deir el Shein 'box', while 90th Motorised and 21st Panzer attempted to envelop the southern half of the British line from the rear. After brushing aside 4th Armoured Brigade's weak attack on their left flank the two divisions came up against the South Africans on the ridge above Deir el Munassib. Night fell without the decisive breakthrough which Rommel had expected.

The major source of this relative failure seems to have been the over-confidence of the Panzer Army commander, and his consequent launching of the attack with inadequate air support. During the first thirty-six hours of the battle the efforts of the Desert Air Force provided vital compensation for the inferiority of the British armour. But this situation could not last.

On the following morning Auchinleck played his only trump, directing the strong 1st Armoured Division against the right flank of II Afrika Korps and the much weaker 1st Army Tank Brigade against the left flank. For a few hours the Germans were in trouble, for while 14th Motorised was blithely making headway towards the coast the two panzer divisions were under attack from both sides by marginally superior forces. For once the British had managed to concentrate against a dispersed enemy.

If Auchinleck had been prone to euphoria – which he was not – these few hours would have been his last chance for indulging in it. For by early afternoon Rommel had brought 15th Panzer forward to support the other two divisions, the Luftwaffe was at last beginning to make its presence felt, and the British attack was beginning to wilt. At 16.00 Auchinleck received the distressing news that 14th Motorised had reached the coast. 50th Division was now cut off inside the Alamein perimeter, and between the Germans and Alexandria the road was virtually empty. This was the moment of decision. Should Eighth Army fight gallantly on to probable extinction, or should it break off the battle and withdraw to the Delta and perhaps beyond?

There was really no choice. Auchinleck ordered 50th Division to break out of its encirclement that night; the 5th Indian and South African divisions, now under pressure from both north and west with the belated arrival of the Italian armoured corps, were ordered to fall back to the north-east. The British armour would once again fight a delaying action, this time between the coast and Alma Halfa Ridge.

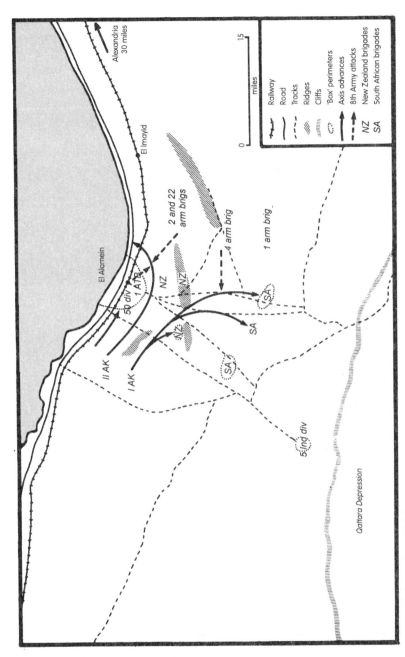

10. Breakthrough at El Alamein

It was easier to issue these orders than to ensure that they were carried out. The battlefield between El Alamein and El Imayid was, by early evening on 24 May, a confused swirling mass of men and vehicles. Darkness fell with the forces of the two sides leaguered in promiscuous profusion across the desert. Soon after midnight 50th Division made its bid for freedom, its columns crashing eastwards through friend and foe alike. Most of the artillery was lost, but the majority of the men made it through to the greater safety of El Imayid.

Rommel too was having his problems turning desires into reality. The RAF had taken such a toll of his supply columns the previous day that yet again the panzer divisions were thirsting for unavailable fuel. It was not until evening on the 25th that he could unleash II Afrika Korps along the coast road towards Alexandria, some twelve hours behind the retreating British. Meanwhile the South African and 5th Indian divisions had somehow failed to receive the order to withdraw issued on the 24th, and by the next day the coast-road option was closed. They pulled back across the open desert towards El Faiyada. Eighth Army, though not destroyed, was now split in two.

Not so *Panzerarmee Afrika*. On the night of 25/26 May the two Afrika Korps rolled east under the moon on the trail of the British. Rommel already had his plan of campaign for the conquest of the area west of the Suez Canal worked out. 20th Panzer, supported by the Italian armour, would drive north-east to encircle Alexandria. The rest of the German armour would strike out east and south-east for the Delta region and Cairo.

Through 26 and 27 May the two armies drove east, their respective columns often intermingling on the same tracks and roads. Many minor actions were fought as commanders suddenly realised that the motley collection of British and German trucks running alongside them belonged to the enemy. But nothing occurred to stop the relentless march to the east. By evening on 27 May 20th Panzer had contemptuously pierced the virtually non-existent Wadi Natrun-Alexandria line and reached the coast four miles east of the city. Alexandria was cut off.

Of militarily greater significance, at around 18.00 the same evening, an armoured column approaching the vital Nile Bridge at Kafr el Zaiyat was mistaken for a British column by the engineers detailed to destroy it. It was in fact the leading column of 14th Motorised, largely equipped with British and American trucks. The bridge was taken intact, and the Germans were across the Nile.

Sixty miles to the south the tanks of I Afrika Korps were approaching the outskirts of Cairo. In the city itself sporadic street-fighting was in progress

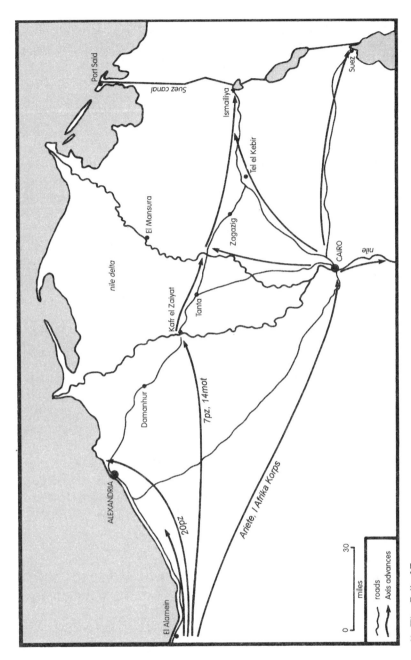

II. The Fall of Egypt

between the British military police and a few Egyptian Army units which had answered the Free Officers' call to revolt. Farouk had disappeared as promised. Egypt was slipping swiftly from the British grasp.

On the morning of 28 May units of 90th Motorised seized, with Egyptian help, one of the Nile bridges in Cairo. This, for Auchinleck, was the final straw. He had been in touch with Brooke, and had been given *carte blanche* to save Eighth Army. The seizure of the Nile bridges and the speed of the panzer advance had ruled out the defence of any line short of the Suez Canal. It was certainly too late to mount any defence of the Delta, as had once been envisaged. Auchinleck took the logical step of sanctioning the retreat to the Canal which was already underway. The South African and 5th Indian divisions, which had lost the race for Cairo with I Afrika Korps, were ordered up the Nile valley. Cairo was abandoned to the enemy.

On the afternoon of 28 May 90th Motorised drove through the centre of the capital to a rapturous reception from its more vocal inhabitants. The Free Officers, whose belated but significant contribution had made them national heroes, were much in evidence. Less heroically, but right on cue, King Farouk and Ali Maher emerged from hiding.

The panzer divisions rolled as fast as fuel supplies would allow along the Suez and Ismailiya roads to the Canal. Rommel was still with them, having declined a room in the famous Shepheard's Hotel booked for him by Egyptian admirers. He had driven past the Pyramids on the previous day – 'larger than I imagined' as he wrote to Lucie – but sightseeing in general would have to wait. That day he received news of his promotion to Field-Marshal.

On the east bank of the Canal the British were siting their guns, scanning the western horizon for the dust-clouds thrown up by the advancing Germans. In London the dreadful news was being digested. The battle for North Africa was over. The battle for the Middle East would soon be underway.

Chapter 7
TSUSHIMA REVISITED

Well, if she gets insulted just because I insulted her!
Groucho Marx

I

In the distant Pacific the two warring navies prepared for what both believed would be the decisive confrontation. In Hiroshima Bay the Japanese admirals bent over maps in the *Yamato* operations room, and worked out the details of Kuroshima's new plan. Haste was the order of the day.

It was a brilliant plan, which for sheer lethal simplicity could only be compared to Manstein's plan for the invasion of France. It is one of the great ironies of the Second World War that both were second-best plans, only adopted when details of the preferred plans became known to the enemy. Both plans also made use of this fact, of the enemy 'not knowing that we knew that he knew'. Both were the product of a gifted professional strategist's dissatisfaction with the predictability of a tradition-bound plan. Both were cast to give full rein to the revolutionary possibilities inherent in new weaponry by men not professionally associated with those weapons. Kuroshima was no more a 'carrier man' than Manstein was a 'panzer man', but both had received support from those who were associated with the new weaponry, in the one case Yamaguchi and Genda, in the other Guderian.

There were also differences of emphasis. Kuroshima's plan perhaps relied more on the 'double-bluff' aspect. The original plan would serve as a feint for the new one, and to this end the broken code was continued in use throughout the month of May. Naturally the information transmitted was somewhat selective. Kuroshima knew that the Americans would expect Nagumo's carriers north-east of Midway, and it was intended to satisfy this expectation. This time, however, the main battle-fleet would be in close attendance. The Americans would also expect a diversion in the Aleutians and a convey of troopships for the seizure of Midway. Both of these would certainly be at sea, but the first without the carriers *Junyo* and *Ryujo* and with severely limited objectives, the second with orders to assault the island only *after* the decisive naval engagement had been fought.

On the other hand, the Americans would not be expecting Nagumo to take his carriers south of Midway Island, in the general direction of the Hawaiian group. This would pull the American carriers south, towards the greatest surprise of all, a second carrier force under Vice-Admiral Takagi moving northwards on an interception course in complete radio silence. If, as seemed possible to Kuroshima, the American carriers retreated to the east rather than seek battle with Nagumo's powerful force, then Takagi's force would be in position to cut them off. Whatever happened the US carriers would find themselves outnumbered and outmanoeuvred, and swiftly dispatched to the ocean floor. And then nothing would stand between the Imperial Navy and the West Coast of America but a few planes on Oahu and a bevy of obsolete battleships in San Francisco Bay.

If Yamamoto's haste was one side of the Pacific coin, an American need to temporise was the other. The 'Two-Ocean Navy' programme, which was designed to give the US Navy preponderance in both the Atlantic and the Pacific, had only been set in motion in late 1940, and the first of the new ships would not be leaving the stocks until the coming autumn. For the next six–nine months the new Pacific C-in-C, Admiral Chester Nimitz, would have to hold off the Japanese with what he had. If he could do so – hold Hawaii and its Midway sentry, keep open the route to Australia – then the balance would begin to swing faster and faster in America's favour. But it would not be easy.

The Japanese preponderance in all classes of warships has already been noted; the American admirals were as aware of this basic fact as the Japanese themselves. The American public – or, to be more precise, the American press – was a different proposition. The pre-declaration of war attack on Port Arthur in 1904 might have been greeted by the American press as a 'brilliant and bold seizure of the initiative', but the identical attack on Pearl Harbor had not been viewed quite so magnanimously. It had been a 'Day of Infamy' and infamy, as all lovers of Hollywood films will know, is always the work of the weak and the cowardly. The Great American Public clamoured for some decisive punitive action against these insolent little yellow men.

Though most of the US naval chiefs were obviously aware that these 'little yellow men' were travelling around in some very large warships it is hard to avoid the conclusion that at some level they shared the public under-estimation of Japanese capabilities. The admirals were worried, but they were not as worried as they should have been. Nimitz's instructions to his carrier admirals on the eve of battle were cautious enough:

> ... you will be governed by the principles of calculated risk, which you shall interpret to mean avoidance of exposure of your forces to attack by superior enemy forces without good prospect of inflicting, as a result of such exposure, greater damage on the enemy.

– but the mere fact of sending four carriers against an enemy force probably comprising twice that number made a mockery of such caution, and suggested a gross American optimism as regards the quality of the Japanese ships and crews, and the brains that directed them. Nimitz should have known better.

There was one mitigating circumstance. In August 1940, after eighteen months of solid work, Colonel William Friedman had broken the Japanese naval code. The code-book at the bottom of Darwin harbour, which Yorinaga had assumed to be the source of this illicit knowledge, had merely confirmed Friedman's findings. The belief that they 'had the drop' on the Japanese provided Nimitz and his colleagues with an enormous fund of false confidence.

The Japanese did not disabuse them, and no suspicions were aroused when messages advancing Operation 'AF' by seven days were deciphered by the Black Chamber Intelligence Unit at Pearl Harbor.

But this change of date did necessitate a change in American plans. Task Force 16, centred round the carriers *Hornet* and *Enterprise*, had not yet returned to Pearl Harbor from its abortive mission to the Coral Sea. Now it would not have time to do so, and for one person this was indeed good news. Admiral William 'Bull' Halsey, the senior American carrier admiral, had a debilitating skin disease and was due for hospitalisation when the Task Force reached home. But now the bed and lotions would have to wait, and Halsey would have the chance to do what he had been itching to do since the attack on Pearl Harbor, to 'chew Yamamoto's ass'.

Similar sentiments, and a similar over-confidence, were also much in evidence as Rear-Admiral Frank Fletcher led the other Task Force (17, comprising the carriers *Lexington* and *Yorktown* with cruiser and destroyer support) out to sea on 23 May. Sailors and fliers were buoyant, eager to get a crack at the despised enemy. Only their commander seemed subdued, and after the war he would explain why:

> There seemed to be a general consensus throughout the fleet that we were some kind of St George sallying forth to slay a particularly nasty dragon. I couldn't escape the feeling that if St George had been half as confident as most of my staff and crews then the dragon would probably have won.

The dragon was already at sea. On 20 May Vice-Admiral Takagi had sailed from Truk in the Carolines with his four carriers – *Shokaku*, *Zuikaku*, *Junyo* and *Ryujo* – and a strong battleship, cruiser and destroyer escort. The same day the Midway assault force had left Saipan, accompanied by four heavy cruisers. On 21 May Yamamoto's Main Fleet had upped anchor in Hiroshima Bay and threaded its way in single file down the Bungo Channel to the ocean. The Commander-in-Chief, as addicted to the *I Ching* as he was to poker, had thrown the yarrow stalks on the eve of departure. The hexagram had been *Hsieh*, 'deliverance'. 'Deliverance means release from tension ... his return brings good fortune because he wins the central position.'

II

Some six days later, at 4.15am on 28 May, Yamamoto's fleet sailed out from under the clouds two hundred miles west-north-west of Midway Island. Light was already seeping across the horizon, the stars fading in the sky above. The commander himself, gazing out from the bridge of the *Yamato*, saw the new day uncover his vast armada of ships. Behind the *Yamato*, their guns bristling, rode the battleships *Nagato* and *Mutsu*; two miles or so to the north another four battleships sailed on a parallel course. Between these two lines of firepower the four carriers under Admiral Nagumo – *Akagi*, *Kaga*, *Soryu* and *Hiryu* – formed a wide rectangle. Across the water their gongs could be heard vibrating, signalling the order to bring the first wave of planes up on to the flight deck. Soon the green lights would be glowing, and the first Zero fighters would take to the sky, there to hover protectively over the launching of the bombers. All around the capital ships a screen of destroyers, augmented to the van and rear by cruisers, kept a wary eye out for enemy submarines. This was the day of reckoning, Japan's chance to win control of the Pacific, to prolong the war beyond the limits of American patience or resolve.

By 05.15 the torpedo-bombers ('Kates') and dive-bombers ('Vals') had formed up in the sky overhead and, surrounded by their Zero escort, disappeared in the direction of Midway. Having launched his bait Yamamoto set out to find his prey. Search planes from the cruisers and carriers were sent out to cover a three hundred-mile arc to the east. In the meantime more fighters were sent aloft to shield the fleet, and Yamamoto settled down to wait for news of the enemy.

240 miles due north-east of Midway the two American Task Forces waited under a clear blue sky. Halsey, with nothing as yet to attack, had only launched his search planes, some two hours earlier, at first light. The Admiral, according to one of *Enterprise*'s few survivors, was as tense as ever on the eve of action, pacing up and down the bridge, cracking nervous jokes about Japanese incompetence. He knew Yamamoto was out there somewhere; he just wanted a precise fix, and then the world would see how the Japanese would fare in a straight fight. Certainly they were past masters at backstabbing, but, he insisted to his staff, once confronted by a resolute enemy they would find they had met their match. One is irresistibly reminded of the late George Armstrong Custer, riding contemptuously into a Sioux and Cheyenne camp whose warriors outnumbered his own by twenty to one. On seeing the huge encampment Custer is said to have exclaimed: 'Custer's luck! We've got them this time!'

Halsey might well have echoed the sentiment at 06.05, as a message came through from Midway Island. The radar there had picked up the incoming Japanese strike force some thirty miles out. Five minutes later Halsey got his precise fix. One of the *Yorktown* dive-bombers launched on search duty had found the Japanese Fleet, 135 miles west-north-west of Midway, pursuing a south-easterly course. The Admiral signalled to his own fleet: south-south-west at full speed. Within three hours he should be close enough to launch a strike.

On Midway Island the American offensive air-strength – Dauntless and Vindicator bombers, Marauders and Avenger torpedo-bombers, high-level B-17 'Fortresses' – had scrambled off the island airstrips and into the sky, setting course for the probable location of the Japanese Fleet. They went without fighter protection; the obsolete Buffalo Brewsters neither possessed the necessary range nor could be spared from the duty of defending the island.

At 06.40 the Japanese planes appeared out of the west, a dark mass of bombers crowned by a misty halo of Zeros. The Buffaloes attempted to

129

intercept the bombers but were cut to ribbons by the fighters; of sixteen flown up only two returned to crash-land in the lagoon. Fuchida led his planes down against the island's installations, into the teeth of spirited American anti-aircraft fire. The fuel installations went up in a sheet of flames, blockhouses disintegrated under a hail of bombs. Most successful from the Japanese point of view, the runways were cratered from end to end. No American planes would be launched from Midway in the near future. The cost was five Kates, three Vals, and a solitary Zero.

150 miles away the motley armada of American planes from the island was approaching Yamamoto's ships. Unfortunately the little cohesion it had once possessed was already a thing of the past, the attack arriving in driblets that the Japanese could fend off without undue exertion. First the torpedo-bombers, coming in low, were subjected to a vicious enfilade from the ships screening the precious carriers and the close attentions of the Zero standing patrol. Only two limped back to Midway, where the lack of a functional airstrip necessitated more crash-landings in the lagoon. Next the dive-bombers arrived, and these too found the defences hard to penetrate, only three piercing through the flak and fighters to unleash their bombs. All three, by accident or design, chose *Soryu* as their target, but drenched decks from three near-misses was the only outcome. The B-17s fared no better, dropping their bombs with great enthusiasm but little accuracy on the twisting ships 20,000 feet below. Optimistic American eyes counted many hits; there were none. The Japanese Fleet had absorbed all that Midway could throw at it, without so much as a scratch.

It was 07.25. From the *Yamato*'s bridge Yamamoto watched his fleet repairing the damage done to its formation. Fuchida had just radioed news of the Midway attack, advising that there was no need for a second attack. The airstrip was out of operation, the Japanese could concentrate on the American carriers they hoped were some 300 miles away to the north-east. Accordingly Yamamoto ordered Nagumo to send the second wave of bombers back below. Barring a calamity there would be time to bring in the returning first strike while the Americans were still out of range. Reinforcements were sent up to join the Zero patrols above the fleet. And then, again, a period of waiting.

By 08.20 Fuchida's planes were setting down on the flight decks, and being rushed below for re-arming and refuelling. Simultaneously the second wave was brought up from the hangar decks, already primed for action against the American Fleet. By 09.00 the process had been completed without any ominous sighting of approaching American planes. There was still no word of the enemy carriers. The search planes should be on the return leg of their sweeps by this time. If the Americans were where they should be, then they would soon be sighted. Either that or things were not working out according to plan. And that would entail some radical rethinking on the *Yamato* bridge.

It did not prove necessary. At 09.24 a report came in from the *Akagi* scout plane – 'a large enemy force'. Ten minutes later came the composition. The force included four carriers, and was steaming south-westward some 120 miles north-east of Midway.

This was it! *Kido Butai*'s planes swept down the flight decks and into the air. This second wave was mostly composed of Pearl Harbor veterans who had been deliberately held back by Nagumo and Genda for this moment. It was the cream of the Navy air arm. Soon over a hundred planes – roughly equal numbers of Vals, Kates and Zeros – were forming up overhead, and soon after 10.00 the order was given by flight-leader Egusa to proceed north-east against the enemy. Twenty of the Zeros remained behind, hovering above the Japanese carriers. Yamamoto did not want Nagumo to take any unnecessary risks, especially with four other carriers moving in from the south. The wisdom of this policy was soon proven. With the Japanese strike force barely out of sight the destroyer *Hatsuyuki* reported a large enemy force approaching from the north. Halsey's planes had arrived.

Since 06.00 Halsey had been hurrying his carriers southwards to get within range of the Japanese Fleet, and by 09.20 his planes were lifting off from the four carriers. The air crews were all as eager to come to grips with the enemy as their Admiral, and flying over the smoking remains of Midway did nothing to lower their blood-pressure.

More than eagerness would be needed. Within minutes of sighting the Japanese armada the American pilots found themselves ploughing through the same dense flak as had greeted their comrades from Midway. The dive-bombers, arriving just ahead of the slower torpedo-bombers, bore the brunt of the nimble Zeros' defensive fire. Only a few broke through to deliver their bombs, and all missed the scurrying Japanese carriers. But their sacrifice had not been in vain. The had drawn the Zeros up, and close to the surface the torpedo-bombers had only to contend with the ships' anti-aircraft fire and the walls of water thrown up by the fleet's heavy guns. As a result three Avengers cut through to launch their torpedoes at the huge bulk of the *Kaga*. One passed narrowly astern, the other two struck close together amidships. The carrier, holed beneath the water-line, shuddered to a halt, listing violently to port. She would take no further part in the battle, and would finally sink that evening.

It was now 10.55, and three flights of planes were airborne: the first American strike returning to its carriers, the first Japanese strike which was nearing those carriers, and the second American strike which had just taken to the air. If this had been all, then Halsey's confidence might have been justified. But it wasn't. Within minutes, some 250 miles to the south, Vice-Admiral Takagi would be launching a first strike from his still undiscovered fleet. His planes would have twice as far to fly as those from the other two rapidly converging fleets. They would be making their appearance in about two hours time.

In the interlude between the launching of their first and second strikes Halsey and his subordinate Fletcher had been exchanging animated signals as to the second group's composition. Halsey, true to his nature and the Japanese expectations, was inclined to throw everything he had at the enemy. Fletcher, showing greater reverence for the cautious aspect of Nimitz's ambivalent instructions, wished to keep most of the fighter strength back for defence against the inevitable Japanese attack. Better to weaken the American attack, he argued, than to lose the carriers. Halsey, uncharacteristically – there is evidence that he was feeling the strain of his illness on this day – agreed to a fatal compromise. Neither enough fighters were sent with the attack to make it count, nor enough kept behind to ensure adequate protection. When Egusa's eighty-odd planes were picked up by the radar receivers a bare eighteen fighters were waiting to engage them.

For the moment the luck went with the Americans. Yamamoto's decision to hold back most of his fighters tended to offset the American decision. Secondly, Fletcher's Task Force, seven miles astern of Halsey's, was shrouded by clouds during the vital minutes and escaped the notice of the Japanese pilots. Furthermore the Japanese failed to divide their force equally against *Hornet* and *Enterprise*, and the latter escaped relatively unscathed. Two bombs hit the edge of her flight deck, two torpedoes passed narrowly by. The fires were extinguished without difficulty.

A half a mile away across the water *Hornet* had not escaped so lightly, having received no less than five bomb and two torpedo hits. The command post had been annihilated, killing the captain and his staff; the elevator had been blown in a twisted heap across the face of the island super-structure. Two other bombs had lanced through the flight deck and on to the hangar deck before exploding. Secondary detonations continued as the ammunition stacks caught in the raging fires. The order was given to abandon the burning, listing ship at 11.45. Over four hundred men trapped

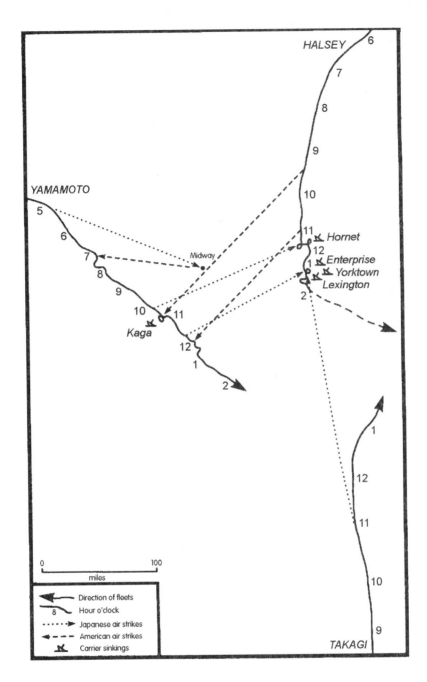

HALSEY
6
7
8
9
10
11
12
1
2

YAMAMOTO
5
6
7
8
9
10
11
12
1
2

Midway

Kaga

11
Hornet
12
Enterprise
1
Yorktown
Lexington
2

1
12
11
10
9
TAKAGI

0   100
miles

→ Direction of fleets
8 ~ Hour o'clock
·····▶ Japanese air strikes
◄─ ─ American air strikes
↘ Carrier sinkings

12. The Battle of Midway

below-decks were unable to comply and went down with the carrier twenty-five minutes later.

The score was one carrier apiece.

By this time Yamamoto and Nagumo had launched a second strike from their three functional carriers, and were preparing to receive the enemy's second blow. News of the *Hornet*'s demise was compensation for the loss of the *Kaga*. The odds, in fact, had shortened. Now it was seven against three, and planes from all seven carriers were now *en route* for the three Americans. It only remained to beat off the last air attack.

The sky above Yamamoto's fleet was clear, and the American pilots had no trouble identifying the three carriers amidst the ring of warships. This advantage was offset, though, by the warning it allowed the radar-less Japanese of the approaching attack. Every available Zero was soon airborne and the scenes of the previous hour were re-enacted. The ponderous torpedo-bombers, this time arriving ahead of the dive-bombers, went down in flames one by one to the combined firepower of the fighters and warships. The dive-bombers, which had strayed off-course, arrived ten minutes later, and the Zeros could not gain altitude quickly enough to prevent several screeching down against *Hiryu* and *Soryu*. The latter managed to escape any serious damage, but three 500 lb bombs hit the *Hiryu*'s flight deck, starting blazing fires. These were extinguished without too much difficulty, but the carrier's ability to launch or receive planes was at an end as far as this operation was concerned. By 12.55 the fleet was once more in formation, the surviving American planes disappearing in the direction of their own carriers. They were not to find them. A hundred miles to the north-east the final act was beginning.

At 12.40 the last of the aircraft returning from the first American strike were touching down on the decks of *Yorktown*, *Enterprise* and *Lexington*. The flight-leaders confirmed their earlier report than an *Akagi*-class carrier had been rendered inoperational, and probably sunk. Halsey informed them that the second strike had reported destroying another carrier. He intended to get the other two.

Fletcher did not agree, and advised a tactical withdrawal. He was not as convinced as his superior – or not so determined to assume – that these four carriers were the only Japanese carriers in the area. Where was the rest of the known Japanese carrier strength? The score at this point was two to one in the Americans' favour; surely this was the prudent moment to withdraw.

Midway would be lost, but in the long run the three surviving carriers were more vital to the defence of Hawaii, and America itself, than one island outpost.

Unknown to either him or Halsey it was too late to avert the incoming attacks. But the fact remains that had Halsey listened to his second-in-command the catastrophe might have proved less complete. He did not listen, preferring to order a third strike on to the flight decks, thereby packing them with planes full of fuel and high explosives. It was an invitation to disaster.

At 13.09 *Yorktown*'s radar – *Enterprise*'s had been put out of action in the previous attack – picked up the Japanese planes closing in from the south-west. The American fighters scrambled into the air, but there was no time to launch the full-loaded bombers.

For the moment it did not seem to matter. The battle in the air went well for the Americans. Yamamoto's caution had deprived the Japanese bombers of sufficient fighter support, radar had given the Americans ample warning, and the less experienced pilots under the veteran Fuchida found it hard to pierce the defences. Only a few hits were scored on the three carriers and none proved crippling. The surviving Japanese attackers turned for home, leaving the Americans with the brief illusion that the battle was going their way.

But at this moment a stunned radar operator on *Yorktown* picked up another flight of aircraft approaching from the south-east. Fletcher's fears had been justified. It must have been little consolation. The fleet was scattered across the sea in the aftermath of the attack; its fighter cover, in any case thinned almost to exhaustion, was dispersed and lacking altitude. The three carriers were virtually naked.

The thoughts passing through Admiral Halsey's mind at this moment will never be known. In minutes his expectations of victory must have turned to the nightmare knowledge of certain defeat. He did not have to suffer such thoughts for long. The Pearl Harbor veterans from *Shokaku* and *Zuikaku* came diving out of the sun at the helpless carriers, lancing in across the waves through the broken screen of covering ships. *Enterprise* was immediately hit by at least five 500 lb bombs – three on the flight deck, one on the bridge, one on the rear of the superstructure – and two torpedoes close together amidships. There were several large explosions in quick succession and one enormous convulsion. A Japanese pilot later likened the sound to that of a motorbike revving up, and then bursting into life. Or, as in *Enterprise*'s case, into death. Within five minutes of receiving the first bomb the ship was on her way to the bottom, the flaming flight deck hissing into the sea. It was the fastest sinking of a carrier in naval history. There were only fourteen survivors.

Yorktown was slightly more 'fortunate'. Also claimed by several bombs and at least one torpedo the carrier shuddered to a halt, listing at an alarming angle. Fletcher had time to order the ship abandoned, and to transfer his flag to the destroyer *Russell*. *Yorktown* went under at 14.26.

A mile away the *Lexington* was also in her death agonies. The target of *Ryujo* and *Junyo*'s less experienced pilots, she had only received three bomb hits. But on decks strewn with inflammable material it was enough. The fires, once started, proved impossible to control, and quickly spread down through the hangar deck. The engines were unaffected, but the engine-room was cut off by the flames. Explosion followed explosion, slowly draining the giant carrier of life. At 14.55 the 'Lady Lex' followed her sister carriers to the bottom.

Their demise was not the end of the battle. In the daylight hours still remaining, and through the next day, the Japanese planes energetically attacked the American cruisers and destroyers as they fled eastwards for the shelter of the planes based on Oahu. Four heavy cruisers were sunk, the last of which, the *Pensacola*, went down at 13.30 on 29 May, some ten miles south of Disappearing Island. It was an apt postscript to the disappearance of an effective American naval presence in the Pacific Ocean.

Chapter 8
FALL SIEGFRIED

What is the use of running when we are not on the right road?

German proverb

I

Chief of the General Staff Colonel-General Franz Halder glanced out of the car window at the sunlight shimmering on the waters of the Mauersee and then turned back to the meteorological reports in his lap. In the eastern Ukraine the roads were drying; another two weeks and the panzers would be mobile along the entire Eastern Front. *Fall Siegfried*, scheduled to begin three weeks hence on 24 May, would not have to be postponed.

The car, *en route* from OKH headquarters at Lötzen to the Führer's headquarters near Rastenburg, left the sparkling Mauersee behind and dived into the dark pine forest. Halder looked at the OKW memorandum. Apparently Rommel was to assault Tobruk the following morning. With the forces at his disposal - forces, Halder reminded himself, that he could well make use of in Russia - he should have no trouble in taking the fortress. And then Egypt, Palestine, Iraq and the meeting with Kleist and Guderian somewhere in Persia? It was possible, perhaps even probable. Halder was not a man given to 'grand plans' - they smacked of amateurism - but he had to admit that this one had more than an air of credibility.

It would have been strange if he had thought differently, for half the 'Grand Plan' was in the briefcase on the seat beside him. Based on the unconsummated sections of *Fall Barbarossa*, drafted by the OKH operations section to Halder's specifications, redrafted to the Führer's specifications, tested by war games at Lötzen, *Fall Siegfried* was designed to end the war against the Soviet Union and create the conditions for the destruction of British power in the Middle East. It was a lot of weight for a single plan to carry.

For five months the front line in the East had barely shifted. The first and most important reason for this was the unreadiness of the Wehrmacht to fight a war in Russian winter conditions. The enemy might have been virtually non-existent on some fronts, but tanks do not run in sub-zero temperatures without anti-freeze, without calks or snow-sleeves for their tracks, without salve for frozen telescopic sights. The supply system could not carry these and other essentials, plus food, clothing, ammunition and fuel a thousand miles from Germany overnight. Something had to be sacrificed, and OKH preferred to forgo a few hundred square miles of snow rather than have its forces freeze to death. As a result of this policy the Germans had suffered few casualties during the winter, either from the winter or the cold.

The second reason for the Army's immobility during these months was a need for time to make up the losses incurred in the summer and autumn of 1941. Compared to the Red Army figures Wehrmacht casualties had been light, but they still amounted to over three-quarters of a million men and a vast amount of hard-to-replace military equipment. The panzer divisions had suffered particularly badly from the appalling road conditions, and many more tanks had been written off in this way than had been put out of commission by enemy action. Bringing these divisions back to full strength occupied the tank-factories and the training instructors for the better part of the winter.

If the condition of the Army necessitated a breathing-space, its leaders were convinced that they could get away with such a period of inactivity. The revised estimates of Soviet strength submitted to Halder by General Kinzel, head of Foreign Armies (East) Intelligence, showed that the 1941 estimates had been grossly optimistic. There had been a fifty per cent error in the manpower figure, and the extent of industrialisation in the areas beyond the Volga had not been realized. But, and here was the encouragement for Halder, Kinzel reported that the losses and disorganisation suffered as a result of the German advance had dealt a temporarily crippling blow to Soviet war industry. It was true that the enemy had managed to evacuate a large number of industrial concerns to the Volga-Ural region, but these could not possibly be fully operational before the summer. It was extremely doubtful, Kinzel concluded, that any significant rise in the Red Army's strength would occur before the autumn. The seizure of the Caucasus oilfields, he added in an appendix, would greatly retard a possible Soviet recovery.

So, Halder had reckoned, the Army in the East could afford to sit still for five months. In that time he had tried to do something about German armament production, though with little success. The German war industry, contrary to popular myth but consistent with the general economic chaos of National Socialism, was, with the exception of its Italian counterpart, the most inefficient of those supplying the war. The whole business, in true Nazi fashion, was divided up between the interlocking baronies which made up the German leadership. These worthies – Todt, Goering, Funk, Thomas at OKW, Milch at OKL – competed for resources, priority, prestige, the Führer's ear, and between them achieved far less than their more single-minded counterparts in Kuybyshev and the West. Halder, who had no aptitude for threading his way through such a jungle hierarchy, could only attempt to win over the head monkey. But Hitler, as already noted, had no interest in such mundane matters as long-term production statistics. Porsche's designs for giant tanks and miniature tanks excited him, but they were only designs. Halder wanted more Panzer IIIs and IVs, not super-weapons for winning the war in 1947. He would get neither. The one time Hitler deigned to speak on the subject it was to assure his Chief of the General Staff that the war would be over by 1943, so there was no cause to worry. How this tied in with Porsche's drawing-board fantasies was not explained. Halder was sent back to Lötzen to scheme the final defeat of the Soviet Union in 1942.

The original *Barbarossa* directive had laid down that 'the final objective of the operation is to erect a barrier against Asiatic Russia on the general line Volga-Archangel', but had made no mention of the Caucasus. Halder, however, was committed to the conquest of the Caucasus by the Karinhall 'Grand Plan' decision. And he doubted if an advance to the Volga would produce results to justify the probable cost. There were no important industrial centres apart from Gorkiy west of the great Volga bend. Accordingly he ignored the Archangel-Volga line, and drafted a plan for the conquest of the Caucasus. Army Group Centre would make only a limited advance, Army Group North would take Vologda and Konosha and so cut the railways which carried Allied supplies from Murmansk and Archangel to the Volga-Ural region. Army Group South, with the bulk of the panzer forces, would move south-eastwards down the Don-Donetz land corridor, secure the land-bridge between Don and Volga west of Stalingrad, and then advance south into the Caucasus.

This plan was presented to Hitler at Berchtesgaden on 4 April. It was not well received. Unknown to Halder, Jodl had also prepared a *Siegfried* and Hitler had found his more amenable. Halder was treated to its salient points, though not the name of its author, and was told to redraft the OKH plan with the following objectives: the Caucasus *and* the attainment of a line Lake Onega-Vologda-Gorkiy-Saratov-Astrakhan. He should bear in mind that a further advance to the Urals might prove necessary.

Hitler gave no reasons for this obsession with miles of steppe and forest. Instead he treated Halder to a lecture on the German need for the Caucasian oil. The Chief of the General Staff noted in his diary that 'the Führer's accident does not seem to have dimmed his appetite for statistics'.

At Lötzen, through the last fortnight of April, Halder's staff struggled to produce a *Siegfried* to the Führer's taste. In the end a three-stage plan was agreed. In the first stage Army Group Centre, augmented by Sixteenth Army and Fourth Panzer Army (all the panzer groups had been upgraded to army status), would attack along the front between the Oka river and Bologoye to attain a line Chudovo-Rybinsk reservoir-Volga-Gorkiy-Ryazan. Having thus secured a salient bound by the Volga and Oka rivers, Second and Fourth Panzer Armies would strike southwards with Fourth Army while Second, Sixth and First Panzer Armies struck east to meet them. Eventually a quadrilateral bounded by Ryazan, Gorkiy, Stalingrad and Rostov would be occupied, the line Hitler demanded manned by the infantry, and the armour released for Stage 3, the conquest of the Caucasus. In the far north Third Panzer Army and Army Group North would be advancing to the ordained Vologda-Onega line.

It was an audacious plan, and made more so by the same lack of reserves with which OKH had launched *Barbarossa*. But that, the dubious Halder reassured himself, had succeeded. The testing of the plan by war game, at Lötzen on 2 May, emphasised the narrowness of the margins but still prophesied success. Hitler proved happy with the new drafting, but could not resist making a few minor alterations. The operation orders were sent out.

On 17 May, the day 20th Panzer reached the coast at Buq-Buq in North Africa, Hitler addressed his Eastern Front commanders at the Wolfsschanze. It was his usual practice to meet them half-way, but Russian distances were great and he had no intention of climbing aboard another plane. He treated the assembled company to a verbose summary of the war situation. Rommel would be in Cairo 'in a few days', the U-Boats were sinking more Allied merchant ships each month than they could build in six, the Japanese were proving too strong for the effete Americans. All that he asked of those present was that they deliver the final crushing blow to the disintegrating colossus in the East. That achieved, the bulk of the Wehrmacht could return to the West, there to offer a decisive deterrent to Anglo-Saxon intervention in the affairs of Europe. The war would be effectively won.

The generals listened to this glowing picture, were given no chance to ask questions, and dispersed. It was the first time most of them had seen Hitler since the accident. 'He looks older,' Guderian wrote to his wife, 'and his left hand shakes terribly.'

II

In Kuybyshev Stalin did not need meteorological reports to know that the period of the spring thaw was drawing to a close: he had only to look out of the window. Soon the Germans would renew their advance, and there seemed precious little chance of stopping the initial onslaught.

But there were few signs of despair, either among the leaders gathered around the table in Kuybyshev's Governor's Palace or among the population at large. The devastating blows dealt by the invader had not split the Soviet Union asunder. Rather, the empty barbarism of Nazi occupation policies had served to emphasise the positive side of Stalin's totalitarianism. Life in Soviet Russia was certainly harsh, but at least the harshness seemed to serve a purpose. The dream born in 1917, that had soured in the succeeding years, seemed more relevant in 1942 than it had since the days of Lenin.

In the vast tracts of occupied Russia, that area of forests and marshland which stretched northwards from the borders of the Ukrainian steppe, the partisans were emerging from their winter retreats. Though still under-organised their presence would be increasingly felt in the months ahead, particularly by those unfortunates detailed to guard the long German supply-lines. In the Ukraine, where the Germans had been initially welcomed as liberators by a significant section of the population, such activity was rendered difficult by the openness of the terrain. But already the cruelties of the occupation had made active collaboration the exception rather than the rule. The loyalty of the non-Russian citizens of the Caucasus, who were yet to learn the realities of German rule, was still to be tested.

On the thousand mile frontier of unoccupied Russia the Red Army awaited the coming offensive. Despite losses exceeding eight million it was still the largest army in the world. It was also one of the worst-equipped and definitely the least-trained. Those few experienced troops who had survived the fires of 1941 were spread too thinly among the copious ranks of raw recruits; only the Siberian divisions of the Far Eastern Army were coherent, well-organised military units. And they had suffered most heavily in the bitter struggles of early winter.

The new Red Army leadership offered some consolation for the poor state of those it had to lead. Most of those who had lost the battles of 1941, whether through incompetence or misfortune, had been replaced. Those in command in the spring of 1942 had either proved themselves extremely adept or extremely fortunate. Much had been learned, many obsolete theories cast aside. Most important of all, given the political realities of the Soviet system, Stalin himself had learnt from his mistakes. No more Soviet armies would be ordered to stand their ground while the panzers cut it from under their feet.

Still, strategic *savoir faire* was of limited use to an army that had a severely limited supply of tanks and aircraft. The excavation of the Gorkiy and Kharkov tank production plants had effectively halved Soviet tank production in the first five months of 1942. The removal of the Voronezh aircraft industry had a serious effect on plane production. Though both tanks and planes were being produced in the Ural region in quantities which would have shocked the Germans, for the coming campaign they were still in pitifully short supply.

So this was the material at Stavka's disposal for averting Hitler's next 'crushing blow'. A large, inexperienced Army, sound leadership, insufficient armour, and an Air Force which could hardly hope to challenge the Luftwaffe for control of the Russian skies. How should it be used?

Just as Hitler and Halder had their list of objectives to gain, so Stalin and Stavka had a list of objectives to hold. Not surprisingly the lists were similar. But fortunately for the Soviet Union, and ultimately for the world, they were not the same. The priorities were different.

The Soviet decisions were taken at a routine Stavka meeting late in the evening of 4 April 1942. Those present included Stalin, Molotov, Shaposhnikov, Timoshenko, Budenny and Zhukov. The last-named argued that the greatest threat to the continued existence of the Soviet Union lay in a German advance beyond the line of the Volga. Behind that river, Zhukov continued, Soviet war industry was being rebuilt. In the cities of the great Volga bend – Kazan, Ulyanovsk, Syzran, Kuybyshev itself – and in those to the east and south, in the Urals, Siberia and Soviet Central Asia, the foundations were being laid for eventual victory. Nothing must be allowed to disturb this construction. Though there was now little hope that the Germans could be pushed back by Soviet arms alone, the growing power of the United States and the continued defiance of Britain would eventually diminish the German presence on Soviet soil. Then these new foundations would prove their worth. As the German power decreased the Soviet power would rise. Then would be the time to march west.

As Zhukov outlined his case Stalin, as was his habit, walked up and down behind the lines of seated generals and marshals, puffing pipe smoke out into the room and occasionally stopping to gaze out of the window at the moonlit Volga. Every now and then a sharp report was audible inside the room, as another stretch of ice cracked in the thawing river.

Shaposhnikov raised the question of the Caucasus. 'Can these industries east of the Volga maintain their production without the Caucasian oil?'

'Of course the retention of the Caucasus is vital,' Zhukov replied. 'But we do not have the forces to defend all those areas that are vital.' He took a memorandum from his attaché case. 'And it seems that the Caucasus is not so vital as the Germans believe, or as we ourselves believed. The oilfields in the Volga-Kama, Ukhta, Guryev and Ural regions are now being developed at the fastest possible speed. According to this report we can survive, at a pinch, without the Caucasian oil. And this is a pinch. The defence of the Caucasus must come second to the defence of the Volga line.'

Stalin, the Georgian, said nothing. Which usually implied agreement. Shaposhnikov was not satisfied. What about the aid from the West? Was it not vital to keep open the southern ingress route, which passed through the Caucasus?

Zhukov reached for another memorandum. 'Work on the new road between Ashkabad and Meshed in northern Persia is well advanced. Of course this road will not have the capacity of the trans-Caucasus route, but it will be better than nothing. The southern ingress route is not the only one. The Archangel railway is carrying a substantially greater volume of goods. And even if Vologda falls – which is likely – the terrain between there and Konosha is most unsuitable for the enemy's armoured formations. We have a much better chance of holding this route open. And even if it were closed, there is still Vladivostok. Unless the Japanese win a great victory over the Americans they will not add to their list of enemies by attacking us in the Far East. If they do, if the worst comes to the worst, we shall have to carry on without outside aid. We will have no choice. But we must hold the Volga line, or there will be nothing left to carry on for!'

The meeting went on into the early hours, but Zhukov's list of priorities was not questioned in principle. The Red Army's dispositions in the following weeks reflected these priorities. The front was now divided into nine Fronts – North, Volkhov, North-west, West, Voronezh, South-west, South, North Caucasus and Caucasus – comprising twenty-six armies or roughly three and a half million men. Half of these armies were attached to only two Fronts, West and Voronezh, holding the centre of the line between the Volga below Kalyazin and Liski on the Don. Of the six armies held in reserve, four were deployed behind these two Fronts. If the Germans intended a straight march east towards the Urals they would have to go straight through the bulk of the Red Army.

III

An hour before dawn on 24 May the German artillery began its preliminary bombardment, and as the sun edged above the rim of the eastern horizon the panzer commanders leaned out of their turrets and waved the lines of tanks and armoured infantry carriers forward.

In the German ranks morale was high. The soldiers had survived the rigours of a winter that would once have been beyond their darkest imaginings, and now it was spring. The leaves were on the trees, the pale sun warmed their feet, their hands and their hearts. The next few months would see this business in the East finished. And then at best there would be peace and home, at worst a more amenable theatre of operations.

The commanders were equally optimistic. Guderian, up with the leading tanks of 2nd Panzer, was later to write:

> Although there was some concern that the final objectives of the summer campaign were not clearly defined, and that this lack of clarity might encourage interference from the Supreme Command (i.e. Hitler), there was little doubt in any of our minds that the war in the East would be concluded before the autumn.

Guderian of course was always at his most optimistic when moving forward, and Second Panzer Army was certainly doing that. On the opening day of the campaign the two strong panzer corps, 24th and 47th, burst through the weak link between the Soviet Twenty-fourth and Fiftieth Armies, throwing the former south towards the Oka and the latter north into the path of von Kluge's advancing infantry. By evening on that day the leading elements of 2nd Panzer had broken through to a depth of thirty miles and were approaching Lashma on the Oka. Fifteen miles to the north 3rd Panzer was nearing Tuma. The Soviet forces facing Second Panzer Army had been comprehensively defeated.

One-hundred-and-twenty miles to the north, on the other wing of Army Group Centre's attack, Fourth Panzer Army was having greater difficulty breaking through the Soviet Fifth Army's positions on the River Nerl. This unexpectedly stubborn resistance forced Manstein, who had relieved the sick Höppner as Panzer Army commander, to shift the *schwerpunkt* of his attack southwards in the early afternoon, and it was not until dusk that 8th Panzer was free of the defensive lines and striking out across country towards the Moscow-Yaroslavl road.

On the following day both panzer armies were in full cry towards the Volga and their intended rendezvous in the neighbourhood of Gorkiy. But that evening the Führer decided to interfere with the smooth unfolding of Halder's plan. To Hitler July 1941 was only three months and a long coma away. He remembered only too clearly how many Russians had escaped from the over-large German pockets around Minsk and Smolensk. Then he had insisted on smaller, tighter encirclements against the opposition of his panzer generals. He did so again now. Watching Guderian and Manstein motoring blithely on across the Wolfsschanze wall-map towards the distant Volga the Führer again feared that the Russians would escape the net. He ordered both panzer armies to turn inwards behind the retreating enemy.

Guderian and Manstein both protested loudly to von Bock. Bock protested diplomatically to Brauchitsch. Brauchitsch protested very diplomatically to Hitler. A day was wasted. The Führer remained unmoved. Brauchitsch said as much to Bock, who passed on the message to Guderian and Manstein. Both duly turned a panzer corps rather than their whole armies inward behind the Russians.

Or so they thought. In fact the Red Army formations, granted an extra day's grace by the arguing Germans, had pulled back beyond the range of the gaping jaws. When Guderian and Manstein's units met east of Kovrov on the evening of 27 May they closed a largely empty bag. The eventual tally of prisoners was a mere 12,000.

Hitler was not disappointed. The low figure, he told Halder, was an indication of the enemy's weakness. Halder was inclined to agree, but the commanders on the spot were not so sure. But in any case only a few days had been wasted, and what were a few days?

In the long term they were to prove rather important. For when Manstein had received Hitler's original directive he had been on the point of ordering 41st Panzer Corps into the undefended city of Yaroslavl. But with the need to close the pocket there had no longer been the forces available. This was unfortunate for the Germans, for Yaroslavl was to cost the Wehrmacht many more lives than those Russians trapped by Hitler's manoeuvre.

Meanwhile the Soviet armies that had escaped encirclement were now back behind the Klyaz'ma river, and Guderian's panzers were held up for a further two days by resolute defence. Then, to the Germans' surprise, the Russians withdrew during the night of 30 May. Apparently they were not

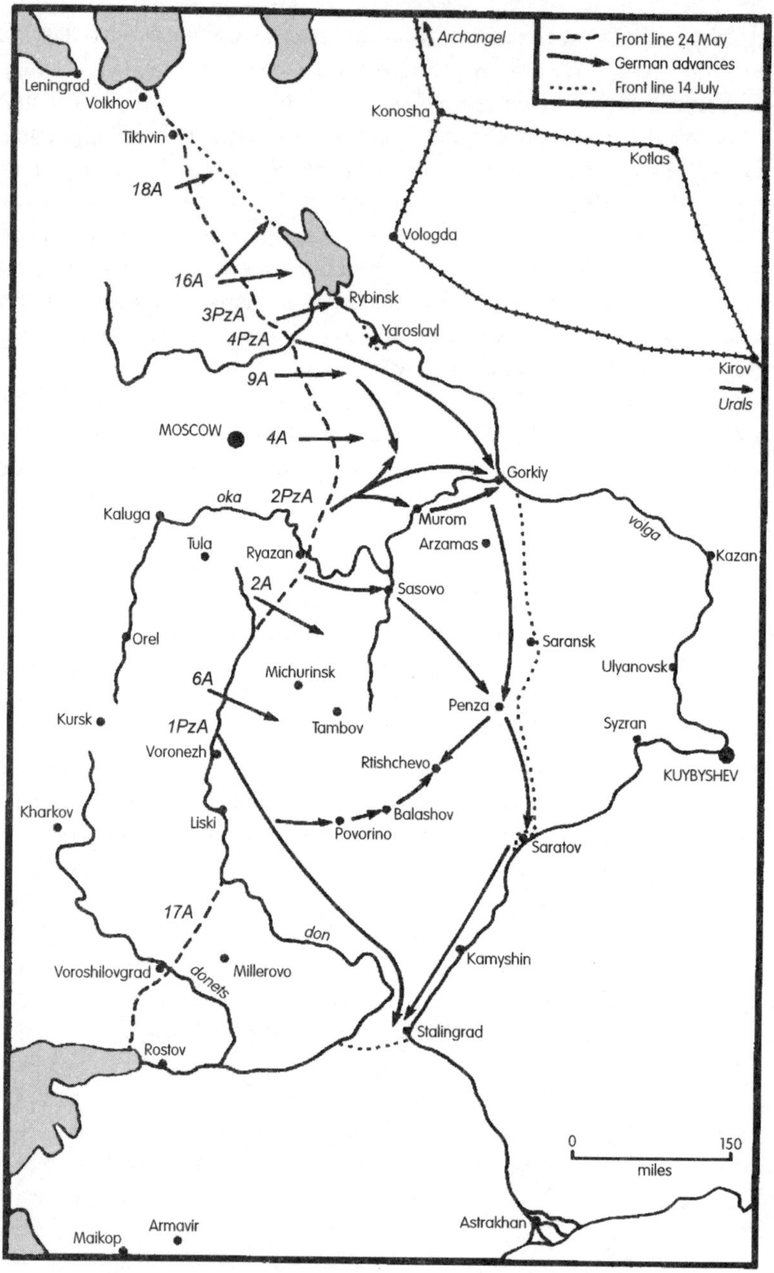
Archangel
Front line 24 May
German advances
Front line 14 July
Leningrad
Volkhov
Tikhvin
Konosha
Kotlas
Vologda
18A
16A
3PzA
4PzA
Rybinsk
Yaroslavl
9A
Kirov
Urals
MOSCOW
4A
Gorkiy
oka
2PzA
Kaluga
Murom
Arzamas
volga
Tula
Ryazan
Kazan
2A
Sasovo
Orel
Saransk
Ulyanovsk
6A
Michurinsk
Penza
Kursk
1PzA
Tambov
Syzran
Voronezh
Rtishchevo
KUYBYSHEV
Kharkov
Liski
Balashov
Povorino
Saratov
17A
don
Voroshilovgrad
Millerovo
donets
Kamyshin
Stalingrad
Rostov
0
150
miles
Astrakhan
Maikop
Armavir

13. Fall Siegfried

going to stand their ground and fight to the last as in the previous year. This new devotion to elastic defence was disturbing.

Fortunately for the Germans the same day offered evidence that the Red Army had not yet shaken off all its bad habits. With that incompetence which the Master Race found more typical of their enemy the Soviet forces in Murom allowed 2nd Panzer to seize the road and rail bridges across the Oka intact. By morning on 31 May a sizeable bridgehead had been established, and the whole of 47th Panzer Corps was being funnelled through on to the right bank of the river. Two days later, as Manstein's tanks reached the Volga north of Gorkiy, Guderian's were cutting the city's road and rail links to the south and east.

Here again Hitler attempted to interfere, though with less success. He forbade Guderian to enter the city; panzer forces were not suitable for urban warfare, and Gorkiy would have to wait for the infantry, still some eighty miles to the west. Guderian, while agreeing in principle, thought it senseless to allow the enemy three or four days to prepare defences in what was virtually a defenceless city. He informed Bock that the order could not be obeyed, as 29th Motorised was already engaged within the city limits. Having done so he ordered 29th Motorised to engage itself within the city limits. Hitler bowed to the apparently inevitable. On 3 June the last Red Army units in the city withdrew across the Volga, and the swastika was hoisted above Gorkiy's Red Square.

It was not yet fluttering above Yaroslavl. By-passed by the panzers when occupation would have been little more than a formality, the city was being feverishly prepared for defence as Ninth Army ponderously approached the flaming chimney beacons from the west. On 3 June the first battles were beginning in the vast textile factories of the ancient city's western suburbs. No one in the German or Soviet High Commands foresaw that Yaroslavl's reduction would take six weeks and cost the Germans 45,000 casualties. The beginnings of this battle were ignored for, with the capture of Gorkiy, all eyes were now fixed on the Oka line, springboard for Stage 2 of *Siegfried*, the great march to the south.

IV

In Kuybyshev Stavka waited. Where would the enemy strike next? Zhukov, who had been Stavka's representative at West Front HQ during the preceding fortnight, had been relieved to see that the Germans were making no attempts to secure bridgeheads across the Volga between Gorkiy and

Yaroslavl. A panzer advance downstream along both banks would have presented formidable problems. But, given that the enemy had eschewed such a tempting opportunity and, further, given that his armour was still concentrated north of the Oka, it seemed most likely that a direct march east across the Volga Uplands was intended. And this was barely less dangerous. Stavka knew that there was no natural line short of the river that the Red Army could hope to hold. All the strength it possessed would be needed to hold the river-line itself. It was re-emphasised to all Front, army and divisional commanders that on no account should they allow their formations to be encircled by the German armoured units; they were to fight, retreat, fight and retreat again, if necessary – and it probably would be – all the way back to the Volga.

In Hitler's Rastenburg HQ, now over 800 miles from the front, little attention was paid to the possible responses of the enemy. As always the German strategic intelligence was as poor as the tactical intelligence was good. The paucity of prisoners taken in Stage 1 was attributed to the Red Army's lack of manpower; reports from the Front that the Soviet formations were showing a new awareness of the tactical values of withdrawal were given little credence. It was estimated that there were approximately 120 Soviet divisions on the line Gorkiy-Sea of Azov, and the Führer expected most of them to fall into the bag during Stage 2. In these early June days the atmosphere at Rastenburg was little short of euphoric. Cairo had fallen, Gorkiy had fallen. The Japanese had won a major victory in the Pacific. Everything was going right. There was no reason why Stage 2 should go wrong.

On the morning of 17 June Army Group Centre rolled forward into the enemy once more. This time Second Panzer Army was on the left wing, Fourth Panzer Army having been moved to the Ryazan area during the second week of the month. The two armies made rapid progress. Such rapid progress in fact that even Halder began to grow suspicious. Prisoners were scarce, the Russians coolly fighting their way backwards. Guderian's tanks rumbled into Arzamas, Manstein's reached the Tsna river south of Sasovo. Second Army took Ryazsk on Manstein's right flank, Fourth Army moved forward between the two panzer armies.

For the next few days the panzers rolled on through pasture lands broken by large stretches of deciduous forest. The stukas swooped down on the retreating Red Army, the tanks sent up their clouds of dust, German commanders examined their inadequate maps by the light of burning villages. All the familiar horror of *blitzkrieg* spread southwards towards the open steppe.

The miles slipped away beneath the panzers' tracks at a rate not seen since the previous summer. On 23 June Guderian's advance units had travelled two hundred miles and were approaching Penza from the north. The next day they met Manstein's vanguard south-east of the town. Another huge pocket had been created. But again the haul of prisoners and equipment was disappointing. And many of those forces which had been caught in the encirclement found little difficulty in breaking through Guderian's thin screen and escaping to the east.

Four hundred miles to the north the struggle for possession of Yaroslavl was entering its third week. Hoth's panzers had secured a bridgehead over the Volga to the east of Rybinsk, and the Army Group North commander Field-Marshal von Leeb had planned to use them to cut off Yaroslavl's communications to the north. But as he was about to set this process in motion Hitler, worried about the long front south of the Don which was held by only Seventeenth Army and the armies of Germany's allies, demanded that Hoth's Panzer Army should part with one of its two panzer corps. Ninth Army would have to continue its struggle for the factories, sewers and cellars of Yaroslavl with insufficient support.

On 23 June the two northernmost armies of Army Group South – Sixth Army and First Panzer Army – joined the drive to the south-east. Kleist's panzers struck east and south-east, towards Balashov and along the left bank of the Don. Simultaneously Manstein and Guderian were preparing to resume their southward march.

Another week passed. On 30 June the pincers closed again, this time outside the railway junction of Rtishchevo. Further east Guderian's panzers, aimed on Saratov, were checked for the first time in the neighbourhood of Petrovsk. The leading units of 2nd Panzer were assailed by a Soviet armoured brigade and suffered unexpected casualties. The continuation of the German advance had to wait for 18th Panzer's arrival the following afternoon. The Soviet tanks melted away to the east.

Guderian continued south, reaching the Volga above Saratov on the morning of 2 July, and cutting the railway entering the city from the west twenty-four hours later. Saratov seemed well-defended, so this time the refractory general obeyed the orders from Rastenburg to place a screen round the city rather than attempt its capture. 47th Panzer Corps moved on down the right bank of the great river. Its tanks had now covered over five hundred miles since 24 May and the strain was beginning to tell. Though losses in action had been negligible, the attritional qualities of the Soviet roads had exerted a formidable toll on the vehicles.

149

In the Wolfsschanze such things were not visible on the wall-maps. All these showed was the relentless march of the German forces. *Siegfried* was succeeding. All was well.

In Kuybyshev, strange though it would have seemed to Hitler and his henchmen, spirits were also rising. The southern thrust of the German armour had brought that same relief with which the French High Command had greeted von Kluck's fatal turn to the south outside Paris in August 1914. Then General Gallieni, the Military Governor of the French capital, had transported troops in taxis to attack the exposed German flank. Stavka had no such options available to it, but the Soviet leaders could bear such inconvenience. What mattered, what really mattered, was that the panzers were streaming southwards, away from the crucial line, away from a swift end to the war in the East.

Their own armies were withdrawing steadily towards the Volga. Though often outflanked by the German armour and pummelled by the screaming Stukas the Red Army refused to break up and die as it had the previous year. Skilful leadership in the field and intelligent use of propaganda played their part in encouraging this fortitude, but the most telling factor was Stavka's simple common-sense tactical directive: fight until threatened with encirclement, and then withdraw. Of course a large proportion of the Soviet forces were encircled at one time or another, but the enormity of space on the steppe and the profusion of forests in the northern half of the battle-zone offered ample opportunities for escape. The German lines were too thin on the ground, the Luftwaffe too thin in the sky, to dominate such a vast area. The major portion of the West and Voronezh Front armies had reached the line Gorkiy-Saransk-Saratov-Stalingrad by the end of the first week of July.

Their retreat left South-west and South Fronts, covering the Don-Sea of Azov line, in an exposed position, and as Kleist's tanks neared the Don-Volga land-bridge west of Stalingrad on 6 July Zhukov ordered the two Front commanders to withdraw their armies south-eastwards to the line of the Don. Hoth's panzer corps, which had just arrived in the 'threatened sector' was ordered back to the north by Hitler, to the exasperation of all others concerned. Seventeenth Army, and the Italian, Rumanian and Hungarian formations, moved forward into the vacuum left by the retreating Russians.

Stage 2 of *Siegfried* was almost complete. On 8 July Guderian's tanks entered the northern outskirts of Stalingrad as Kleist's moved in from the south-west. After two days' skirmishing the Red Army fell back across the mile-wide Volga. Upriver Sixth Army was fighting its way into Saratov. The central section of the line Archangel-Astrakhan had been reached. As Ninth and Third Panzer Armies prepared for the final onslaught on Yaroslavl, Eleventh, Seventeenth, First Panzer and Second Panzer Armies deployed for the invasion of the Caucasus.

And after that the Middle East. Rommel, the troops in Russia were told rather prematurely, was about to cross the Suez Canal. Soon they would be joining hands with him somewhere in Arabian Nights' country. For the enemies of the Reich nemesis was clearly at hand.

Chapter 9
FEEDING THE FLOOD, RAISING THE DYKES

An ambulance can only go so fast.
Neil Young

Cairo/Tel el Kebir

Mussolini had made his triumphal entrance into Cairo on 12 June, and after spending three days in the Abdin Palace tutoring King Farouk in fascist theory and practice he had returned to Rome. The Duce was somewhat disappointed in the lukewarm reception he had received from the Egyptian populace; he would have been more so had anyone been tactless enough to inform him of the rapturous acclaim accorded to Rommel in the previous week.

Farouk, once free of Mussolini's overbearing presence, devoted himself to self-congratulation. He considered he had handled the whole business rather well. His national popularity had reached new heights, his friend Ali Maher was forming a government. A new era had formed for the two inseparables – himself and Egypt.

But the King was fooling himself. The only thing the Germans and Italians had yet found to agree on was the irrelevance of Ali Maher's government. Both Axis partners hoped for an Arab revolt against the British east of Suez, and so loudly proclaimed their support for the ideals of Arab nationalism. But in reality, as their actions were to show, they cared as much for Arab liberation as they cared for a Jewish homeland. Words were one thing, the accelerating breakdown of the Egyptian economy, already heavily strained by years of British occupation, was something else entirely. Each ally took what he could lay his hands on before the other did. This race for booty both disenchanted the

152

'liberated' Egyptians and caused serious friction between the two Axis partners.

By mid-June Rommel was sick and tired of the political squabbles resonating through Cairo's new corridors of power, and of his souring relationship with Count Mazzolini, the new Italian Civil Commissioner. The Field-Marshal moved to new military headquarters at the abandoned British Tel el Kebir air-base, leaving the junior von Neurath to suffer in his place. Back in the desert Rommel hoped to be left alone by the politicians. He was to be disappointed.

On 23 June a rather important visitor arrived at Tel el Kebir. Hajj Amin Muhammed el-Husseini had been one of Arab nationalism's leading lights since the early 1920s, when he had played a large part in inciting anti-Jewish riots in the British mandate territory of Palestine. The British, with that priceless ambivalence which seemed to guide most of their actions in divided Palestine, first sentenced him to ten years *in absentia* and then appointed him Grand Mufti of Jerusalem, the most senior religious position in the province. Husseini soon manoeuvred himself into the Presidency of the Supreme Muslim Council, and thus acquired control over extensive political and religious funds. In the next fifteen years he used these to plague the mandate territory with his own brand of opportunistic anti-Zionist extremism.

The Palestine Arab Revolt, which began in 1936, forced him to flee the country, but he had already secured contacts in both the outside Arab world and the chambers of Axis power. Through 1940 and 1941 he played a significant role in fomenting the Iraqi rebellion, and after its failure he moved on to Tehran with similar schemes in mind. When the British and Russians moved into Iran two months later he fled to Turkey disguised as the servant of the Italian envoy. From there he reached Rome, and eventually Berlin. In the two Axis capitals he urged Axis-Arab collaboration in driving the British and the Jews from the Middle East.

Eventually, in April 1942, Husseini reached Berchtesgaden and the Führer. Here his contacts with the Abwehr and the SS stood him in good stead. Hitler had already perused the Abwehr report on him, prepared by one Professor Schrumpf, an Alsatian doctor practising in Cairo. The Mufti, Schrumpf declared, was not really an Arab at all. He was a Circassian, an aryan. 'Owing to the operation of the Mendelian law and the inherited ancestral traits, Circassian blood began to predominate in his family . . . this is important from a psychological viewpoint since pure Arab blood could first of all not have been so consistent and systematic in the struggle against the English and the Jews; he would certainly have been bought off. What is more, that Caucasian or Aryan blood enables us to expect from the Mufti in the future the faithfulness of an ally of which pure Arab blood would be incapable.'

This was all very impressive, particularly in view of the Arabs' low rating in the *Mein Kampf* race hierarchy. Hitler was certainly impressed. In one of those rare sentences which say volumes about the reasons for the Nazi failure, the Führer noted that the Mufti's 'exceptional cleverness' made him 'almost equal to the Japanese'.

Hitler, however, was not one to let empathy get the better of him when German interests were involved. The Mufti's request for German support to realise his dream – a united Jew-free Arab nation – could not be granted. Or at least not yet. Surely, Hitler argued, the Mufti realised the difficulties of the German position. There were the Italians, the French and the Turks to consider. When the war was over things would be different. But for the moment the most he could offer in public was a general statement of sympathy for Arab aspirations. In private he could promise the Mufti 'the decisive voice in Arab affairs' once the war had been won. When the German spearhead reached Tbilisi in the southern Caucasus, then 'the hour of Arab liberation' would be at hand. The volunteer 'German-Arab Legion', now training in the Ukraine, would join the German spearhead for the march on Basra. During that march it would swell into an enormous army of liberation.

This, the Mufti agreed, was an exciting prospect. But would it not be better to move this unit to North Africa? When Egypt was liberated the volunteers could be used to excellent effect in Palestine.

Hitler thought not. 'The supply channels to North Africa are already over-loaded,' he told Husseini. This, though true, was not the only reason for Hitler's refusal. He wished to keep the Legion in Russia, where it would be more firmly under his control. The Mufti left Berchtesgaden with no more to show for his Circassian blood than long-term promises.

But he had not given up hope. Reaching Egypt soon after Mussolini he eventually secured an appointment with the reluctant Rommel. At Tel el Kebir he explained his desire that the Arab Legion fight alongside Rommel's legendary Panzer Army. The Legion's presence, he told the Field-Marshal, would do much to ease the Panzer Army's passage through Palestine, Transjordan and Iraq. Perhaps Rommel would take it up with the Führer, perhaps even recommend such a course?

Rommel was polite. He would mention it, he said. In fact he did nothing of the kind. He did not like the Mufti – 'a tricky sort of customer,' he told Lucie; 'I didn't trust him an inch' – and he had enough trouble coping with the allies he already possessed. A military man to his bones, Rommel was as averse to thinking about such things as most members of his dubious profession. He was interested in military problems, in getting his army moving again, in leaving Egypt behind. And this was proving difficult enough.

The basic problem, as usual, was supply. There were seven basic necessities: food, water, fuel, ammunition, repair facilities, human replacements and mechanical replacements. Food and water presented no problems as long as the Panzer Army remained in Egypt, but the other five were all in short supply. The British, thanks to Auchinleck's insistent thoroughness, had left little behind them intact.

They had also effectively denied the Axis partners the use of Alexandria's port. Three weeks before Egypt's fall, Auchinleck, with exemplary foresight, had ordered the finding and preparing of a blockship to sink in the harbour entrance. This had been accomplished, and the last of the port facilities destroyed, the day before Balck's panzers had encircled the city. Since Port Said had also been badly damaged, and was still under British fire, Axis supplies continued to be unloaded at Benghazi and Tobruk for transportation along the long desert coast-road. The distance involved and the shortage of motor transport made this a slow and agonising process for the impatient Rommel.

It was not his only problem. OKH informed him that only one more infantry division could be sent to Egypt. There would be only a few new tanks, and no replacement engines. The little armour the chaotic German armament industry could manage to produce was all earmarked for the Eastern Front. The 400 tanks remaining to *Panzerarmee Afrika* after the victorious but costly conquest of Egypt would have to suffice for the breakthrough to the Persian Gulf. Fuel was also in short supply; most of the Reich's precious reserves were being used to eat away Russian miles. It would be ironic, Rommel told his Chief of Staff, General Bayerlein, if lack of oil prevented them from reaching the oilfields.

But there was nothing one could do about such things, other than send demand after unanswered demand to the desk-bound generals at Lötzen, and undertake a fruitless trip to Rastenburg in early July. On that occasion Hitler listened patiently, recited a string of uncheckable statistics, presented Rommel with his Field-Marshal's baton, and sent him back to Egypt. The only consolation was a week spent with Lucie at their Heerlingen home.

Back at Tel el Kebir Rommel waited for the supply problems to sort themselves out and worked on his plans for the continuation of the advance. The Panzer Army's objective was obvious enough – the head of the Persian Gulf. The problem was how to get there. There was a limited choice of routes once Sinai had been traversed, either the Haifa-Baghdad road or the Aleppo-Baghdad railway. But this could be decided later. First the Suez Canal had to be crossed. The bridging equipment was expected to arrive shortly, and it was not thought that the British would make a determined effort to hold the eastern bank. They were only deploying a skeletal force; the Sinai roads could not supply a larger one. The British would make their stand on the other side of the desert, at the gates of Palestine, where the Axis supply routes would be stretched.

There was one way round this desert bottleneck: a seaborne assault on the Levant coast. But this would have involved the prior seizure of Cyprus and the full participation of the Italian Navy. The first was ruled out by Hitler's decision to use Student's paratroopers elsewhere, the second by lack of fuel.

There was also the problem of the two divisions and two brigades which the British had withdrawn up the Nile Valley, and which were now being adequately supplied through Port Sudan and Port Safaga on the Red Sea coast. This force, largely composed of infantry, offered no serious threat to Axis control of lower Egypt, but it could not just be ignored. A covering force would have to be left behind. Rommel wished to leave the Italians. This would both allow him to use his full German force and rid him of his troublesome and ill-equipped ally.

Mussolini was not of the same mind. He insisted that at least *Ariete* take part in the cross-Sinai attack. The Middle East was, after all, in the Italian sphere of influence. Hitler agreed to *Ariete*'s inclusion. He did not want to anger the Duce and, in any case, what harm could it do? *Ariete* would be accompanied by five German divisions and under the direct command of his favourite field-marshal. Rommel, though far from convinced, was forced to accept the Führer's decision. 90th Motorised and 21st Panzer, both of which had suffered heavily in the May battles, would be left behind. The remaining four German divisions, *Ariete* and the newly-arrived 164th Division would make up the new Panzer Army Asia.

This grandly-named Army was not likely to live up to its name before mid-August. In the meantime Rommel would have to wait, to worry about the time granted to the British, and to watch, from a respectful German distance, as the Egyptian economy succumbed to hyper-inflation.

Wolfsschanze

If the steady erosion of Germany's pro-Arab façade was noticed amidst the medieval Prussian forests no one seemed to care too much. At the

Wolfsschanze it was all smiles through June and July. *Fall Siegfried* was consuming the Russian steppe, *Panzerarmee Asien* was poised to drive the British from the Middle East. By mid-July even Yaroslavl had fallen. In the Wolfsschanze canteen bets were being placed. Rommel was seven to four on favourite to reach Baghdad first; Guderian a mere two to one against.

While his armies flowed across the maps Hitler had developed an obsession with oil. He read all he could find on the subject, and watched all the available films in the Wolfsschanze cinema-room. By the end of July he had mastered the theory and theoretical practice of finding oil, drilling oil, transporting and refining oil. He knew at least as well as the British just how dependent they were on the Iraqi and Iranian oilfields. He thought he knew – though his information was two years out of date – how dependent the Russians were on the Caucasian oil.

All this oil now seemed within the Wehrmacht's grasp. Two months, three, perhaps even four. But no more than that. In his late-night monologues the Führer imparted visions of a Reich swimming in the black fluid. 'An empire that is not self-sufficient in oil could never survive,' he told all and sundry. The middle Eastern and Caucasian oilfields would be one of the three pillars of the thousand-year Reich, along with the vast agricultural lands of the Ukraine and German industrial genius. With such a material basis beneath them the German people could let their spirits soar, could realize the true potential of the *volk* soul.

Within the context of such euphoric visions the Führer sought to bring the war to its inevitably triumphant conclusion. It was little more than a matter of playing out time. The Russian problem had been, or soon would be, conclusively solved. The British problem likewise. Perhaps it would be necessary to mount an invasion of England in 1943 – personally he doubted it. The British would sue for peace while they still had some of their empire left, before the Japanese gobbled up India.

This over-confidence, or 'victory disease' as the Japanese called it, was to have important, perhaps crucial consequences. Hitler drew one conclusion from the imminence of victory – he did not need allies. When German arms reigned supreme from Narvik to Abadan, from the Urals to the Pyrenees, then all of them – Italians, Japanese, Finns, Hungarians, Arabs – would have to make their own way in a German world. Of course he would always have a soft spot for the Duce, and there was no need to annoy him unduly at this stage. Hence the agreement to the inclusion of *Ariete* in the ranks of Rommel's Panzer Army Asia. But allowing the Italians the whole of the Middle East in their sphere of influence – that had been over-generous. The boundaries would have to be withdrawn in a manner that more faithfully reflected the two allies' respective contributions to the conquest of the area.

The Japanese could not be dealt with in this way. They were more powerful and they were further away. When Raeder had come to him in February with his plans for concerted action in the Middle East-Indian Ocean area it had seemed that the military advantages of Japanese help would outweigh the political disadvantages of a Japanese presence. But over the following months the equation had see-sawed. By April the Japanese had been demanding tripartite Axis declarations of independence for the Arab World and India. This was quite unthinkable. Worst of all, Mussolini had supported the Japanese, presumably as a feeble attempt to counter German predominance. Such anti-German groupings within the Axis would have to be stopped. The Japanese would have to be held at a long arm's length.

Fortunately this was now possible without doing any damage to the military situation. The British were going to be driven from the Middle East whether or not the Japanese Navy cut their Indian Ocean supply lines. So Japan should be encouraged to concentrate its efforts in the Pacific, to reducing the American Navy still further. This would keep the Americans' eyes off Europe, weaken the Allied hold on the Atlantic, and leave Germany a free hand in the Middle East. Accordingly Raeder was instructed to 'discourage' Japanese intervention in the Indian Ocean area, and to minimise German-Japanese co-operation as tactfully as he saw fit. The 'grand plan' would be a purely Teutonic affair.

London

While serving as Commander-in-Chief Middle East, General Wavell had noted down his reasons for believing that Germany would lose the war:

1. Oil, shipping, air power and sea power are the keys to this war, and they are interdependent.
   Air power and naval power cannot function without oil.
   Oil, except very limited quantities, cannot be brought to its destination without shipping.
   Shipping requires the protection of naval power and air power.
2. We have access to practically all the world's supply of oil.
   We have most of the shipping.

We have naval power.

We are potentially the greatest air power, when fully developed. *Therefore we are bound to win the war.*

Or so it seemed in 1940-1. But by the summer of 1942 the other side of the same coin was becoming equally apparent. In mid-July General Brooke noted in his diary:

> All the motive-power at sea, on land, and in the air throughout the Middle East, Indian Ocean, and India is entirely dependent on the oil from Abadan. If we lose this supply, it cannot be made good from American resources owing to shortage of tankers and continuous losses of these ships through submarine action. If we lose the Persian oil, we inevitably lose command of the Indian Ocean, and so endanger the whole India-Burma situation.

A report from the Oil Control Board confirmed Brooke's realistic assessment. If Abadan and Bahrein were lost, the report concluded, nearly thirteen and a half million tons of oil would have to be found from the US and other sources. An additional 270 tankers would be needed to carry this oil, and they did not exist.

The British *had* to hold the Middle East against the strong enemy thrusts converging on the Persian Gulf from the north and the west. The defence of the Iraqi-Iranian-Gulf oilfields came second only to the defence of Britain and its Atlantic lifeline in the War Cabinet's list of priorities. Certainly the prospect of losing these oilfields did a wonderful job in concentrating the British mind. One member of the War Cabinet noted that 'the gravity of the situation is such that the PM has stopped pressing for his Norwegian project. This, I suppose, is some consolation.'

There was no such solace for Auchinleck. He had presided over the most humiliating series of reverses suffered by a British army in living memory. It mattered little that the responsibility was hardly his, that the interference from his superiors and the crushing superiority of the German force had rendered defeat inevitable. It mattered even less that his decision to evacuate Egypt and so save Eighth Army, rather than fight a glorious but hopeless battle in the Delta Region, would prove one of the most crucial decisions of the war. He had lost. The troops needed new leadership, a new source of confidence. Auchinleck had to go. On 6 June the relevant telegram arrived from Whitehall. General Alexander would take over the Middle East Command, General Montgomery, on Brooke's insistence, the leadership of Eighth Army. General Wilson would remain in command of

159

the 'Northern Force', comprising Ninth and Tenth Armies in Syria, Iraq and Iran.

Reinforcements were being assiduously sought for Alexander to pass on to his army commanders. There were three possible sources. General Wavell agreed to part with two divisions from India, on the grounds that a Japanese offensive in northern Burma could not take place before the monsoon ended in October and might not take place at all. A further three divisions were to arrive from England; one was already rounding the Cape, the others were to be shipped out in transport originally earmarked for either a cross-Channel or North-west Africa operation. The third source was the United States Army. Roosevelt had already offered three hundred Sherman tanks; now the deployment of American troops in the Middle East was being considered.

In the Indian Ocean the British were doing their utmost to ensure that all these reinforcements would reach their destination. The port of Diego Suarez in Madagascar had been occupied in May, and through the early summer Somerville's Eastern Fleet was being reinforced as fast as was possible. The battleships *Renown* and *Duke of York* had both arrived in May, a third carrier, *Illustrious*, was expected in July. The British were not to know that this fleet would never be tested, that a combination of German discouragement and Yamamoto's strategic preferences would inhibit renewed Japanese naval action in this area.

But perhaps the most important legacy of Egypt's fall was the change in Bomber Command policy decreed by the War Cabinet. Bomber Command's single-minded devotion to the strategic bombing of Germany was proving a luxury that Britain could no longer afford. A chorus of protest had started to grow when Malta succumbed to the Luftwaffe while the British bomber force was busy attacking the German railway system. With Egypt's fall this chorus grew too loud to ignore, and it was decided to shift some of the strategic bombing force to the Middle East. New airfields in Iraq and Iran were prepared for their arrival.

All roads in the British Empire now led to the Middle East. And none towards France or North-west Africa. The War Cabinet realised that there could be no Second Front in 1942, nor probably in 1943. This realisation had to be passed on to Britain's two major allies, both of whom saw the Second Front as the main priority of the moment. Churchill and Brooke would go to Washington to explain matters to their suspicious American counterparts; Cripps and Wavell would travel to Kuybyshev and break the bad news to Stalin.

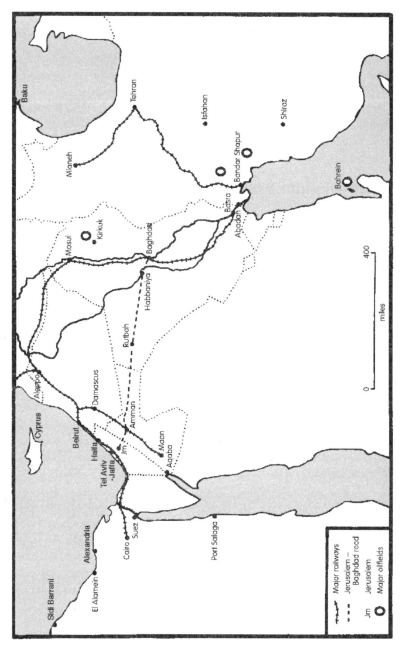

Baku

14. The Middle East Theatre

Places labelled on map: Baku, Tehran, Mianeh, Isfahan, Shiraz, Bandar Shapur, Basra, Abadan, Bahrein, Kirkuk, Mosul, Baghdad, Habbaniya, Rutbah, Aleppo, Damascus, Amman, Maan, Aqaba, Jm (Jerusalem), Jaffa, Tel Aviv, Haifa, Beirut, Cyprus, Alexandria, Sidi Barrani, El Alamein, Cairo, Suez, Port Safaga

Legend:
- Major railways
- Jerusalem – Baghdad road
- Jm Jerusalem
- ⊙ Major oilfields

0   400
miles

Washington DC

In June 1942 the war had come home to America in a welter of anger and bitterness. Like its Pacific enemy the United States was not a country accustomed to setbacks, let alone defeats as crushing as that suffered at Midway. Now Hawaii was at risk. The whole western seaboard was at risk. The most powerful nation in the world had been humbled by the *Japanese*.

In the war councils of the American administration the 'Germany first' policy agreed in January was also at risk. The two service chiefs, General Marshall and Admiral King, were as aware as the British that the latter's Middle Eastern reverses involved the indefinite postponement of a cross-Channel assault on the European mainland. However, they did not deduce from this that US forces should be committed in the Middle East. On the contrary, both men, and particularly King, saw in the postponement of European action a chance to commit more American forces in the Pacific. The American population shared their enthusiasm for a new 'Japan first' policy.

Roosevelt fortunately disagreed. He had committed the United States to assist the British against Germany, and the fall of Egypt made that more necessary, not less so. Naturally the security of American soil – Hawaii and the West Coast – had the highest priority, but that was a matter for the Navy. There would certainly have to be a temporary shift of naval forces from the Atlantic to the Pacific, but that was all.

Churchill and Brooke arrived to join in the argument on 19 June, splashing down on the Potomac in the sea-plane which had carried them across the Atlantic. Brooke was brought up to date by Dill before talking to Marshall and King, while Churchill retired to Roosevelt's country residence at Hyde Park for a tête-à-tête with the President.

Both the British leaders reiterated the basics of the strategy agreed in earlier meetings. The two powers were to launch a counter-offensive against Germany in the West as soon as their 'essential interests' in other areas had been secured. These 'essential interests' included the Iraqi-Iranian oilfields, which were now threatened. Until such time as the threat receded 'Sledgehammer' was impossible. As Brooke put it: 'Precious shipping and resources cannot be directed to one end of the Mediterranean when strength was needed to defend the other.'

His audience was not particularly appreciative. King sat silent, his face a study in obstinacy. He had already decided that American resources should be directed to the Pacific, not to either end of the Mediterranean. Marshall was more generous. He said that he recognised the difficulties of the British position, the immensity of the burden they were bearing. But he asked Brooke and Dill to take into account the strong desire of the American public for action against the Japanese.

At Hyde Park Roosevelt, who had probably done more for the American public than any President since Lincoln, listened diplomatically to Churchill and confirmed his personal commitment to the 'Germany first' policy. He hoped Churchill would share his view that the retention of Hawaii and the safeguarding of the US-Australia sea-route were also 'essential interests' of the Allied powers. He admitted to the British Prime Minister that he was under considerable pressure from his service chiefs to commit greater American forces in the Pacific. He would have to give them something, and that something would have to be naval forces, including the two US carriers currently in the Atlantic. He realised that this would place a strain on the Atlantic lifeline, but there were no alternatives.

Churchill concurred gratefully. He said that *Illustrious*, now *en route* to the Indian Ocean, could be recalled to the Atlantic to fill the gap. But what could the Americans offer the Middle East? An armoured division? Planes? Roosevelt admitted that he did not know what was available. They would have to ask Marshall the following day.

Next morning the two leaders returned to Washington by train. There they found that Marshall had been largely won over by a combination of Brooke's persuasiveness and the knowledge that, for the moment, there was no way the US *could* commit most of its resources in a Japanese-held Pacific. Admiral King, though unrepentant, had admitted defeat. The British had got their way, and the rest of their visit was spent in sightseeing and hammering out the details of the US commitment in the Middle East. Several squadrons of US bombers would be flown out to Iran, and at least one of the armoured divisions previously earmarked for North-west Africa would be shipped to Basra as soon as possible. Churchill and Brooke left Washington on 27 June feeling more optimistic than they had eight days before.

Kuybyshev

The British party had arrived at Kuybyshev on 17 June. It was warmly welcomed, Molotov leading the soldiers and diplomats to a convenient hangar for a caviare and vodka lunch. This was the high-point of the visit.

That evening Cripps saw Stalin. The Soviet leader reluctantly conceded that there could be no Second Front that year, but then offended Cripps by accusing the Royal Navy of cowardice in stopping the Arctic convoys. He appeared 'unruffled' by the new German offensive, but refused to give any details of the Red Army's strength. He doubted whether the Germans would reach the Volga. He was also afraid that the American failure in the Pacific might encourage the Japanese to attack the Soviet Union. It was all rather vague and, as far as Cripps was concerned, most unsatisfactory.

Wavell was receiving no more joy from Shaposhnikov. When asked whether he was confident that the Red Army would hold the Caucasus, the Soviet Chief of Staff could only reply that he 'did not think' the Germans would succeed in breaching the mountain barrier. Wavell found this 'did not think' profoundly disturbing, but could elicit no more detailed information. The Russians expressed interest in Tedder's offer of British air support in the defence of the Baku area but were reluctant to reach any hard-and-fast agreements. Time would tell, they repeated over and over again.

Many Russian shrugs and glasses of vodka later the British departed for home. They were little the wiser for their visit. The Soviet Union was still in the war, its leaders *seemed* confident. But who could tell? Wavell told Alexander that 'we shall only know for certain how strong the Red Army is in the Caucasus when we spot the first panzer column crossing the Persian border.'

Baghdad/Rafah

General Alexander arrived in Baghdad to take over the Middle East Command on 14 June. He had already played a large part in organising two relatively successful retreats, to Dunkirk and the Chindwin. It was hoped that he would not be organising a third, from Iraq.

Auchinleck had chosen Baghdad as the new Middle East Command HQ before his dismissal, and Alexander confirmed the choice. From the City of the Arabian Nights he expected to oversee both the maintenance of internal security in the British-occupied Middle East and the shifting of war material from the disembarkation port of Basra to the fighting fronts. Baghdad was of course a long way from the prospective front in Palestine, but Alexander was not a man who liked to interfere in the day-to-day running of the armies under his overall command. It was his job, as he and his commanders saw it, to funnel through the men, planes, motor transport and supplies to where they were needed most.

The maintenance of internal security was now clearly a military matter of some importance. It was also beset with growing difficulties. In the aftermath of Egypt's fall the Middle East seemed to many like a dynamite dump with any number of fast-burning fuses. In Jerusalem, Haifa, Damascus, Baghdad, Tehran and other major cities the whispers of Arab and Persian rebellion were gathering themselves into a roar. Swastikas appeared on walls, thinly-disguised pro-Axis reports appeared in even the previously loyal newspapers. The reliability of the British-trained Arab units was no longer taken for granted. To the British the celebrated Fifth Column seemed truly ubiquitous.

They clamped the lid down tighter than before. Conscious of their vulnerability the British security forces resorted to measures which they described, in true national style, as 'stern but fair'. To the Arabs they seemed merely harsh, and a further reminder of their subordinate status. They did not share the British view of the war as a crusade; they knew little of the plight of Europe's Jews, only that several hundred thousand of them had appropriated land in Palestine. To the Arabs the British were fighting for the right to maintain their global empire, and there was nothing noble in that. But they were not yet ready for rebellion. They waited, as their counterparts in Egypt had waited, for the Germans to engage their well-armed occupiers, before making too overt a move of their own.

The British stepped up the propaganda war. Much was made of the escalating chaos in Egypt, and of the imperial designs of the Italians, who the British knew were anathema to the Arabs. The latter were not initially impressed; it would be several weeks before the same news reached the Fertile Crescent through a more reliable source – their own people. In those days of June and July it was British repression and Arab caution that kept the area behind the fighting fronts relatively quiescent.

Alexander's other major task was the supplying of his armies. In losing Suez the British had lost half their port capacity, and now only Basra (which could handle 5000 tons a day) and Aqaba (250 tons) could be used for supplying the armies east of the Canal. The latter, moreover, was well within range of the new Luftwaffe bases in the Suez Canal Zone.

So all depended on the 5000 tons coming into Basra. Not all of it was destined for the British; over ten per cent was loaded on to the Trans-Iranian railway for shipment into Russia. Nor could the other ninety per cent be brought to Baghdad, since the single-track Baghdad-Basra railway could only carry 3900 tons a day. One of Alexander's first decisions on taking over the Middle East Command was to order a crash-doubling of the tracks. But this would take an estimated three months.

The problem worsened at Baghdad. The road to Haifa could only handle 1200 tons, enough for five divisions. The railway to Aleppo could take slightly more, but it unfortunately ran through Turkish territory and could not be relied upon. In Palestine there were enough supplies stored to maintain seven divisions for ninety days. The conclusion to be drawn from all these figures was that Eighth Army, in the prevailing situation, could only maintain seven divisions in Palestine for six months. Unless something was done in the meantime demand would exceed supply after that period. Alexander set out to see that something was done.

General Bernard Montgomery had arrived in the Middle East on the same plane as Alexander. The two men had known each other for a long time, and as very different people often do, got on very well together. As a military 'team' they worked well; Montgomery's problems had always been with superiors (he had trouble recognising them as such), and Alexander was content to keep well in the background.

In June 1942 he gave Montgomery, with Churchill and Brooke's backing, only one firm directive. He was not to indulge his well-known penchant for heroics. There was to be no 'we stay here, dead or alive' defence of Palestine. It was Iraq and Iran which were vital to Britain, and it was Montgomery's job to see that Alexander had time to prepare their defence. A dead Eighth Army would benefit no one but Rommel.

Churchill, as usual, had also been more specific. 'My ideas for the defence of Palestine and Syria,' he telegrammed Eighth Army's new commander, 'are roughly not lines but a series of localities capable of all-round defence blocking the defiles and approaches.' Brooke was less free with advice. Montgomery knew Palestine well – he had served there twice before, in 1930-1 and 1938-9 – and Brooke thought he could be trusted to work out his own defensive strategy. He was confident that Montgomery, as long as he restrained his enthusiasm, would demonstrate the same energetic drive in slowing Rommel's advance as he had shown in evacuating 3rd Division from Belgium two years before.

In Palestine Eighth Army was slowly recovering from its traumatic flight. The better part of five divisions had successfully escaped across the Suez Canal, but all the base workshops had had to be left behind, suitably wrecked, in Egypt. The Red Sea had not parted for their transportation. Now, in late June, the South Africans were still manning the east bank of the Canal to prevent the Germans from making too easy a crossing, while the survivors of 1st and 2nd Armoured Divisions (with only ninety-five tanks between them), 50th Division and the New Zealand Division were organising themselves in north-east Sinai. The RAF had extricated itself with less difficulty, and was now filling up the ninety available airfields in

Palestine, Cyprus and Syria. But the airforce too had lost most of its repair facilities, and the nearest available were at Habbaniyah in Iraq. Morale, generally speaking, was abysmal.

The saviour was on his way. After talking with Alexander and his newly-inherited staff in Baghdad, Montgomery travelled west across the desert towards Palestine. On 19 June he arrived in Jerusalem, and on the following day motored down to Eighth Army HQ at Rafah. He quickly made an impression on both his corps and divisional commanders and the dispirited troops. The men who had 'lost Egypt', and were glumly preparing to lose Palestine and whatever lay behind it, were made acutely aware that their new commander had no intention of losing anything. 'Rommel will not, repeat *not*, go through this Army,' Montgomery told them. 'He is almost at the end of his tether, and we're going to be there when he reaches it.' Three days after Montgomery's arrival, as if on cue, the first fifty of 120 new tanks arrived from Basra. The new commander of Eighth Army left no one in any doubt that he was personally responsible for this welcome shipment.

There is no doubt that Eighth Army, as a collective entity, responded favourably to the little man's bravado. Not that there was much time to think about such things. Suddenly lying around in the sun had given way to intensive training and construction work. Montgomery had decided that the six divisions at his disposal – 44th Division was due to arrive from Basra in mid-July – would try to hold, for as long as possible, the strong positions at Jiradi-Rafah and Umm Katef on the two main entry routes into Palestine. Rommel would have difficulty getting round either of these positions since they were flanked by either sea, high ground or soft sand. And he would have 'a real fight on his hands' to get through them.

Brooke agreed, but was concerned about the possibility of a German seaborne invasion in the rear of this line. Montgomery correctly discounted this. He had seen for himself in England the problems involved in mounting such operations, and in any case the RAF and the small naval force which operated under its protective cover in the eastern Mediterranean would soon put a stop to any such nonsense. As if to conclude the argument he cabled Brooke: 'Rommel is a land animal; all Germans are land animals.'

Still, even Montgomery had to admit that these land animals might break through his lines, and other defensive positions were being prepared south of the Jerusalem-Jaffa railway for Eighth Army to fall back to. Further back still, along the Litani river and the Golan Heights to the north and in the mountains behind the Jordan river to the east, more construction work was underway. Alexander was not so confident as Montgomery that Eighth Army would stop Rommel short of the Iraqi border.

One thing was certain. If Rommel did take Palestine the British were determined that he should derive as many headaches from this troublesome land as they had. In the previous two years the British authorities had been inundated with offers of help from the various Zionist organisations. Each had been spurned on the grounds that the military advantage to be gained would not compensate for the political cost to Britain's post-war plans. But by the summer of 1942 post-war plans were becoming a luxury. The Arabs had demonstrated their deplorable and total lack of loyalty to His Majesty; the Jews, whatever they thought of Britain – which wasn't much – were obviously not about to collaborate with the Germans. A tacit truce had already been agreed between Menachem Begin, the new leader of the Irgun Zvi Leumi terrorist organisation, and the British Commissioner. Fifteen hundred youths from the *kibbutzim* were already receiving instruction in guerrilla warfare from the British Army. On 23 June British representatives met with leaders of the Jewish *Yishuv*, notably David Ben-Gurion, Golda Myerson and Moshe Sharrett, to expand the area of military co-operation. The 24,000 Jewish police in Palestine were to be given more and better arms, and regular units were to be formed for both counter-Arab and counter-German action. The Jewish leaders were also promised, in the strictest confidence of course, that their sharing in the struggle would reap a post-war reward. There would be no further restrictions on Jewish immigration into Palestine. Presumably in this case the British Government was less interested in securing the loyalty of the Jews – they would have fought willingly in any case – than in paying back the Arabs for their lack of this precious quality.

Whatever the motives for this dubious promise, it was hoped in Whitehall that the new degree of British-Jewish military co-operation would slow the German advance to an appreciable degree. In London it was estimated that Rommel might take anything from three weeks to four months to reach the Iraqi border. If it could be the latter then there was a good chance he would arrive too late. American and RAF reinforcements would by then have arrived in strength.

In the north General Wilson's force was still considerably smaller than that at Montgomery's disposal. But the enemy was many more miles away. At the worst he might cross the Soviet-Iranian border in late August, which would leave two months before winter set in and put a stop to mobile operations in the mountains of northern Iran. Even during those two months the panzers would find it hard to move swiftly or far. Roads were few and bad, winding interminably through mountain passes which offered great possibilities for successful defence. Consequently Wilson was putting his faith in infantry and air power. By late August he hoped to have received the 2nd and 5th Divisions from India, the 51st and 56th Divisions from England, the 1st American Armoured Division from across the Atlantic, and heavy RAF reinforcements from a variety of sources. New airfields were under construction at Zahedan, Mirjaveh and Kerman in south-eastern Iran; here the bomber squadrons so begrudged by Bomber Command would be based.

Through July and August Wilson could do little but wait. He knew that two panzer armies and two infantry armies had entered the Caucasus from the north. It all depended upon how much of them emerged at the other end. And on how soon. And on the attitude of Turkey.

Ankara

Shortly before his death in November 1938 Mustafa Kemal, the founding-father of modern Turkey, had looked ahead to the war he was sure would soon engulf the world he was leaving behind. 'Stay on England's side,' he had advised his successors, 'because that side is bound to win in the long run.'

The new leaders of Ataturk's state had done their best to follow his advice, and in 1939 Turkey signed a treaty of alliance with England and France which committed her to joining the forthcoming war should it spread to the Mediterranean. And although the speed of France's fall gave the Turks second thoughts about actually fulfilling these obligations, their policy of neutrality retained a strong pro-Allied bias.

The German invasion of Russia changed all this. Now the minority pro-Axis lobby, which included Army Chief of Staff Fevzi Cakmak, found itself allied to the nation-wide anti-Russian lobby. As far as most Turks were concerned the Germans had picked a good enemy. When a leading Turkish general visited the Eastern Front and reported back that all that remained of Russia was its snow, the nation as a whole breathed a grateful pro-Axis sigh of relief. During 1942, as the war drew closer to the Turkish frontiers, it became apparent to both the Turks and the world that Hitler might soon find himself a new ally in Ankara.

The Allies redoubled their efforts to buy the Turks off. The British offered fighter squadrons they did not have, the Americans lend-lease they could not ship. The Germans too made promises – definite ones of arms deliveries, vague ones of territorial rewards – which were equally spurious. The difference was that the German promises were riskier to refuse. If their armies in Egypt and the Caucasus joined hands in Iraq then Turkey would be encircled, and forced to dance to Hitler's tune. It would surely be better, argued newspapers like the pro-Axis *Cumhuriyet*, for Turkey to dance willingly and receive her just reward.

The Turkish President, Ismet Inönü, was still determined, if possible, to remain faithful to the testament of his old friend Ataturk. He suspected that Turkey was doomed to enter the war that was lapping around her shores, and that sooner or later sides would have to be chosen. But better later than sooner. Inönü believed, despite appearances to the contrary, that the Axis powers would lose the war. But he needed an Allied victory to convince his people. In the meantime he had to compromise. He informed the British that they were no longer free to use the vital Aleppo-Mosul railway for transporting war materials, adding in private that he had no choice if he wished to stay in power. If the Caucasus could be held, he told the British Ambassador, if Rommel could soon be defeated, then Turkey could stay out of the war. If not, then at the very least he would be forced to allow the Germans transit rights across Turkish territory. When all was said and done, if the British could not beat the Germans then Turkey would have to join them.

Chapter 10
HIGH NOON OFF PANAMA

There is less in this than meets the eye.
Tallulah Bankhead

I

The Japanese Fleet returned in triumph to Hiroshima Bay on 13 June. The American carriers had been destroyed, Midway Island occupied after a bitter four-day struggle. It was a modern-day Tsushima, celebrated throughout Japan as a victory for the virtues of the Japanese way and as a defeat for the godless materialists on the other side of the ocean.

But the cost to the Japanese carrier force had been high. *Kaga* was at the bottom of the Pacific; *Hiryu*, torpedoed by a US submarine during the voyage back to Japan, would take six months to repair. *Akagi* and *Soryu*, though hardly damaged, needed extensive replacements of aircraft and pilots. The other carriers would not return for some weeks. *Shokaku* and *Zuikaku* had sailed for the south immediately after the naval engagement to take part in the previously postponed Coral Sea operation. *Junyo* and *Ryujo* were still at Midway, waiting while the island's airstrips were made ready to receive their planes. So all in all it would be at least six weeks before *Kido Butai* could again operate as a coherent striking force.

For Yamamoto, once more relaxing aboard *Yamato* in Hiroshima Bay, it was an opportunity for taking stock. The crushing victory he had just secured had not brought the Americans cap-in-hand to the negotiating table. He had never really believed that it would. Midway was only one of a series of hammer-blows designed to weaken American resolve. Each of these blows paved the way for another. Where should the next one be struck?

Before the Battle of Midway Yamamoto had been reasonably sure of his answer to this question. Despite his airy promises to Kuroshima in early May the Japanese Commander-in-Chief had never seriously considered an all-out assault on the British position in the Indian Ocean. Japan's primary enemy, the only one which could stand between the nation and its destiny on the Asian mainland, remained the United States. Even after Midway this could never be forgotten. The next blow, and the one after that, must be aimed at American power, at American resolve, until the Americans themselves were forced to call a halt to this war.

Yamamoto's next priority was Oahu, the most important of the Hawaiian Islands. It stood at the centre of the Pacific chess-board. Pearl Harbor was *the* central Pacific naval base, the funnel through which American military potential would be poured into the Pacific bottle. Without Oahu, without Pearl, the Americans would have to mount their Pacific operations from the distant coast of the American continent, a formidable if not impossible task.

The Japanese capture of Oahu would also be a psychological blow of enormous proportions. Midway had been too far from the United States. It had been a naval tragedy and another island occupied. But there were many islands, and navies could always be built again. Midway had brought bad news, traumatic news, of the war home to America, but it had not brought the war itself. That was what was needed. The occupation of American soil, of American bases, of American civilians. Oahu.

Even before Midway, Ugaki and Yamamoto had canvassed support for such an operation, but the Army had refused to supply the necessary troops and the Naval General Staff had denounced the plan as being too hazardous. Now, with such a victory behind him, Yamamoto hoped that he could obtain the troops and the go-ahead from his naval superiors. He was soon to be disillusioned.

The Army saw matters in a different light. It always had. Japan, an island power with continental aspirations, had produced two services of equal status and power which looked in opposite directions. While the Navy directed its energies eastward towards the Pacific and its American enemy, the Army looked west towards China, its ever-reluctant bride. Soliciting the co-operation of this bride was the Army's eternal task; that, and fighting off the other noted rapists of the underdeveloped world, the great powers of continental Europe and Anglo-America.

The Navy's role, according to the Army, was basically secondary. It consisted of securing the Army's lines of communication between the home islands and the conquered territories, and of fending off naval interference from the other great powers. In 1905 this had meant little more than controlling the Straits of Japan, and though by 1942 the role had expanded geographically – south towards the protection of the vital oil, east against the air-sea threat posed by the United States – in essence it remained the same. Japan's destiny lay on the Asian mainland, not amongst the myriad coral atolls of the Pacific. Action in the latter zone served action in the former, not vice versa.

The glorious victory at Midway was interpreted in this light by the Army leaders. The Navy was doing its job, holding off American interference in the vital Chinese warzone. It would have to continue to do this job, until such time as the Army had made China a fit place for Japanese to live in. For this latter task the Army needed all the divisions it had. Or nearly all of them. It was recognised that certain army units would have to be deployed alongside the Navy – the Pacific was an amphibious, not a purely oceanic setting – but their number would have to be small. The Japanese Army was not an infinitely expendable resource.

The struggle in China continued. Little progress had been made in the seven months since Pearl Harbor. In Chungking Generalissimo Chiang Kai-shek still defied the Japanese, despite the loss of the Burmese end of his road to the outside world. In the north-central provinces of Shensi and Shansi the activities of the communist partisans under Mao Tse-tung were becoming more rather than less troublesome. The Japanese invaders were still wading in thick treacle.

What could be done to solve this painful problem? Blind to the realities of the situation the Japanese, in true Western style, sought to solve an internal problem by juggling with the periphery. They convinced themselves, despite evidence to the contrary, that the Chinese would give up their struggle if completely cut off from external aid.

One source of this aid was India. An air-lift was now supplying Chiang Kai-shek from bases in Assam. Throttling this route at its source would involve the invasion of India, an operation which would involve the participation of the Navy and perhaps also Japan's Axis partners.

There were many in the Japanese Army leadership who welcomed the idea of co-operation with Germany in the Middle East/India area. Unfortunately their enthusiasm was not shared by either the Navy or, more important, the German Führer. German policy was becoming increasingly anti-Japanese in the summer of 1942. Even before Midway it had been an ambivalent mixture of reluctant admiration and vague distaste. Ciano noted in his diary that the latter was gaining the upper hand in the months that followed Yamamoto's great victory:

> It is all very well for the Japanese to win because they are our allies, but after all they belong to the yellow race and their successes are gained at the expense of

the white race. It is a leitmotiv which frequently appears in the conversations of the Germans.

The Germans were slightly more tactful in the presence of their 'yellow' ally, but the Japanese were not fooled. If Ribbentrop's charm was not transparent enough for them, then the steadfast German refusal either to offer or receive practical suggestions for joint activity was an obvious enough indication of Japan's status in German eyes. When the Japanese proposed a jointly sponsored declaration of independence for India and the Arabs the Germans simply ignored them. All offers of military co-operation in the Indian Ocean were spurned. The heirs of the Rising Sun got the distinct impression that they were being brushed off.

So, with neither Navy or Axis support forthcoming, the Army was forced to abandon its cherished Indian offensive. Its leaders were forced to turn their attention to the other imaginary source of Chinese resolution – Soviet support of the Chinese partisans. Joining the war against Russia had been a possibility since *Barbarossa* began, and now, in the summer of 1942, it seemed both practical and necessary. The new wave of German victories in May and June had worn down Soviet strength still further; the new wave of German hostility towards Japan made it imperative that the latter secured its natural rights in eastern Siberia while it was still possible. The Kwangtung Army was ordered to update its invasion plans.

At an Imperial War Cabinet meeting on 5 July the Army announced and defended its decision. The conquest of eastern Siberia would both facilitate the conquest of China and provide much-needed *lebensraum* for Japan's crowded Empire. It would finally eliminate the Soviet Union from the war. Simultaneously the Germans would be pushing the British out of the struggle. And the United States would not be able to fight on alone against both Germany and Japan.

Yamamoto, who was not present at the meeting, strongly disagreed with the Army's chosen course of action. He believed that the divisions earmarked for Siberia could be used to better strategic effect against Oahu. But he received no support from the Naval General Staff, who still considered that the Oahu operation was far too hazardous. Nor was this the worst of it. On 16 July Yamamoto was informed that the three smaller carriers – *Ryujo, Junyo* and the new *Hiyo* – would be needed in the Sea of Japan to support the Army's operation against Vladivostok. Which left him with only *Kido Butai*'s four large carriers for the continuation of the war against the United States. He had to do something with them, or the momentum gathered at Midway would be lost. Denied the chance to attack Oahu, Yamamoto began to consider more daring possibilities.

II

Shortly before 06.00 on 7 August the green lights glowed on the decks of *Hiyo*, *Ryujo* and *Junyo*, and the Kates and Vals sped past them and into the air. Once in formation they flew off to the north. Forty miles ahead of them the Russian city of Vladivostok was welcoming the first rays of the morning sun. To the Japanese pilots the huge red orb in the east seemed like a vast replica of their flag strung across the horizon.

At 06.45 the first bombs rained down on Vladivostok harbour, sinking two Soviet cruisers of the moribund Pacific Fleet and three American merchantmen flying the Soviet flag.

At almost the same moment six divisions of the Kwangtung Army moved into the attack at two places on the Manchurian border, near Hunchun, scene of border fighting in 1938, and at the point 120 miles further north where the Harbin-Vladivostok railway crossed the frontier. Three hours later a further seven divisions of the Kwangtung Army, also in two groups, moved forward in western Manchuria, into the semi-desert region around Buir Nor where the Soviet, Mongolian and Manchurian borders join. The objective of these divisions was the large Siberian town of Chita, two hundred miles to the north-west, at the junction of the Trans-Siberian and Chinese Eastern Railways.

The Japanese declaration of war, following at the usual discreet distance behind the commencement of hostilities, was delivered to the Soviet ambassador in Tokyo at midday. Imperial Japan had taken the final reckless plunge.

In the Harbin HQ of the Kwangtung Army its commander, General Umezu, radiated confidence. His crack army, shunted into the wings of the war since 1937, would at last have the chance to prove its devotion and virility to the Sun God reigning in Tokyo. The defeats suffered in the border 'skirmishes' of 1938–9 had been forgotten.

They would soon be remembered. Considering the smallness of the force at his disposal – a mere seventeen divisions – Umezu's confidence was astonishing, and only explicable in terms of the 'victory disease' prevalent at all levels of the Japanese Armed Forces in early August 1942. The Kwangtung Army's intelligence work was wholly incompetent; it was reckoned that there were eight Red Army divisions east of Chita, but in fact there were fifteen, and they were commanded by one of the war's greatest generals – Konstantin Rokossovsky, the future victor of Mutankiang, Vladimir and Smolensk. Stavka had sent him east to take command of the remnants of the Far Eastern Army in mid-July, and he had talked with Zhukov on the eve of his departure from Kuybyshev. The two generals had agreed that Vladivostok would be impossible to hold, but that any further loss of territory should and could be avoided.

If General Umezu had been privy to this conversation he might have been better prepared for what was to follow in August. But instead he interpreted the rapid progress of the armies converging on Vladivostok as further confirmation of Soviet weakness. The three divisions following the railway, spearheaded by the famous 'Gem' Division, fought their way into Voroshilov on the Trans-Siberian only four days after crossing the border. Vladivostok was effectively cut off from the rest of the Soviet Union, and on 13 August the battle for the city began, the Japanese ground forces receiving ample air support from the aircraft based in Manchuria and the carriers still lying forty miles offshore. There was little doubt that the city would fall within a week.

But in the west the Japanese were running into trouble. The attack along the dry Khalka river-bed from the railhead at Halun-Arshan met the same fate as the almost identical sortie launched in 1939. The numbers on each side were roughly equal, but the Soviet forces were qualitatively far superior. The Japanese had no heavy tanks, no medium tanks to match the T-34s, and none of that battle-sense won by the Soviet tank-crews in close encounters with the German panzers. After advancing fifty miles across the arid flats towards Buir Nor the four divisions of the Japanese left wing were simply routed by Rokossovsky's brilliantly executed armoured encirclement. The right wing fared no better. Three days later, in the area of Kharanor, it received a similar thrashing.

General Umezu's confidence was rather strained by these defeats, but his spirits were slightly restored by the surrender of the small Soviet force still in Vladivostok on 19 August. Japanese losses had been heavier than expected however, and after two divisions had been entrained for the west to bolster their ailing comrades on the Mongolian front there only remained three depleted divisions for the march on Khabarovsk, some four hundred miles up the Trans-Siberian. By the end of the month they had covered forty of them, reaching the small town of Sibirtsevo. They were to get no further.

The military leaders in Tokyo had grossly under-estimated the Red Army in the Far East, and had grossly overestimated the ability of their own forces, hitherto used exclusively against either non-industrialised nations or

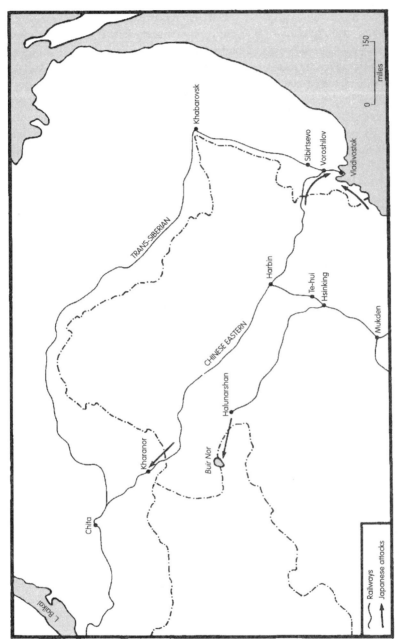

15. Japan Attacks the Soviet Union

Western armies fighting in unfamiliar surroundings, to overcome a Western army that was fighting in its own back-yard and with superior weaponry. The spirit of *banzai* could not compensate for the disparity of strength.

The decision to attack the Soviet Union, which had been taken for opportunist rather than sound strategic reasons, was to prove the worst legacy of the 'victory disease' engendered by Midway and earlier triumphs. It won the Japanese nothing but the city of Vladivostok and the consequent blockage of the American-Soviet supply route. This might have proven its worth given time, but time was never on the side of Japan. On the debit side the attack on the Soviet Union ruled out the reallocation of the Kwangtung Army to other theatres, and it tied down a large portion of the Japanese Army's Air Force at a time when Japan was crucially short of planes and trained pilots. The last slack had been taken up; the Japanese Army had lost its flexibility.

And as for the three carriers used against Vladivostok – their absence was soon to be dearly felt elsewhere.

III

While battle had raged through the streets of Vladivostok *Kido Butai* had been passing close by the spot from which, nine months before, it had opened the war against the United States. This time only four carriers – *Akagi*, *Soryu*, *Shokaku* and *Zuikaku* – were rolling and pitching in the North Pacific waves, but other factors had proved more constant. Admiral Nagumo was still pacing across his bridge expressing anxiety. Admiral Kusaka was still reassuring him.

This time Kusaka had less cause for optimism, for *Kido Butai* was not the force it had been. Victory had taken its toll, and both Genda and Fuchida were worried about the quality of the pilots drafted in to replace those lost at Midway. Japanese training programmes had been crippled by the shortage of aviation fuel, and these replacement pilots had not enjoyed the many hours aloft that had been granted their predecessors. This was all the more serious in that the battles to come would probably prove harder than those already past. Genda and Fuchida tried to suppress their doubts as they pored over the maps of Los Angeles and San Diego in the *Akagi* operations room.

Yamamoto, denied the chance to hit Oahu, had decided to give the Americans a lesson in vulnerability by hitting the Californian coast. The choice of San Diego as a target was obvious enough; it was the biggest US

Navy base on the West Coast. Los Angeles, to Yamamoto, represented something more intangible. In his years as Naval Attaché in Washington the Admiral had learnt, or thought he had learnt, a great deal about the American character. Americans were a nation of materialists and a nation of dreamers living in uneasy conjunction. He had decided to attack both, the material in San Diego, the dream in Los Angeles.

It would be risky. Surprise, though essential, might well prove elusive. *Kido Butai* would have to pass through the Hawaii-West Coast sea-lanes without being detected. Once within range of its targets the fleet would be vulnerable to attack from shore-based aircraft. Withdrawal would have to be swift indeed. Once out of reach of these aircraft *Kido Butai* would be safe, for according to Japanese Intelligence the US Navy only possessed one remaining carrier, the *Ranger*. And since their agent in Panama had not reported this carrier's passage through the Canal, it was assumed that she was still in the Atlantic.

Through the second week of August the carriers sailed on undetected at the maximum speed allowed by the accompanying oil tankers. The search-planes flew a 180-degree arc to a distance of 300 miles ahead of the fleet, and several times the carriers changed course to avoid being sighted by merchant ships. By early morning on 18 August they were approaching their destination, a point some two hundred miles off the Californian coast, equidistant from Los Angeles and San Diego. So far everything was proceeding according to plan.

As the sky lightened in the west the planes left the decks of the four carriers. Both cities were to be attacked simultaneously, to maximise the element of surprise and to give an exaggerated impression of Japanese strength. Tomonaga was to lead the planes from *Shokaku* and *Zuikaku* against Los Angeles, Fuchida those from *Akagi* and *Soryu* against San Diego.

On the American coast a sleepy radar operator in San Diego picked up the incoming flight but assumed it was composed of American planes. There was no particular reason for this assumption, save the general expectation that the Japanese were about to attack Oahu and an understandable refusal to believe that Yamamoto would have the temerity to attack the sacred soil of continental America. In Los Angeles the radar operator seems to have been completely asleep; no other satisfactory explanation has ever been found for the complete failure to detect the enemy approach.

Fuchida's planes swept into the attack at 07.15. Their sole target was the naval base in San Diego Bay, and to their joy the Japanese pilots discovered that once again the American warships were unprotected by torpedo nets.

179

Their old friends the battleships *Pennsylvania* and *Maryland*, which had been under repair in the dockyards ever since Pearl Harbor, were once again sent to a shallow harbour floor by Japanese bombs and torpedoes. The battleship *Mississippi*, the cruisers *Vincennes*, *Chicago* and *Minneapolis*, and several destroyers suffered similar fates.

The attackers did not escape unscathed. Though the AA defences had little reason to congratulate themselves the American fighters, once airborne, took a heavy toll of the Japanese planes. Nearly a third of Fuchida's force failed to return to the waiting carriers.

Over Los Angeles Tomonaga's attack was inflicting less material damage but wreaking untold havoc in the wonderlands of the American psyche. Turning in from the sea along the crest of the Santa Monica Mountains, the Japanese bombers homed in on the eccentric target Yamamoto had chosen for them – the Hollywood dream factory. The Warner, Universal and Walt Disney studios, strung out along Ventura Boulevard, were hit by numerous bombs. One of them killed the well-known director Michael Curtiz in his car at the Warner studio gates; another destroyed all the prints of his latest film, *Casablanca*, in the Warner editing rooms. As a minor concession to military rationale, the Japanese planes also attacked the Lockheed aviation factories three miles further north in the San Fernando valley. With rather less deliberation a stray bomb knocked the H and the WOOD from the famous Hollywood sign, leaving, or so Oliver Hardy was later to claim, a splendid memorial to his talents in the night-time sky. And with splendid irony another Japanese bomb destroyed the cinema at which John Huston's *Across the Pacific* had opened the previous week.

By this time the American fighters had belatedly scrambled into the air from their Long Beach and Los Alamitos airfields, and several stray members of the attacking force were brought down over the city. But by and large Tomonaga's force had disappeared before the population of Los Angeles was aware of its arrival. The panic only set in later. For weeks afterwards, nervous citizens would either scan the sky for unfriendly planes or form standing patrols on the beaches, their eyes peeled for the inevitable Japanese invasion barges.

By 11.00 Nagumo's carriers had recovered all the planes that were going to return, and *Kido Butai* was making top speed into the south-west. For the next forth-eight hours it was attacked spasmodically, and with little noticeable effect, by shore-based American planes of all shapes and sizes. By nightfall on 20 August Nagumo believed his fleet was safe, from both attack and detection. He ordered a change of course to the south-east.

Nagumo did not know that ten miles behind him, its low silhouette hidden by the horizon's curve, the American submarine *Cuttlefish* was doggedly trailing his giant carriers. At midnight on 20 August her captain reported the Japanese change of course.

IV

Contrary to Japanese belief the US Navy possessed three operational carriers in August 1942, not one. Two of them, moreover, were in the Pacific. *Saratoga*, though badly damaged by a torpedo in January, had not, as the Japanese happily assumed, been sunk. In June it had re-emerged from the San Diego repair yards and was now in Pearl Harbor. Neither was *Wasp* where the Luftwaffe had said it was – at the bottom of the Mediterranean. In fact this carrier had passed through the Panama Canal in early July, unnoticed by the local Japanese agent, who was languishing in an American military prison in the Canal Zone. His codebook was still in use however, as the American intelligence authorities relayed comforting but false information to Tokyo. *Wasp* had also required extensive repairs, and had only been passed fully operational the previous week. It had sailed for Pearl only forty-eight hours before Fuchida's planes appeared over San Diego harbour.

So Admiral Nimitz, still Pacific C-in-C despite the Midway debacle, had something to play with. When the news of the Californian attacks reached him in Hawaii he acted with commendable speed. *Saratoga* was leaving Pearl Harbor before the morning was over; she was to rendezvous with *Wasp* in the vicinity of Clipperton Island, some eight hundred miles off the Mexican coast.

Nimitz did not know where Nagumo was going, but he suspected the worst. Though the reports coming in from *Cuttlefish* suggested that *Kido Butai* was returning home via the southern Pacific, the American C-in-C feared a Japanese strike against the Panama Canal. He was right, but it would be two nerve-wracking days before *Cuttlefish* reported Nagumo's change of course and confirmed Nimitz's suspicions. From that moment on the question was – could the Japanese carriers be overtaken? It seemed likely that *Kido Butai*, operating at such distance from its bases, would be moving slowly to conserve fuel. If so, then there was a chance.

The Japanese carriers, once beyond the reach of shore-based aircraft, had indeed reduced speed for that reason, but not to the degree Nimitz was hoping for. He had assumed that the maximum speed of the accompanying tankers – around twelve knots – would be the maximum speed of the fleet. He was mistaken. The tankers had been left behind after a last refuelling on the morning of 22 August; more were waiting farther to the south, having sailed from Truk at the beginning of the month.

Aboard *Kido Butai* spirits were high. Another great victory! They had attacked the American mainland with relative impunity! In the operations rooms the maps of San Diego and Los Angeles had been returned to the map-drawers, and those of the Panama Canal Zone brought out for intense perusal. Genda and the flight leaders studied the paths to be taken by the torpedo-bombers as they homed in on the giant gates of the Pedro Miguel and Miraflores locks.

The destruction of these gates, Yamamoto had discovered in consultation with Japanese engineers, would put the Canal out of action for many months. Allied trade would be gravely impeded, and additional strain placed on an already precarious shipping situation. It would also make it harder for the US Navy to switch its ships from ocean to ocean at short notice. But the main rationale behind the Canal attack was psychological. The mere fact of a successful Japanese strike against an American installation 9000 miles from Japan was what counted. Surely the enemy would realise from this the impossibility of winning the Pacific war.

Aboard the Japanese ships the days went by. The rough and cold northern Pacific was a long way behind them now, and the crews relaxed in the bright tropical sun. *Kido Butai* was over 7000 miles from Japan, further than it had travelled in the Ceylon operation. Even Nagumo had almost ceased his worrying, a fact which caused Kusaka a certain amount of anxiety.

On the morning of 26 August the fleet rendezvoused with the tankers sent out from Truk and took on another week's fuel. By evening on the following day *Kido Butai* was one hundred miles due west of Coiba Island, 450 miles from the Pacific end of the Panama Canal. Genda went over the attack plans with the flight leaders one more time.

At 06.00 on 28 August the carriers were lying fifty miles off the wide entrance to the Gulf of Panama. The planes were speeding down the flight decks and into the sky. Once again Mitsuo Fuchida would lead them into the attack. Soon after 06.30 the 120 Japanese planes moved off in formation, the dawn to their right, Panama straight ahead.

Three hundred miles to the west Rear-Admiral Frank Fletcher stood on the bridge of the *Saratoga* and watched the same dawn ease the darkness away.

His force comprised the two carriers *Wasp* and *Saratoga*, the battleships *Washington* and *North Carolina*, five cruisers and seventeen destroyers. It was almost within striking distance of where Fletcher assumed the enemy had to be. His search-planes were about to be launched; he assumed that the Catalinas based at Fort Amador in the Canal Zone would already be in the air. Soon there should be news.

The American fleet was observing complete radio silence, and there was one important fact of which Fletcher was unaware. *Ranger*, the sole US carrier in the Atlantic, had been relieved of escort duty and rushed south across the Caribbean to join the battle. It had arrived at the Atlantic end of the Canal in the early hours of that morning, and was due to pass through to the Pacific the following night.

There would not be time. At 07.10 *Ranger*'s captain received two pieces of information. One of the Catalinas had found the Japanese fleet, and the Canal Zone radar installations, on full alert for several days, had picked up an incoming flight of enemy planes. The only naval battle in history to span two oceans was underway.

The Canal Zone's AA defences had been greatly strengthened in the months that followed Midway, and the radar warning had given the USAF plentiful time to scramble, so Fuchida's planes received a lively welcome. The Vals and their Zero escort were assailed by American fighters – mostly Wildcats – high above the Canal Zone, and both sides suffered heavy losses. Far below the raging dogfights the Kates were flying through a hail of flak towards the Pedro Miguel locks. Two broke through to launch their torpedoes against the lower gates, both of which were severely damaged. But since the locks were empty and the upper gates also closed there was no uncontrollable rush of water. The one torpedo dropped inside the locks exploded harmlessly when it hit the shallow bottom. As his surviving planes turned back to sea a frustrated Fuchida radioed Nagumo that there was need of a second strike.

The Admiral, waiting for such news with Kusaka on the *Akagi* bridge, agreed to launch one. There was no likelihood of US naval forces in the area, and his fleet could protect itself against the Panama fighters. The search-planes from the cruisers *Tone* and *Chikuma* had been out on patrol to the east and south since 06.30, and had found nothing but empty ocean. The sky was still clear. At 08.15 Nagumo ordered the second strike-force into the air.

Unknown to the Japanese theirs were not the only planes hurtling down a carrier's flight deck. At around 08.25 *Ranger* was launching its fighter- and torpedo-bombers from a point five miles off Colon in the Atlantic Ocean. They flew across the isthmus, passing on their left the fire and smoke left by Fuchida's raid, and ventured out into the Gulf of Panama.

At around the same moment Admiral Fletcher was listening to the clanking of the *Saratoga* lift as it brought the armed planes up from the hangar deck. The distance between his task force and the Japanese was rapidly closing. Fletcher offered a silent prayer of thanks for the blanket of cloud which seemed to be accompanying his eastward passage.

From the viewpoint of the *Akagi* bridge these clouds were still no more than a line across the western horizon, and Nagumo and Kusaka were pre-occupied with watching the recovery of Fuchida's returning planes. Soon after 09.30 Kusaka went down to talk with Fuchida himself, leaving Nagumo to fret on his own. The Admiral noticed the clouds on the horizon. They were coming nearer. Could the *Tone* search-plane have missed something out there to the west?

'What *could* it have missed?' asked the sarcastic Kusaka on his return. 'A fleet of American carriers? All but one were sunk at Midway! And if that one is out there, we shall have no trouble in destroying it.'

The logic seemed sound to Nagumo, but before he had time to ponder the question further some disquieting news came in. A flight of approaching bombers was reported by the northernmost Japanese destroyers. As the Zero patrols above the fleet sped north to intercept this menace, Nagumo and Kusaka asked each other where it had come from. It could only be the mainland. But what were carrier planes, Dauntlesses and Devastators, doing in Panama? Could that one carrier be in the area?

For the next ten minutes the two Admirals considered this question, as the flak and the Zeroes dealt with *Ranger*'s planes. No great damage was suffered; only *Soryu* was hit by a bomb and the resultant fire was easily extinguished.

Nagumo's problems were not yet over, however, for now he received news from Tomonaga. The second strike on Panama had been as unfortunate as the first. The American air defences were still unbroken, the lock-gates were still unbreached, and there was need for a third strike.

Nagumo now found it difficult to take a decision. There were too many imponderables. Kusaka tried to assist him. The first strike should be ordered back on to the flight deck, he urged. If there was an American carrier in the area – which he doubted – then Fuchida's planes could be sent to destroy it. If not then a third strike could be launched against the Canal. *Kido Butai* had not come 9000 miles to be baulked by a pair of lock-gates.

Kusaka's confidence restored Nagumo's. He agreed with his Chief of Staff. Unfortunately their conversation had taken ten minutes, and they would prove the most important ten minutes in *Kido Butai*'s glorious but short career.

Wasp and *Saratoga* had launched their planes soon after 09.00. Fletcher had learnt something from the Midway battle, and he had sent the slower torpedo-bombers off ahead. They would pull the fighter defences down to the surface, and so maximise the chances of the dive-bombers.

Fletcher knew he was outnumbered two to one in carriers and planes, but he also knew that he had surprise on his side. And this time there was none of that false confidence which had preceded Midway; the crews knew what they had to do, knew that it was going to be extremely hard, and that they were going to do it anyway.

By 10.55 the flight decks of the four Japanese carriers were almost full of planes loaded with high explosives. At that moment a fresh flight of enemy aircraft was sighted moving in from the west. This time there were more of them. Where were all these planes coming from? A chill of desperate uncertainty passed through the minds of the Japanese sailors.

The American torpedo-planes bored in towards the Japanese carriers, through the vicious flak and the marauding Zeroes. One by one they went down, eliciting murmurs from Nagumo in praise of their reckless gallantry. 'The Americans must be feeling desperate today,' muttered the more prosaic Kusaka. Nagumo did not answer. Perhaps a dumb foreboding was growing in his consciousness. The torpedo-bombers had at least scattered his fleet, and the Zeroes had all been pulled down close to the water. Nagumo looked up, in time to catch the first glimpse of the American dive-bombers dropping out of the sun. Nemesis had arrived. It was 11.10.

The 500 and 800-pound bombs lanced into the flight decks of all four carriers, tearing huge holes and starting blazing fires. The fuel and explosives in the densely-packed planes ignited. The Japanese firefighting teams were unable to contain the spreading flames. Burnt men lay screaming in agony amidst the charred corpses of their comrades.

Some of the bombs had passed clean through the flight decks to explode on the hangar decks below. These triggered off more multiple explosions as the fires spread to the bomb and torpedo racks. Fuel lines ignited, sending rivulets of flame washing across the decks of the listing carriers.

None of them had been hit by torpedoes, and none were damaged below the water-line, but only *Shokaku*'s engines and rudder were still working at

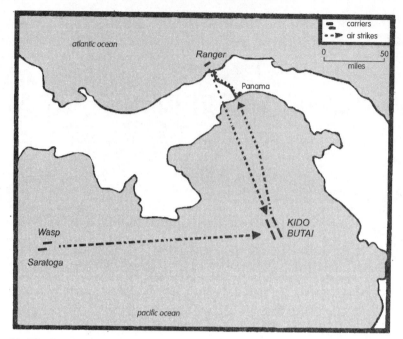

16. The Battle of the Panama Gulf

14.00, and only she would still be tenuously afloat at the end of the day. The still-burning hulk of this famous carrier would be sunk by its own destroyer escort on the following morning.

Nagumo and Kusaka had abandoned the stricken *Akagi* within thirty minutes of the attack. From the bridge of the battleship *Kirishima* they watched the carriers of *Kido Butai* burn. Pearl Harbor, Ceylon, Midway, California – it had been a glorious morning. But now it was past noon, and the sun was commencing its downward turn. The Rising Sun would rise no more.

Chapter 11
PANZERS THREE MILES FROM JERUSALEM

It may be a fire, tomorrow it will be ashes.
Arab proverb

And we shall save Jerusalem
From Rommel's grubby German hands.
Eighth Army ditty, September 1942

I

Through the last week of July and the first fortnight of August Field-Marshal Rundstedt's Army Group South had been moving south across the four hundred miles of open country between the Don and the Caucasus Mountains. Eleventh Army had crossed the Kerch Strait into the Kuban and was fighting its way down the Black Sea coast. On its left flank the stronger Seventeenth Army was marching in the wake of Kleist's panzers towards the northern end of the mountain highway that led across to Sukhumi. In the centre, astride the main road and rail communications, First and Second Panzer Armies pushed south towards the Georgian Military Highway and the Caspian littoral respectively.

The distances involved were immense, supply a continuous problem, but the German advance was living on its own momentum. Across the dry steppe, through fields of waving corn and man-high sunflowers, towards the distant cloud above snow-capped Mount Elbruz, the German tide flowed forward, leaving its customary trail of burning villages, rotting corpses, and vehicles which had finally succumbed to one bad road too many.

The German High Command had estimated that there were twenty Russian divisions in the Caucasus, but so far they had seen little to substantiate such a figure. Small groups of Red Army soldiers and tanks hindered the panzer spearheads at all the difficult river-crossings, but melted away into the south once the Germans had secured bridgeheads on the southern banks. In Lötzen it was thought that the Red Army would make its stand at the entrance to the mountain passes; until then the problems were all logistic ones – water, vehicle maintenance, the ever-recurrent shortages of fuel.

The last-named had not been alleviated by the capture of the Maikop and Grozny oilfields, on 2 and 12 August respectively. Both had been put out of action by the retreating Red Army. The oil storage tanks had been destroyed and all vital plant equipment removed. It would be several months before any of the precious black fluid could be brought to the surface, always assuming that the German supply network could stand the additional burden of moving the necessary equipment.

This was well appreciated in Kuybyshev, and preparations were already being made for the destruction of the Baku fields. If, as was now feared, the Red Army failed to hold the line of the mountains, the Germans would find no functional oil-wells on the other side.

The Caucasus was only one of three fronts on which the Soviet Union was fighting for its life. The Japanese attack in the Far East, though no surprise, had been thoroughly depressing. The relative ease with which Rokossovsky had thrown back the invaders in the Mongolian border region was encouraging, but the closing of Vladivostok, at a time when the volume of American aid coming in through the port was rising steeply, was a hard blow. And successful or not, the war in the Far East was now tying down twenty Red Army divisions.

These could well have been used on the third crucial front, forty miles south of Vologda. Since the final fall of Yaroslavl in mid-July 3rd Panzer and Sixteenth Army had been trying to reach the important railway junction. The strong Red Army positions on the Danilov ridge had been successfully stormed on 24–25 July, but little further progress had been made in the weeks following. This front was now acting as a magnet to the German and Soviet High Commands; both were throwing in reserves they could ill afford, raising the stakes without changing the ratio of forces.

It was not yet apparent, but the dangerous game in progress south of Vologda was more dangerous to the Germans. The bulk of the panzer force was now tied up either here or in the distant Caucasus, leaving the long line from Gorkiy to Stalingrad manned almost exclusively by infantry formations. This was only safe as long as the Red Army had no armoured reserve.

It was building one. Soviet industry, after all the problems involved in the vast removal programme, was at last getting back into its stride. New tanks and planes were starting to pour steadily off the Ural and Siberian assembly lines. In Kuybyshev this was felt to be a trump card. Regardless of the likely fall of the Caucasus this card would be there to play. As long as Hoth could be held south of Vologda for another two or three months, then the long winter nights would see a resumption of the Arctic convoys and the alleviation of the most worrying shortages. And then, perhaps, advantage could be taken of that long thin German line stretching from Gorkiy to the south.

In the Wolfsschanze such eventualities were not under consideration. Victory was still taken for granted. Certainly Halder was getting worried, and Hitler was getting more than annoyed, at the time it was taking to accomplish this inevitable victory. By mid-August Vologda was proving more than an irritation or a nuisance, it was a symbol of German frustration.

This feeling was deepened in the third week of August by the stubborn Russian resistance in the Ordzhonikidze region, at the northern end of the Georgian Military Highway. By 19 August Kleist's panzers had been battering their armoured heads against a wall for five days without making more than an appreciable dent. Hitler, a thousand miles away in his forest lair, ranted and raved and attacked the furniture. Halder, with rather more thoughtfulness, began to consider the unwelcome possibility of another winter of war.

II

In the first week of August Rommel had finally bridged and crossed the Suez Canal. The South African battle-groups had withdrawn across Sinai in good order, and the full might of *Panzerarmee Asien* moved forward in their wake along the coast and Bir Gifgafa roads. The British airstrips at Jebel Libni, Bir Rod Salim and El Arish were repaired and enlarged to accommodate Rommel's Luftwaffe support. The German supply corps began the arduous task of carrying the necessary supplies across eighty miles of desert. By 16 August Rommel felt ready to attack.

The British were dug in behind the extensive minefields on the two main roads leading into Palestine. The New Zealand Division and 1st Armoured

Division held the narrow Jiradi defile and the vital Rafah crossroads ten miles further to the east. 50th Division and 2nd Armoured Division were deployed astride the Umm Katef bottleneck on the inland route. The South Africans and the green 44th Division were in reserve. Montgomery was determined that the Germans would have to fight for every inch. 'He has no more divisions than we have' he told his divisional commanders, 'let's hit him for six!'

Early on 17 August 20th Panzer attempted unsuccessfully to rush the Jiradi Pass. Only a few tanks broke through the defending New Zealanders' fire, and these were destroyed at the eastern exit by the Grants of 1st Armoured Division. Rommel realised that he would have to flush out the defenders position by position, and the dismounted 14th Motorised began this task that afternoon. Both sides suffered heavily in the numerous hand-to-hand encounters.

The Germans were making little more progress on the inland route. A frontal attack by 7th Panzer on the Umm Katef defences floundered in the minefields and was beaten back. Cruewell's attempt to outflank the position by pushing 15th Panzer down the El Quseima road came closer to success; the German tanks were only halted by 4th Armoured Brigade and the timely arrive of a South African brigade.

The Germans seemed to be finding it difficult to operate without the luxury of an open desert flank. Or so Montgomery complacently believed. But unfortunately for the British the German commander was aloft in his Storch reconnaissance plane, searching the terrain for a way out of his dilemma. He found one. On the night of 19–20 August 15th Panzer advanced slowly along the dry bed of the Wadi Hareidin, considered impassable by the British command, and turned north into the soft underbelly of the Rafah crossroads defensive complex. Through the morning a confused tank battle was fought in the dunes south of the crossroads, and 1st Armoured Division, despite inflicting heavy losses on 15th Panzer, was thrown back in the direction of Rafah town. This allowed Cruewell to lead a battle-group north-west through Kfar Shan to the eastern end of the Jiradi defile. The 4th and 5th New Zealand Brigades were now trapped between Cruewell's tanks and a renewed push by 14th Motorised from the west. Several frantic hours followed before nightfall allowed the New Zealanders the chance to break out along the coastline to the east.

The northern flank of the British position was crumbling. Montgomery realised as much, and threw in the reserve 44th Division between Rafah and Khan Yunis as a temporary stop-gap. But worse was to come. 7th Panzer's tank regiment had been fed along the Wadi Hareidin in 15th Panzer's tracks, and on reaching the Palestine frontier turned south towards El Auja, fifteen miles behind the British position at Umm Katef. This was one of Rommel's finest moves, a classic example of the double encirclement enacted from a central thrust. It nearly paid off. Unfortunately for Rommel *Ariete* proved unequal to the task of completing the encirclement. Advancing up the El Quseima road the lightly-armoured Italian tanks were severely punished by the heavier Grants and Shermans. While the South Africans doggedly resisted 7th Panzer's advance above the El Auja road, 50th and 2nd Armoured Divisions evacuated Umm Katef and pulled back to the east and safety. Rommel was left cursing the presence of *Ariete* and the consequent absence of 21st Panzer. Who needed allies?

The Red Army could have done with some help. Field-Marshal Rundstedt, in an attempt to break the deadlock in the Caucasus, had loaned Kleist one of Guderian's panzer corps. The additional divisions had made all the difference. After a day-long battle for the small mountain village of Kazbegi, the motorised infantry and the Stukas had at last cleared a path for the tanks through the upper Terek valley, and by evening on 20 August 9th Panzer had penetrated the entrance to the Krestovyy Pass. Next morning the panzers were rumbling down into the heart of Georgia, a mere sixty miles from Tbilisi.

Four days earlier units of Seventeenth Army had captured the port of Sukhumi, trapping two Soviet armies between themselves and the advance of Eleventh Army down the Black Sea coast. On the other German flank Guderian's spearhead had been making similar good progress, reaching Kuba, a hundred miles from Baku, on 20 August.

Now was the moment, thought the Führer, for his masterstroke. On the morning of 21 August, as the 9th Panzer crews threw snowballs at each other in the high mountains, Student's Airborne Corps, fresh from its Maltese triumph, took off from airstrips in the Grozny area. Its mission was to capture the lucrative Baku oilfields intact.

This operation, code-named *Schwarz Gold*, was ill-conceived and ill-prepared. Everything had been rushed. Intelligence of both the terrain and the local Red Army strength was inadequate. The airborne officers and troops were insufficiently briefed. There was not enough fighter support; Luftflotte IV was fully engaged on the Georgian Military Highway. Student protested that the operation was suicidal, but to no avail. Hitler was in no mood to listen. 'The Reich cannot do without the Baku oil,' he told the Airborne leader. The Germans could not afford to trust the local Azerbaijan population to protect their main source of wealth, nor could they risk

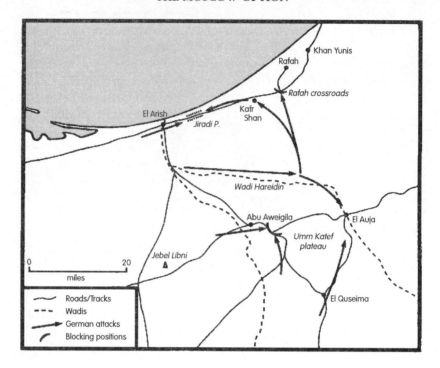

17. Breakthrough into Palestine

Guderian arriving too late to prevent the destruction of the vital installations. There could be no repetition of the Maikop and Grozny experiences. Surprise was essential, Hitler insisted. There was no time for exhaustive preparations, and in any case there was no need. There could not be more than a handful of Russian battalions in Baku. And Guderian would be arriving in thirty-six hours at the most. All Student's men had to do was to land without breaking their legs and then stand guard around the largest wells. What could go wrong?

Everything. There were four divisions of the Soviet Ninth Army in Baku, and another three blocking Guderian's path at Kilyazi, fifty miles to the north. It would be four days before the panzers arrived.

They were four long days. Student's paratroopers dropped out of their Ju52s, on to the Aspheron peninsula, and into a panorama of exploding oil installations. General Tyulenev, commanding the Caucasus Front, had issued the demolition orders at dawn that day.

There was no chance for the *fallschirmjager* to interfere with the destructive process, for no sooner had they landed than they were assaulted

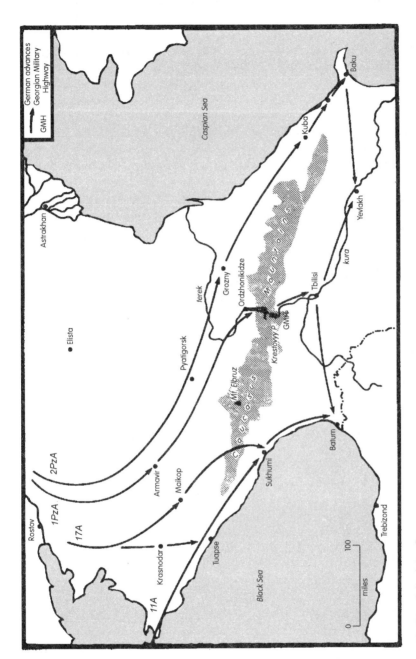

18. The Fall of the Caucasus

by Red Army infantry and tanks. The drop had not been well concentrated, and isolated German pockets of varying size were soon struggling for survival against a numerically superior enemy.

The next day brought some relief, for a nationalist demonstration inside the city swiftly escalated into a fully-fledged Azerbaijan revolt, and the Red Army found its hands full. But Student's force would never be the same again; by the time Guderian's tanks arrived on the evening of 23 August the *fallschirmjager* had suffered forty per cent casualties. The Airborne Corps destroyed on Cyprus in May 1943 had already been crippled outside Baku.

Hitler's rage at the failure of *Schwarz Gold* was only slightly mollified by Kleist's triumphal entry into Tbilisi on 23 August. The Red Army had already been driven from the city, partly by local Georgian nationalists, mostly by the imminence of the German arrival. NKVD men liberally adorned the lampposts of Pushkin Street.

Leaving these scenes of celebration behind, 3rd Panzer Corps turned west towards the Black Sea and 48th Panzer Corps east down the Kura valley. At 16.30 on 26 August the latter met the leading units of Guderian's 46th Panzer Corps at Yevlakh. The Caucasus had been effectively conquered. The only Black Sea port still held by the Red Army was Batum, close to the Turkish border, and that too would fall within a few days.

It was now time, Hitler thought, for the Turks to make up their minds. On 27 August he dispatched his last offer to the dilatory leaders in Ankara. If Turkey joined the Axis they could regain the lands stolen by the Allies in the 1920s – Armenia and Mosul. If not . . . the consequences were unstated, but unlikely to be pleasant.

III

It was late in the evening of 28 August. Franz von Papen, ex-Chancellor of Germany and now Ambassador to Turkey, waited outside Ismet Inönü's study in the Presidential Palace in Ankara. He had been waiting for some time, and trying to make sense of the muffled argument raging on the other side of the closed door.

At 10.35pm the door opened and out stepped Chief of Staff Fevzi Cakmak and Assistant Chief of Staff Asim Gunduz. The former was smiling, the latter grim and tight-lipped. Von Papen felt relief. The Turks were joining the war!

The Ambassador was ushered into Inönü's sumptuous study. The President looked exhausted. Obviously his arguments, and those of his supporter Gunduz, had failed to make any impression on Cakmak. Von

Papen wondered what the Chief of Staff had threatened the President with. His resignation, or something more? The resignation would have been enough.

Inönü gestured von Papen into the seat facing his desk. 'We will declare war on the Soviet Union at midnight tonight,' he said. 'In an hour and twenty minutes,' he added, looking at his silver pocket watch. 'Doubtless the British and Americans will declare war on us before too many hours have passed by.'

Inönü looked out of the window. Von Papen wondered why he could never get accustomed to the idea of a Turk having a silver pocket-watch. 'You will not regret this decision,' he said. 'Turkey will regain its former glory. In . . .' Inönü cut him off. 'I am not interested in former glories,' he said in German. 'And I sincerely hope we do not regret this decision. You have spoken with Cakmak? You know the arms we need, and how fast we need them?'

'They will begin to arrive in the next fortnight,' von Papen replied. 'I have the personal assurance of the Führer.'

'Then so be it,' said Inönü. 'We shall meet again in the morning, when your new military attaché arrives.'

The German Ambassador took his leave. Inönü swivelled his chair round to face the large window, and looked out across the darkened capital of the new Turkey built by his friend Ataturk. The die had been cast. There had been no choice. For weeks he had waited for a sign, for an Allied victory, for something with which to convince his people that the Allies would win the war. He still believed they would. But there had been no sign.

Inönü could not know, as he watched the last lights of Ankara winking out, that half a world away the first of *Kido Butai*'s doomed carriers was sliding beneath the tropical waves off Panama.

The following morning, some eight hundred miles to the south-east, General Alexander was drinking a morning cup of coffee with R.G. Casey on the latter's veranda in Baghdad. The morning reports from Eighth Army were remarkably good, considering the situation. The losses in the frontier battles had been slight, and the troops' morale, according to the ever-optimistic Montgomery, was still high. They knew they had dealt Rommel a few good blows, and the increasing evidence of the RAF's mastery of the Palestinian skies was boosting spirits. Next time they would stop Rommel once and for all. There would be no triumphal German entry into Jerusalem.

Alexander took Monty's optimism with a healthy dose of salts, but he had other corroborative evidence. Air-Marshal Tedder's reports affirmed the growing power of the RAF, and also noted the difficulties being experienced by the Luftwaffe in providing Rommel's Panzer Army with adequate protection from its makeshift bases in Sinai. Apparently one panzer division had been badly mauled from the air the previous day on the Beersheba-Hebron road. Perhaps it was too early to make firm judgements, Alexander told Casey, but the military situation seemed to be 'past its worst'.

Casey hoped so. The political situation, he told the General, was as satisfactory as could be expected, and also likely to improve. The long hiatus between Rommel's capture of Egypt and his advance into Palestine had been most beneficial to the British cause. The Germans and Italians had found time to disagree on just about everything, and in the process to wreck Egypt's fragile economy. 'The Egyptians are growing disenchanted very quickly,' Casey said. 'There are even unconfirmed reports of armed clashes between the Free Officer group and the Italian military police.'

The Minister of State warmed to his subject. 'You see, the important fact is not that the Egyptians have realised that Farouk and Ali Maher are Axis puppets, but that the Arabs in Palestine, Syria and Iraq have realised it too. Now most of the sensible ones are feeling decidedly ambivalent about the prospects of liberation served up on a German plate. For the moment they are waiting to see which way the wind blows. If we can stop Rommel short of Jerusalem then I think most of the Arab leaders will remain neutral. Of course a few fanatics will shoot the odd British soldier and blow up the odd building, but the ones who matter will sit tight and try for the best bargain. Naturally we're offering all we can - vague promises of a plebiscite in Palestine, full independence for all and sundry once the war is over.

'We were lucky that the Iraqi rebellion happened last year rather than this, and that we had the chance to put all the dangerous characters out of the way. Nuri es-Said will stick with us through thick and thin, and he's popular with everyone but the Iraqi Army. We've disarmed them. The same goes for the Shah of Iran. He'll do what we tell him to do as long as the Germans don't appear in front of his palace in Tehran.

'The only leaders that got away last year were Rashid Ali and the Mufti. The Mufti's in Egypt, and having trouble with the Italians. Rashid Ali, as far as we know, is in the Caucasus with his three hundred Arab volunteers, but the Germans will be holding him on a tight rein. And it seems that he and the Mufti are not on the best of terms. Now that the Turks are entering the war the Germans will have a lot more trouble on their hands, though presumably they're not yet aware of it. The Turks will want Armenia from the Russians, and they've doubtless been promised the Mosul region by the

Germans. They asked us for it, but we refused. And we have proof to show the Iraqis. The Germans don't seem to realise that they can't expect to have Turkey as an ally and still get support from the Arabs. The same goes for Azerbaijan. They seem to have accepted an independent Azerbaijan republic – a puppet of course – without considering how it'll go down in Tehran. Persian Azerbaijan had been hankering after its independence for years, and the Shah knows it only too well. The Germans, for all their talk about the power of nationalism, seem completely unaware of its importance outside Germany. They have made a right mess of their Middle East policy.'

Alexander heard Casey out with a great deal of interest. Though nearly fifty-one he was very much one of the new-style soldiers, who appreciated the importance of the political dimension in warfare. If the Germans were, as Casey suggested, losing the political battle for the Middle East, then the military task of the British would be that much easier. Montgomery's optimism had already been discussed; in the north as well, Alexander reported, the situation was looking more hopeful. The German spearheads would probably cross the Russian frontier in the next few days, but the British forces deployed to meet them would not be easily shrugged aside. It was unlikely that the Germans could throw more than four panzer divisions across the border. They were far from their bases, they had been campaigning for over four months, and their supply problems would be almost insuperable. And the terrain would not suit them. In such mountainous country the panzers would be confined to the roads, and the roads were terrible. There were now five infantry divisions and three armoured brigades deployed to stop them, and Alexander had high hopes that they would do so.

On this optimistic note the two were interrupted by the sound of a ringing telephone. Casey went inside, to emerge a few minutes later with a broad smile across his face. 'The Yanks have given the Japanese a thrashing off Panama. They've sunk four carriers. Now that's what I call good news!'

The news reaching Field-Marshal Rommel in Hebron was not so pleasant. In the near future a high-ranking SS officer would be arriving to discuss 'German policy in occupied Palestine' with him. This did not sound good. Rommel had already heard disturbing stories, from Balck and the other officers who had served in Russia, of SS activities in the occupied territories of the East. He did not much care to know more. Still less did he want such 'activities' on his own doorstep. With a conscious effort the Field-Marshal turned his thoughts to a more amenable topic – the coming battle.

This would be the decisive one. The British had escaped his trap on the frontier, but they could not be so lucky twice. If he could puncture their new and hastily-constructed defensive line, then Eighth Army, he was certain, would break up. The road to Jerusalem would be open, and within a few days the panzers could be across the Jordan and on their way into Iraq. And out of this country. Palestine as a battleground did not appeal to Rommel. 'It feels strange to see the name Bethlehem on a divisional order,' he wrote to Lucie. He would rather be in Iraq. The SS could catch up with him there!

In the early hours of the following morning Winston Churchill sat deep in thought in front of a dying fire in his Chequers bedroom. He knew the next few days would decide a great deal. Perhaps the outcome of the war, certainly his own political future.

After the Egyptian debacle he had won a motion of confidence in the House of Commons by only forty-four votes. A pathetic majority, hardly a majority at all. Yet even this vote exaggerated his current popularity in the country as a whole. He had considered resigning. But in favour of who? Eden could never cope with the responsibility, and he knew it as well as Churchill did. Which left only Cripps, who was so eager to get his hands on the levers of power. A clever man, but not a national leader. No, he could not resign in favour of Cripps.

And in any case what could Cripps, or anyone else, do differently? Some of his critics accused him of interfering too much with the military, others of not interfering enough. Some said he didn't understand that this was a people's war, not a Victorian war waged by the upper classes and their obedient cannon fodder. But had he not spoken for the people in 1940 as no other man could have done?

It was fortunate that Egypt had fallen so fast. There had been no time to take breath, no time for the critics to make it a resignation issue. He felt sorry for Auchinleck, who he knew had done his best. That was the way of the world. Eighth Army needed fresh blood at the top, and if Montgomery succeeded then Auchinleck himself would be the first to applaud. The next few days would decide. If Jerusalem fell then Montgomery would be sacked. And so, very probably, would he.

A million miles away from the later summer calm of Chequers advance units of the Turkish Army were crossing the Soviet border in the regions of Yerevan, Leninakan and Batum. Only in the last-named did they meet with serious resistance, mostly from the sailors of the Soviet Black Sea Fleet.

The Fleet itself was at sea. The imminent German-Turkish seizure of Batum would deprive it of the last available port, and escape from the Black Sea through the Turkish-controlled Dardanelles was out of the question. Soon after dawn on 29 August the skeleton crews aboard the one old battleship, five cruisers and fifteen destroyers lit the fuses to the charges that would send each ship to the bottom. As they sailed south towards Trebizond in their motor-torpedo boats – even Turkish hospitality was preferable to German – the Soviet sailors watched ship after ship explode in columns of flame. It was an historic moment: a new record for tonnage scuttled in a single hour.

IV

Through the final week of August both armies in Palestine feverishly prepared for the resumption of battle. Eighth Army was holding an east-west 'line' – in reality a series of blocking positions on the north-south roads – some five miles to the south of the Jaffa-Jerusalem road. This 'line' was well-chosen. The road behind it facilitated the shifting of forces from one end to the other, the roads through it were few and far between. In the eastern sector the terrain was extremely difficult for the motorised warfare at which the Germans excelled.

Three of the armoured brigades were deployed along the east-west road, around Ramle, Latrun and outside Jerusalem; the fourth was stationed on the Jerusalem-Hebron road to the south of Bethlehem. The infantry formations were further forward, dug in on the north-south roads passable for the German armour.

Rommel wished to attack as soon as he could, even though his Army was far from ready. There was a serious shortage of fuel, and the Panzer Army had only 335 tanks in running order, 85 of which were Italian. Bayerlein pointed out that another 70 would have come through the mobile repair ships by the second week of September, and urged the Field-Marshal to wait. But Rommel, urged on by both his superiors in Lötzen and his own desire to deny the British a breathing-space, refused. The Panzer Army would attack at first light on the last day of the month.

The need for haste also influenced his strategy. The sensible course might have been to concentrate on clearing the Levant coast, and so allow supply by sea. But Rommel thought this would take too long. He intended to pierce the centre of the British line and get his panzers round behind Jerusalem, astride the British supply route from Jordan. This was more likely to cause a speedy British collapse.

15th Panzer, which had been reduced to fifty-five tanks in the Rafah crossroads battle, would advance up the coast road with *Ariete*; 7th Panzer, minus its tank regiment, and elements of 164th Division would move north towards Bethlehem on the Hebron-Jerusalem road. Both these attacks would be essentially diversionary. They would tie down strong British forces on the two flanks while the main German force – 20th Panzer, 7th Panzer's tank regiment, and 14th Motorised – would break through the centre. It would take the old Roman highway north-east from Ashkelon, cross the main Jaffa-Jerusalem road at Latrun, and climb up the hill road to Ramallah. From there it would command the high ground above Jerusalem, and be in a good position to cut the British supply artery at Jericho.

On the morning of 31 August the panzer engines burst into life once more, and Balck's tanks led the main force north along the road to Latrun. At the Sejed level-crossing it met resistance from units of 44th Division, but after an hour or so the tactical skill of the German tank-crews and their heavy Stuka support cleared the panzers' path. To the west and east, on the coast and Bethlehem roads, the Germans were also pushing forward.

By early afternoon Montgomery had realised that the central threat was the most dangerous. He ordered the two armoured brigades of 1st Armoured Division to support the 4th South African Brigade at Latrun. By early evening elements of six divisions were fighting for control of the vital Latrun crossroads. On the two flanks the weaker German attacks were being held without undue difficulty.

Through that night and the following day the battle raged on around Latrun without the Germans achieving their desired breakthrough. The terrain made outflanking impossible, the RAF were proving more than a match for the Luftwaffe, and the Shermans just issued to 1st Armoured Division – they had been 'borrowed' from an American-Soviet shipment at Basra – were making their mark on the panzers.

On the evening of 1 September Rommel decided to change his tactics. After dark he pulled 20th Panzer and 14th Motorised out of the Latrun battleground and sent them on a fifty-mile night march. By dawn they were ready to attack on the Hartuv road.

At around 07.00 garbled reports of 'enemy tanks attacking' reached Montgomery's HQ from the 6th South African Brigade at Hartuv. Half an hour later Balck's tanks had shrugged the South Africans aside and were approaching the Jerusalem-Jaffa road. By 08.00 they were astride the road, and striking into the heart of the British position.

In Montgomery's HQ there was a brief moment of panic. The panzers were turning east toward Jerusalem! But Rommel had not abandoned his basic strategy, and it was soon apparent that the Germans had turned north up the ridge between Maale Hamisha and Kastel. By 11.00 Balck was in Biddu, an hour later entering the village of Nebi Samuel. To his right the panzer general could see the Holy City spread out beneath him.

Twelve miles to the west the defenders of Latrun had realised the new weakness of the German forces in front of them. The British armour began to push 7th Panzer's weakly supported tanks backwards. But this enjoyable activity was soon halted, as crisp new orders flowed in from Montgomery. A crisis might be brewing, but Eighth Army's commander was not about to be stampeded. 'Rommel has stuck his neck out,' he told General Ramsden. 'Let's wring it!'

Montgomery also had a better card up his sleeve than Auchinleck had ever had. The 1st US Armoured Division, originally earmarked for North-west Africa, was moving up the road from Jericho to Ramallah, having arrived at Basra some ten days before.

This Rommel did not know. Nor was he to find out for several hours. His first crisis of the day arrived at noon, as 14th Motorised, left to hold open 20th Panzer's supply route at Abu Gohash on the main road, found itself assailed from east and west by British armoured formations. Rommel considered pulling back 20th Panzer, but was naturally loth to do so. Instead he decided to reinforce 14th Motorised from the two flanking German forces, a company of tanks from 15th Panzer and a rifle regiment from 7th Panzer. It was the wrong decision.

14th Motorised was under attack by both 2nd and 4th Armoured Brigades, over 150 tanks. By 14.00 the two British brigades had linked up on the main road, and the Germans had been forced out to the north. Now both 14th Motorised and 20th Panzer were cut off behind the British 'line'.

This was serious for Balck's division, for it was rapidly running out of fuel. At 14.15 the leading tanks had reached the Tel el Fut crossroads, three miles above Jerusalem, to find 22nd Armoured Brigade deployed across its line of advance. A vicious tank battle ensued, with almost 120 tanks exchanging fire at close quarters in the hilly terrain astride the Jerusalem-Ramallah road. At first the German division, better supported by infantry, appeared to be gaining the upper hand. At 14.45 the ever-optimistic Balck assured Rommel that he would be in Jerusalem by nightfall.

Fifteen minutes later Balck received a shock. American tanks had been sighted on the road to the north, only a mile away. There was no time to withdraw; Balck could only hope to turn half of his force around to face this

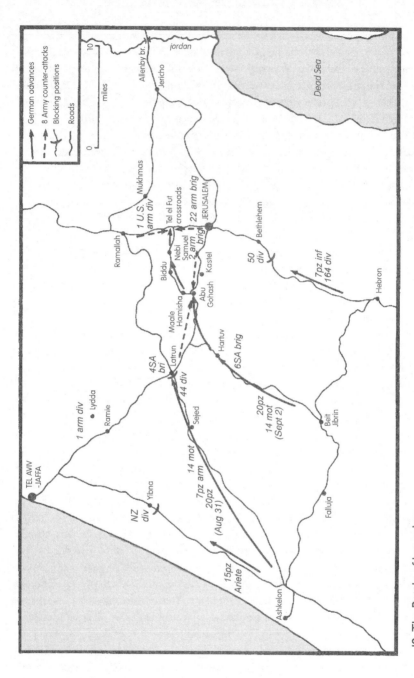

19. The Battle of Jerusalem

new threat. At 15.09 American and German tanks exchanged fire for the first time in World War Two.

It was an unequal struggle. The German division, though more experienced tactically, was so heavily outnumbered as to make defeat inevitable. By 17.00 over seventy-five of Balck's tanks had been destroyed, and Rommel's spearhead had been blunted and torn apart. Ten miles to the south-west those soldiers of 14th Motorised trapped north of the British-controlled main road were escaping to the south without their heavy equipment. The tanks of 15th Panzer, which had been hurrying to their rescue, were halted by the combined efforts of the South Africans and the RAF in the Elah valley, scene of David's unlikely triumph over Goliath. Panzer Army Asia, if not completely defeated, had been comprehensively stopped. Rommel would be in no state to reach Iraq that autumn. All German hopes would now have to rest on the army debouching from the Caucasus.

V

Guderian's Second Panzer Army had resumed its southward odyssey several days earlier. 24th Panzer Corps was moving down the Caspian coast, 46th Panzer Corps was climbing up into the mountains *en route* for Tabriz. This was hardly an overwhelming force, but it was all the roads could carry, and Kleist's Panzer Army had been left behind in the Caucasus.

The ninety-five tanks of 24th Panzer Corps made steady progress, crossing the Persian frontier, against negligible opposition from retreating Red Army units, on 29 August. Through the following day the panzers rolled on through Azerbaijan villages decked with welcoming flags. On 31 August they entered the Persian district of Gilan, rumbling between the rice paddies and the sea towards Rasht. Here the welcome was less rapturous, but there was no overt resistance. On 2 September, after a day spent waiting for fuel, the tanks moved into low gear for the steep climb up to the Iranian plateau. They were 150 miles from Tehran.

The stronger 46th Panzer Corps – it had been reinforced with the SS *Das Reich* and 25th Motorised Divisions – was having a harder time. Units of the Soviet Forty-fourth Army were well dug in behind the Araxes river frontier, and it took Guderian two days to dislodge them. It was not until 1 September that his advance units entered Tabriz, capital of Azerbaijan separatism, to a tumultuous welcome.

This was the day that 20th Panzer was crushed at the Tel el Fut crossroads, but OKH did not see fit to inform Guderian; all he received was exhortations to hurry. The panzer commander protested that the armoured columns would outrun their air support, but his superiors in Prussia were not impressed. There could be no substantial Allied air strength in northern Persia, Hitler told Halder; it was obviously all in Palestine. Which explained Rommel's problems. It was clearly the duty of Second Panzer Army to draw away this British air strength by attacking with all the necessary vigour.

Freiherr von Geyr, commanding 24th Panzer Corps, knew different. On 3 September his leading division, 3rd Panzer, had run into the British 2nd Division's forward position on the Rasht-Qazvin road, south of Rudbar village in the spectacular pass cut by the Safid Rud river. There was no way round this position, and as the head of the German column engaged the defenders, the long and stationary tail came under incessant attack from the RAF. The planes included Bomber Command Lancasters, operating from the new airfields in south-eastern Persia. Their crews certainly found the twisting mountain road a smaller target than Cologne, but their presence in itself was depressing enough to the Germans, and in several cases their bombs started land-slides which blocked the road. And while the panzer crews were busy moving boulders General Wilson was moving 23rd Armoured Brigade up from Zanjan to reinforce the hard-pressed British infantry. There would be no easy breakthrough for the Germans in this sector.

On 6 September Guderian's other corps left Tabriz in two separate directions. The General, though pressed by Hitler to mount strong offensives towards both Tehran and Basra, had decided to ignore the Persian capital. 24th Panzer Corps was already in trouble, and the British and Russian forces facing 46th Panzer Corps on the Tehran road were holding an extremely strong position in the mountains south of Tabriz. Guderian decided to send a blocking-force down this road, while the rest of the Corps moved west and south towards Iraq.

So 25th Motorised and a company of tanks from 18th Panzer were sent down the Tehran road as a military scarecrow, while Guderian himself led 2nd and 18th Panzer, *Das Reich* and 29th Motorised down the Miandowab road between Lake Urmia and Mount Sahand. Through 6 September the tanks rolled onward, meeting no opposition. Perhaps someone in the German ranks pointed out that over there, to the right, was the original 'Treasure Island', Shahi in Lake Urmia. There the great Hulagu Khan had been buried with a host of concubines and untold riches. Hulagu, the grandson of the great Genghis Khan, had taken Baghdad, rolled the Abbasid Caliph up in a carpet and had him trampled to death by Mongol ponies. Perhaps they would do the same to General Alexander!

Guderian doubted it. With each passing day Baghdad seemed further away. The roads were appalling, mechanical failures never-ending. The RAF seemed to be everywhere. His own force, which had now marched nearly fifteen hundred miles since May, was dwindling. And all the help he got from Rastenburg was complaints about the lack of speed.

On the afternoon of 7 September 29th Motorised reached the overgrown village of Miandowab. Now another choice had to be made. Air reconnaissance showed that strong British infantry formations were holding the passes to the south on the Kermanshah road. They could not be ignored. Another blocking force would have to be detached to cover the flank of the main force as it drove west into Iraq. 29th Motorised was left behind to hold the Miandowab road junction and repair its broken vehicles.

Das Reich took the lead. The Iraqi frontier was only seventy-five miles of twisting 'road' away. Mosul and Kirkuk were a further hundred miles beyond. The distances were becoming surreal. But once across the frontier the panzers would find themselves on more amenable ground, on the north-eastern corner of the flat Mesopotamian plain.

Through 9 September the panzers rattled along the broken road, through Kurdish villages surrounded by vineyards, through the dry and dusty hill country south of Lake Urmia. They were now enjoying some measure of air protection from the Luftwaffe squadrons hastily installed at Tabriz, but the RAF was no less noticeable. Late that afternoon Guderian was informed that British bombers had destroyed the Araxes bridges on the frontier. Now there would be more trouble with supplies.

Two hundred miles to the east 24th Panzer Corps was making no progress whatever. A frontal attack by 3rd Panzer and 10th Motorised had been thrown back on 8 September. Geyr asked for Luftwaffe support, but was informed that all available planes were needed to protect Guderian's column.

By early morning on 10 September the latter was approaching the Iraqi frontier. The 6th Indian and 1st Polish Divisions were holding the crest of the Shinak Pass. An attempt by 2nd Panzer's tanks to rush the defences failed, and through the morning and afternoon the SS infantry sought to carve a passage for the waiting panzers. The fighting was bitter and inconclusive. At one stage a way was cleared, and several German tanks broke through the narrow pass. But descending the western slope, the vast Mesopotamian plain laid out before them, these tanks were assailed by 8th Armoured Brigade's new Shermans and subjected to the full wrath of the RAF. On the crest the battle continued through the night, both sides sustaining heavy casualties. But as the sun rose the sky again filled with

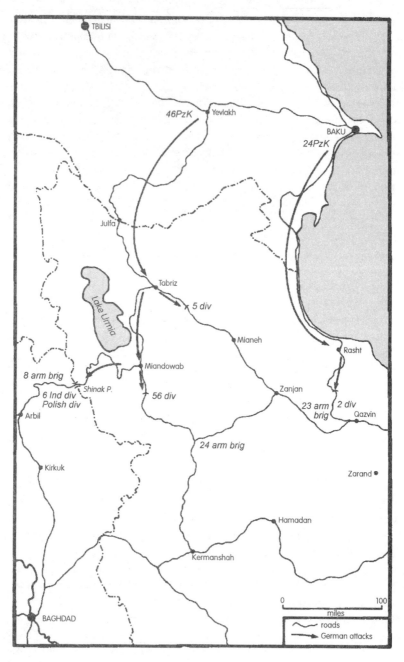

20. Northern Persia: September 1942

British planes, as the squadrons based in Arbil, Kirkuk and Mosul flew round-the-clock missions in a bid to break the German spearhead. By midday 46th Panzer Corps had only twenty-two tanks remaining.

It also had no path of retreat. At 11.00 Guderian received news of British armour advancing up the Kermanshah road towards Miandowab. Three hours later he heard that 29th Motorised, the crack division which had spearheaded his drive on Moscow, had abandoned Miandowab and was retreating in disorder up the road to Tabriz. His troops would not be bathing in the Persian Gulf that autumn. There would be no meeting with Rommel, no easy end to the war in 1942. On that September afternoon, on a mountain two thousand miles from Berlin, the 'Grand Plan' no longer looked so grand.

VI

The attempt to apply *blitzkrieg* on a trans-continental scale had failed. It was bound to do so. For just as National Socialism was a stop-gap solution to the problems of Thirties capitalism, so *blitzkrieg* was never more than a stop-gap answer to the military problems of continental war. It could only work over a limited period of time; it could only be sustained, as was now obvious, over a limited area of space. A panzer company had to keep moving in order to survive; this was basic tactics. The same was true of a panzer Wehrmacht. Once stopped it was doomed, vulnerable at every point of the territory it had traversed with such apparent ease.

Nazi Germany was the supreme example of economic realities being bent to the political will. But however strong the restraining hand, economic realities cannot be indefinitely denied. Such a society lives on its expansionism, on consuming the lands, the work and the lives of others. It lives on its own momentum, until the momentum dies, and then it begins to consume itself. Such a society has nowhere else to go.

The peculiarities of Nazism also played their part. The feudal character of the leadership – short-sighted, competitive, inhuman – hindered the full development of the armament industry which fuelled the expansionist impulse. It was also destined, sooner or later, to stifle the initiative of its only potential opponents, the generals in the field. The virulent racism which festered at the heart of Hitler's *weltanschauung* made it inevitable that Nazi Germany would only win 'friends' through the exercise of overwhelming force. Germany could offer other nations nothing, and this was eventually realised even by those who either welcomed or wished to welcome the Wehrmacht as an agent of their own liberation.

By September 1942 resistance to Nazi rule was growing throughout the length and breadth of Hitler's empire, from France to central Russia, from Norway to Palestine. The need to occupy continuously each newly conquered territory led to a further weakening of those Wehrmacht forces ranged against the growing power of the Allied nations. There was no military solution to this problem. And so long as National Socialism ruled Germany there was no political solution either. Nazi Germany was beaten.

In September 1942, this was apparent to few. The atom-bombing of Stuttgart and Nuremberg, the generals' coup, the Army-SS civil war – all were still three years in the future. But if the defeat of Nazi Germany can be traced back to the roots of Nazism itself, the moment of military destiny can be traced back to those nine September days of 1942, when the seemingly endless flow of the panzer tide was halted outside Jerusalem and on the crest of a mountain pass on the Iraqi-Persian frontier.

Epilogue
12 SEPTEMBER 1942

Our small group of socialist exiles spent the summer of 1942 in Mexico City, walking the sordid streets and sitting outside cafés devouring the news from Russia, the Middle East and the Pacific. We talked endlessly about the war and the possible shape of an eventual peace. We discussed, hearts in our mouths, the implications of a Nazi victory. Some, myself included, argued that it would not alter the broad development of history, that in the long run Nazism could no better solve the problems of capitalism than the more moderate versions of bourgeois rule it seemed destined to replace. Once Hitler had run out of wars the whole thing would burst apart, and the Nazis would be overthrown by their own swollen population.

Others disputed this view. They argued that the Germans would never run out of wars, that they would drag the whole of humanity back to the stone age. In the process they would of course destroy the material basis of the socialism to which we had all dedicated our lives.

Fortunately we never did learn which of these café-schools of thought was correct. But in that summer of 1942 they did seem real alternatives, it did seem, in Berlier's melodramatic but apt phrase, as if 'the insane would inherit the earth'. It was not until the German armies were halted in September of that year that we began once more to believe that sanity would prevail.

Victor Serge, Ten Years in Exile

As dawn broke over Tokyo Admiral Nagumo's fleet was still, courtesy of the International Date Line's irrefutable logic, sailing through yesterday. The remnants of *Kido Butai* had travelled nearly six thousand miles since their traumatic encounter with fate off Panama, and were now fifteen hundred miles due north of Tahiti, more than half-way to the Truk naval base in the Carolines.

Despite the relative proximity of Gauguin's island, Admiral Nagumo was not thinking of grass-skirts and sun-kissed palm beaches. He was still wondering how he was going to apologise to Yamamoto for his disgraceful defeat. Four carriers, two hundred and fifty planes and almost as many airmen had gone to a watery grave in those agonising hours on 28 September, and Nagumo knew as well as anyone that they could not be replaced. And who was responsible? He was. The more pragmatic Admiral Kusaka had argued him out of committing hara-kiri but now, as the Equatorial Current eased his shrunken fleet homewards, Chuichi Nagumo could not escape the feeling that pragmatism had its limits.

Isoruku Yamamoto, aboard *Yamato* in Hiroshima Bay, had other things to think about than Nagumo's responsibility for the new situation. He was trying, with no little difficulty, to convince himself that the loss of the Combined Fleet's four largest carriers, though a great blow, need not necessarily prove a decisive one. *Hiyo*, *Ryujo* and *Junyo* were already on their way to the south-west Pacific to take part in the Samoa and Fiji operations. *Hiryu* would be ocean-worthy again in December. Could Japan retain her ascendancy in the Pacific against a resurgent America? Yamamoto fervently hoped so. It was only the facile optimism of his staff officers that the great admiral found truly unbearable.

Five thousand miles to the west on that same September morning Mordechai Givoni, a nineteen year-old member of the Irgun Zvi Leumi, lay face-down on the flat roof of a two-storey house on the outskirts of Hebron. He was dressed in a white Arab burnous. Below him the road from Beersheba ran left into the centre of the city. To his right the hills of Judaea shifted in the early-morning haze. In the distance he could see a German staff car winding slowly up the incline towards him. The accompanying motor-cyclists were wearing black uniforms.

In the car itself SS Obersturmführer Eichmann stared bad humouredly out at the parched landscape. At least the flies kept off when one was moving. He hoped he would see Rommel that day, finish his business in this accursed Jew-ridden country, and get back to the comfort of his desk in Vienna. He watched the first houses of Hebron looming to greet him.

Mordechai Givoni's eyes did not leave the car. He cradled the rifle against his shoulder, took careful aim at the head of the SS officer in the back seat, and pulled the trigger. He had been a crack-shot since he was ten.

In Ankara Marshal Cakmak was reporting to President Inönü. 'Our troops have reached the new frontier in the Caucasus,' he told Inönü. 'All resistance has been crushed.'

'All resistance?' asked Inönü, raising his eyebrows. 'That doesn't sound like the Armenians.'

'All *organised* resistance. It is true that there is still the occasional incident. But these have no importance. The population is not yet fully resigned to its new status. As you say, the Armenians have always been a stubborn people. A few local leaders have refused to co-operate, a few renegades have taken to the mountains. But we have taken hostages, made an example of a few hotheads. It is only a matter of time.'

'Yes, of course,' said Inönü, in a tone that implied the opposite. 'And the Tigris offensive – are the preparations proceeding according to schedule?'

'There are difficulties,' Cakmak conceded with obvious reluctance. 'The British have mastery in the air. They have tanks and we do not. We are waiting for the German deliveries. They were expected to begin this week, but apparently there have been unavoidable delays.'

'Yes, I thought there might be,' Inönü muttered to himself.

The same subject was under discussion in a well-known restaurant on the Potsdammerstrasse in Berlin, where Albert Speer and Franz Todt were sharing a working lunch. They were having a depressing conversation. Speer's paper napkin was covered in calculations, and none of the answers looked very promising.

'You will have to tell the Führer that it cannot be done,' he told Todt. 'There is no way it *can* be done. We are producing barely enough tanks and planes to cover our losses. At the present rate of production increase, if we can get Goering's agreement and SS approval, both of which are extremely unlikely, we can supply the Army with two thousand new tanks, mostly Panzer IIIs and IVs, in 1943. The enemy will be producing ten times as many. Something has to be done, and quickly. You must make the Führer understand this. As for the Turks, they will have to fight with their bare hands.'

'I hope that is the only bad news I have for him,' said Todt. 'But I doubt if it will be. There is a meeting tomorrow to discuss the exploitation of the Caucasian oilfields. My experts tell me that it will be nine months before we are taking any decent quantity of oil out of the ground. That would be bad enough. But, it seems, even if we get it out of the ground there is no way to transport the wretched stuff. The pipelines have all been destroyed, the railways are already working at full capacity, and all the available tankers are carrying Rumanian oil up the Danube. The Führer is not going to be pleased with whoever has to tell him all this!'

In Kuybyshev General Zhukov sat in the back of the black limousine that was taking him from the airport to the Governor's Palace. He had just returned from a visit to the Vologda Front HQ, and General Yeremenko had assured him that his armies would hold the German advance. Zhukov was pleased to be bringing such good news.

He skipped through the thin pages of the *Pravda* he had picked up at the airport. More good news from the Japanese front intermixed with more dire promises of retribution for the small reactionary cliques which had betrayed Georgia and Azerbaijan to the enemy. But not, Zhukov reminded himself, the oilfields. It would take the Germans months to repair the damage, and by then ...

An hour later he was reporting to the assembled Stavka on the Vologda situation. It was not the only good news the Soviet leaders heard that evening. Six divisions had been extricated from the Caucasus across the Caspian, and units of another two were fighting with the British in northern Persia. The Meshed-Ashkabad road was near completion – supplies would be rolling in from the south once the Persian situation was stabilised. Most encouraging of all was Voroshilov's report on armament production. The factories evacuated to the Urals and elsewhere were again working at peak capacity. From now onwards they would be producing two thousand planes and two thousand tanks per month.

The meeting lasted until dawn on the following day. The reason for its unusual length was simple. For the first time since the Germans crossed their frontier the Soviet leaders had a growing operational reserve. Attack was now one of the options. Stavka, unused to such military luxury, argued long and hard as to how they should use their new-found riches.

General Walther Model had recently succeeded General Hoth as Commander of Third Panzer Army. That morning he was moodily drinking a cup of coffee in his Danilov headquarters. The telephone rang on the other side of the room, and a few seconds later an orderly approached Model.

'It is Field-Marshal Brauchitsch from Lötzen, Herr General.'

Model grimaced, and walked slowly over to the telephone.

'Good morning, Herr Feldmarschall,' he said. 'What can we do for you this morning?'

Brauchitsch affected not to notice Model's insubordinate tone. 'The Führer would like your appreciation of the situation on the Vologda front, Herr General. He is particularly perturbed at the apparent lack of progress in this sector and ...'

Model cut him off. 'I submitted a full report to General von Küchler only yesterday.'

'Naturally, General von Küchler's views are being ascertained,' Brauchitsch continued smoothly, 'but the Führer is also eager to know the views of the army commanders in this particular sector. General von Küchler, as you know, has other responsibilities to take care of.'

'Yes, yes . . . my view, as outlined in my report, is that the situation here is quite disastrous. The reinforcements we have received are quite inadequate. The new tank engines promised for early August have still not arrived. No one seems to know where they are. Fuel stocks are low, and deliveries are not keeping pace with consumption. The Russians are contesting every square yard of land as if it were their last and, according to our intelligence reports, the number of their formations in this sector is growing at an alarming rate. I could be more precise . . .'

'No, that will suffice Herr General. What the Führer particularly wishes to hear from you is an estimated date for the capture of Vologda.'

'I have failed to make myself clear,' Model said, in a tone heavily laced with sarcasm. 'As the situation stands at this moment there is every possibility that we shall *not* capture Vologda.'

'The Führer will not be pleased to hear such a pessimistic evaluation!'

'I am sure the Führer would prefer to know the truth of our situation here. An underestimation of the difficulties facing Army Group North can only hinder him in the exercise of his judgement.'

'Of course,' Brauchitsch replied rather stiffly. 'But I feel he may not be completely satisfied that Army Group North is doing its utmost to overcome these difficulties. In any case, I shall report your opinions to him. Good day, Herr General.'

Model replaced the telephone, a look of disgust on his face. 'Office-boy!' he muttered under his breath.

That afternoon Hans Fischer was brewing tea in the small concrete blockhouse by the railway line. Twenty metres away the tracks crossed a tributary of the Tsna river in an area of dense pine forest. Fischer and his three companions had been detailed to guard this bridge, one of several hundred between Germany and the Volga front, and so safeguard the passage of the trains carrying essential supplies from one to the other. It was a boring job.

Ten minutes earlier Fischer had sent Cullmann to fetch Dietz and Haller. The tea was now ready. Where were they? Fischer went outside. No one was in sight. 'Heinz!' he called out, fighting back a rising sensation of panic.

It was his last word, as an arm grasped him round the waist and a knife bit into his throat.

Lev Susaikov dropped the dead German, wiped his knife on his trousers, and waited. After a few minutes he was sure that there were no others. He beckoned his three comrades out of the pines. Across the railway bridge he could see the others also emerging from their cover.

The partisans fixed and wired the explosives. It took fifteen minutes. Then they scrambled down the embankment to the river's edge and waited. Half an hour later a train appeared. At the centre of the bridge the front wheels of the locomotive hit the detonators. The wooden trellis exploded in a dozen places. The locomotive, and twenty flat-cars loaded with Panzer IVs, slid gracefully down through a cloud of smoke into the river.

In Baghdad two representatives of an older world were sipping their pre-dinner cocktails on Casey's veranda.

'We've been distributing Arabic translations of some of Hitler's more telling utterances,' the Minister of State was saying. 'The Arabs are finding out that according to old Adolf they come just above the Jews and the monkeys in the Nazi pecking order. That should make them think twice about the beneficence of the Third Reich.'

'Only the ones that can read,' joked Alexander.

The easy-going nature of this conversation was not being echoed at the Second Panzer Army HQ in Tabriz. Guderian had arrived at midday, having flown back from Shinak Pass in his Storch. There was no time for cocktails. The German situation in northern Persia seemed to be coming apart at the seams. First the failure to take the Pass the previous morning, then the debacle at Miandowab, and now news of British attacks on the main road south of Tabriz. The bridges on the frontier were still down. The Luftwaffe was still conspicuous by its absence. No supplies were getting through. No fuel, no ammunition, no reinforcements. All Guderian found waiting for him in Tabriz were fresh exhortations from OKH in Lötzen. 'Fast-moving formations should advance to Kermanshah and cut the main Baghdad-Tehran highway.' Did these people understand what was happening here? Had they seen these 'highways', or the state of the 'fast-moving formations'? Had they any idea how this order was supposed to be carried out?

Rommel would have understood Guderian's rage. He also received orders from OKH. But that particular evening he had other matters to concern him. His eminent SS guest had apparently been assassinated in Hebron.

The Field-Marshal arrived back in the city late that evening. The building reserved for his staff was surrounded by SS personnel, and the dead body of Adolf Eichmann was resting, as if in state, on the dining-room table.

Bayerlein was waiting for Rommel. He pulled him into the operations room and shut the door. 'They've gone berserk,' he half-shouted. 'They rounded up about four hundred Arabs, took them out of the town, and mowed them down with machine-guns. We are we going to do?'

Rommel sat down, took off his cap, rubbed his eyes. 'Did they catch the assassin?'

'No, of course not. They couldn't catch anyone. Most of the Arabs they killed were women and children. And it must have been a Jew who did it anyway. The SS can't tell the difference.'

'How many of them are here in Hebron?'

'SS? About forty.'

'Right. We'll arrest their commander, Hauptsturmführer Hanke. I'll suggest to OKH that he be court-martialled, and the rest of them disciplined. I expect I'll be told to mind my own business, but this is still an OKH area; the SS have no right to take action without my agreement. And I certainly would not have agreed to this madness. We'll have every Arab in the Middle East gunning for us after this.'

Rommel walked up to his sleeping quarters. Through the window he could see a bright crescent moon rising above the houses of Hebron. It had been a hard day. And a more decisive one than he yet knew. His reaction to the SS reprisal massacre would spark off a major crisis in the Army's relationship with its Führer. Rommel himself would not escape unscathed. By the end of the year he would be commanding a panzer army on the Eastern Front.

At the Wolfsschanze Hitler had emerged from his bed at the customary afternoon hour to hear of Eichmann's assassination in Palestine. According to his adjutant the Führer took the news with apparent indifference. If so it was one of his pre-storm calms. After glancing through the situation reports from Russia he summoned Brauchitsch from Lötzen.

The Field-Marshal arrived an hour later. He had not yet heard of Eichmann's unfortunate demise, and had no idea of the reason for this peremptory call to heel.

Inside the map-room Hitler was studying the deployment of divisions on the Eastern Front. 'The SS *Totenkopf* Division is to be transferred immediately to Palestine,' he said, without looking up. 'How soon can this be accomplished?'

In a more prudent mood Brauchitsch would have picked a suitable figure out of his hat and left it for Halder to argue the matter at a later date. But on that particular afternoon the Field-Marshal was not feeling prudent. The tone of his conversation with Model was still irking him. This time he would stand up to Hitler.

'SS *Totenkopf* is needed for the forthcoming Vologda attack, Mein Führer. General Küchler is already of the opinion that his forces are insufficient for the tasks allotted them. I do not think . . .'

Hitler's mood snapped. 'All I hear from General Küchler is excuses. There are insufficient forces. There is insufficient fuel, insufficient ammunition. Insufficient everything. It's all I hear from you generals. "We can't make it." You can't make Vologda, you can't make Jerusalem. Any minute now I shall be hearing from General Guderian that he can't make Baghdad. And why can't you make it? I'll tell you why. You lack the necessary will. It is cowardice, that's what it is. And you hide this cowardice behind obsolete strategic ideas. All this General Staff training, it is only an exercise in caution. Moscow – you had to take Moscow. Though Moscow is nothing, one more city, that's all. And as a result the Russians are still fighting. If you had attacked in the south as I had ordered we would have been in the Caucasus six months ago, and there would have been none of these problems.'

Hitler paused for breath. Brauchitsch waited for the tirade to continue. But to his surprise the Führer now spoke calmly, in an almost friendly fashion.

'It has been a great responsibility. I realise that. You are tired, no longer able to perform the tasks that are necessary. What we need now is a pitiless dedication to National Socialist principles, not the professional ability that is learnt in the staff colleges. I am the only one who can lead the Army in this manner, so I am relieving you of your command.'

'As you wish, Mein Führer.'

Brauchitsch departed. The Führer of the German Reich turned back to the huge wall-map. The armies of the Wehrmacht were chess-pieces spread across his global board. Now the world would be given reason to tremble.

In England 12 September was a fine late summer day. At Lords the cricket season came to a close, with the Australian Air Force trouncing the RAF by 277 runs. Across North London Tottenham were hitting six goals past Charlton Athletic. In Doncaster Sun Chariot won the St Leger at nine to four.

General Brooke had not noticed any of this. He had, as usual, been working all day, and looking forward to a Sunday at home with his wife. He was just preparing to leave when a summons arrived from the Prime Minister. Apparently there were vital matters to discuss.

Within an hour Brooke was seated in the back of a car *en route* for Chequers. It had been a hard week, but a satisfying one. The Americans were beginning to arrive in strength at last, both in Britain and the Middle East. They had already dealt the Japanese a sharp blow off Panama. And the Germans had been stopped by Monty and Jumbo Wilson. Leaning back in his seat, freed from the minutiae of work, Brooke felt a sense of relief. Though his mind warned him that it was not yet time for unrestrained optimism, he could not help feeling that the worst was over. 'We are going to win,' he murmured to himself.

At around 9.30pm the car pulled in outside the front entrance of Churchill's residence. The PM, resplendent in his green and gold dragon dressing-gown, ushered Brooke into his study. 'I've been thinking about the reconquest of Egypt,' he exclaimed, as Brooke lowered himself into the proffered armchair.

NOTES AND REFERENCES

(Facts amidst the Fiction)

The proverbs quoted at the head of chapters 2, 4(Kuybyshev), 4(Tokyo), 4(Berchtesgaden), 8 and 11 are all to be found in the *International Thesaurus of Quotations* (Penguin, 1976). The other chapter quotes come from the following sources – *Prologue*: from 'Pledging My Time', *Blonde on Blonde* (CBS, 1966); *chapter 1*: quoted in Werth, A. *Russia At War* (Barrie and Rockliff, 1964); *chapter 3*: quoted in Watts, A. *The Way of Zen* (Pelican, 1962); *chapter 4 (London/Washington)*: from 'The Note-Books', *The Crack-Up* (Penguin, 1965); *chapter 5*: from *The Waltz*; *chapter 6* quoted in Bryant, A. *The Turn of the Tide* (Fontana, 1965); *chapter 7*: a joke not used in the final screened version of *Go West*, quoted in Adamson, J. *Groucho, Harpo, Chico and sometimes Zeppo* (Coronet, 1974); *chapter 9*: from 'Ambulance Blues', *On the Beach* (Reprise, 1974); *chapter 10*: from *Penguin Dictionary of Modern Quotations* (Penguin, 1971).

The 'Eighth Army ditty' and Victor Serge quote heading chapter 11 and the Epilogue are purely fictitious.

Very selective bibliographies of certain topics appear below under the relevant chapters. Certain books, however, do not fit into convenient geographical categories, and some that I have relied upon extensively are: Liddell Hart, B. *History of the Second World War* (Cassell, 1970); Parkinson, R. *Blood, Toil, Tears and Sweat* (Hart-Davis MacGibbon, 1973); Bryant, A. *The Turn of the Tide* (Fontana, 1965); Roskill, S. *The War At Sea (vol 2)* (HMSO, 1957); Bekker, C. *The Luftwaffe War Diaries* (Macdonald, 1967). Other relevant histories published in the intervening period include: John Keegan, *The Second World War* (Century Hutchinson, 1989); R.A.C. Parker, *Struggle for Survival* (OUP, 1989); Richard Overy, *Why the Allies Won* (Pimlico, 1995) and Ian Kershaw's outstanding two volume biography *Hitler* (Penguin, 1998/2000).

NOTES AND REFERENCES

Prologue

I

Churchill is supposedly reading the report submitted by the Thompson Committee on 15 July 1941. The intercepted Japanese message is quoted in Feis, H. *The Road to Pearl Harbor* (Princeton, 1950), p. 249. All other quotes are from *The Times*, *New York Times* and *Daily Mirror* of 4 and 5 August 1941.

II

The meeting at Novy Borrisov did indeed occur, and ended as inconclusively as described. Dr Werner Sodenstern is a fictitious character. Hitler had confirmed Goering as his successor on 22 June 1941.

Chapter 1

The three basic sources I used for the purely military side of the German-Russian war were: Seaton, A. *The Russo-German War* (Barker, 1971), Carell, P. *Hitler's War on Russia* (Harrap, 1964); Clark, A. *Barbarossa* (Hutchinson, 1965). Richard Overy's *Russia's War* (Penguin, 1998) is a good recent history of the conflict.

I

Quotes from Führer Directives 21, 32, 33 and 34 are taken from *Hitler's War Directives* ed. Trevor-Roper, H. (Pan, 1966). The findings of the Zossen war-game are reported in Goerlitz, W. *Paulus and Stalingrad* (Methuen, 1963). The German supply situation in the summer of 1941 is exhaustively discussed in Leach, B. *German Strategy against Russia* (Clarendon, 1973).

II

The situation in Moscow in the summer and autumn of 1942 is described in Werth, *Russia at War*; Cassidy, H. *Moscow Dateline* (Houghton Mifflin, 1943); Mann, M. *At the Gates of Moscow* (Macmillan, 1963). Edvard Radzinsky's *Stalin* (Sceptre, 1997) is one of several recent books which make use of the newly-accessible Soviet archives to throw fresh light on the war years.

Chapter 2

Principal sources used for North African War: Playfair, I.S.O. *The Mediterranean and the Middle East Vol III* (HMSO, 1963); *The Rommel Papers* ed. Liddell Hart, B. (Collins, 1953); Barnett, C. *The Desert Generals* (William Kimber, 1960); Moorehead, A. *The Desert War* (Hamish Hamilton, 1965); Carell, P. *The Foxes of the Desert* (Macdonald, 1960); Strawson, J. *The Battle for North Africa* (Batsford, 1969); Connell, J. *Wavell* (Cassell 1964/9) and *Auchinleck* (Cassell, 1959); Mellenthin, F.W. *Panzer Battles* (Cassell, 1955).

II

Rommel's war with the insect world is quoted in *The Rommel Papers*, pp. 149-50.

III

Churchill's telegram to Auchinleck, and the latter's reply, are quoted in Churchill, W.S. *The Second World War Vol 6* (Cassell, 1964) pp. 23-4.

Chapter 3

For the events leading up to the Pacific War see particularly Feis, H. *The Road to Pearl Harbor* (Princeton, 1950) and Toland, J. *The Rising Sun* (Cassell, 1971).

I

The telegram delivered to von Ribbentrop is quoted in Feis, *Road to Pearl Harbor*, p. 329.

Chapter 4

Kuybyshev
The evacuation of Soviet industry is described in some detail in Werth, *Russia at War*.

Tokyo
Captain Yorinaga is a fictitious character, but the information he gathers together was actually available to the Japanese Navy in the spring of 1942.

Chapter 5

The attack on Malta is based upon contingency plans discussed in Playfair, *Mediterranean and Middle East*; Bekker *Luftwaffe War Diaries*; Edwards R. *German Airborne Troops* (Macdonald and Jane's, 1974); Kesselring, A. *Memoirs* (William Kimber, 1953); *Ciano's Diaries 1939-43* (Heinemann, 1947).

I
Lieutenant Johnston is a fictitious character.

Chapter 6

II
The Middle East Defence Committee Report was actually submitted on 9 May 1942, and is quoted in Playfair, *Mediterranean and Middle East*, p. 203.

III
Principal sources consulted for the political situation in the Arab world were: Hirszowicz, L. *The Third Reich and the Arab East* (Routledge and Kegan Paul, 1966); Schechtman, J. *The Mufti and the Führer* (Yoseloff, 1965); Stephens, R. *Nasser* (Pelican, 1971); Sadat, A. *Revolt on the Nile* (Wingate, 1957); Warner, G. *Iraq and Syria 1941* (Davis-Poynter, 1974).

VI
German/Italian occupation policy in Egypt is based on plans discussed by Hirszowicz in chapter 12 of *Third Reich and Arab East*.

VII
Rommel's conquest of Egypt is based on the plans he drew up shortly before the First Battle of Alamein. See the sketch-map on p. 259 of *The Rommel Papers*.

Chapter 7

My version of the Battle of Midway naturally relies on the numerous accounts available of the real battle. The best of these is Fuchida, M. and

Okumiya, M. *Midway: The Battle that Doomed Japan* (Hutchinson, 1957). Another book I relied on was J.D. Potter's biography of Yamamoto, *Admiral of the Pacific* (Heinemann, 1965). A good recent account of the Pacific War can be found in Dan van der Vat's *The Pacific Campaign* (Touchstone, 1992).

I

Nimitz's pre-battle instructions are quoted in Smith, P.C. *Midway* (NEL, 1976), p. 56.

Chapter 9

Cairo/Tel el Kebir
The good Dr Schrumpf is quoted in Hirszowicz, *Third Reich and Arab East*, p. 263.

Wolfsschanze
Hitler's obsession with oil is mentioned by Carell on p. 578 of *Hitler's War on Russia*.

London
Wavell's appreciation is quoted in Strawson, *Battle for North Africa*, p. 18. The Brooke quote is taken from Bryant, *Turn of the Tide*, p. 366.

Baghdad/Rafah
The British defence of Palestine is based on contingency plans discussed by the War Cabinet's Joint Planning Staff, now available as War Cabinet paper CAB79. For discussions between the Palestinian Jews and the British authorities in the real war see Hurewitz, J.C. *The Struggle for Palestine* (Norton, 1950).

Ankara
For Turkey's role in the real war see Von Papen, F. *Memoirs* (Andre Deutsch, 1952); Lewis, B. *The Emergence of Modern Turkey* (OUP, 1968); Hostler, C.W. *Turkism and the Soviets* (Allen & Unwin, 1957).

NOTES AND REFERENCES

Chapter 10

I

Quote from *Ciano Diaries*, 10.3.42. For other indications of souring German-Japanese relationships see entries for 14.4.42, 21.4.42 and 24.4.42.

IV

The Japanese did in fact believe that *Saratoga* had been sunk.

Chapter 11

II

The 'impassable' Wadi Hareidin was used by General Yoffe's division to split the Egyptian defences in June 1967.

IV

The mountain track leading up from the Jaffa-Jerusalem road to the villages of Biddu and Nebi Samuel was used by both Richard the Lionheart in 1191 and Uri Ben Ari's armoured brigade in June 1967.

Epilogue

Mordechai Givoni, the German railway guards, the Soviet partisans, and Hauptsturmführer Hanke are all fictitious characters.

Other Greenhill books on World War II include:

RED STAR AGAINST THE SWASTIKA
The Story of a Soviet Pilot over the Eastern Front
Vasily B. Emelianenko
ISBN 1-85367-649-7

AT THE HEART OF THE REICH
The Secret Diary of Hitler's Army Adjutant
Major Gerhard Engel
ISBN 1-85367- 655-1

TANK RIDER
Into the Reich with the Red Army
Evgeni Bessonov
ISBN 1-85367-671-3

BLOOD RED SNOW
The Memoirs of a German Soldier on the Eastern Front
Günter K. Koschorrek
ISBN 1-85367-639-X

LUFTWAFFE OVER AMERICA
The Secret Plans to Bomb the United States in World War II
Manfred Griehl
ISBN 1-86267-608-X

THE RECONSTRUCTION OF WARRIORS
Archibald McIndoe, the Royal Air Force and the Guinea Pig Club
E. R. Mayhew
ISBN 1-85367-610-1

Greenhill offer a 10 per cent discount on any books ordered directly from us. Please call 0208 458 6314 or email sales@greenhillbooks.com.

For more information on our other books and to enter our 2006 draw to win military books worth £1000, please visit www.greenhillbooks.com. You can write to us at Park House, 1 Russell Gardens, London NW11 9NN.